ISLAM, MODERNITY AND ENTREPRENEURSHIP
AMONG THE MALAYS

Islam, Modernity and Entrepreneurship among the Malays

Patricia Sloane

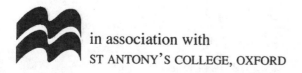
in association with
ST ANTONY'S COLLEGE, OXFORD

First published in Great Britain 1999 by
MACMILLAN PRESS LTD
Houndmills, Basingstoke, Hampshire RG21 6XS and London
Companies and representatives throughout the world

A catalogue record for this book is available from the British Library.

ISBN 0–333–71275–7

 First published in the United States of America 1999 by
ST. MARTIN'S PRESS, INC.,
Scholarly and Reference Division,
175 Fifth Avenue, New York, N.Y. 10010

ISBN 0–312–21300–X

Library of Congress Cataloging-in-Publication Data
Sloane, Patricia, 1957–
Islam, modernity, and entrepreneurship among the Malays / Patricia
Sloane.
p.   cm. — (St. Antony's series)
Includes bibliographical references and index.
ISBN 0–312–21300–X (cloth)
1. Entrepreneurship—Malaysia.   2. Capitalism—Malaysia.
3. Islam—Economic aspects—Malaysia.   I. Title.   II. Series.
HB615.S63 1998
338'.04'09595—dc21   97–38805
                                                                      CIP

This book is printed on paper suitable for recycling and made from fully managed and
sustained forest sources.

10   9   8   7   6   5   4   3   2   1
08   07   06   05   04   03   02   01   00   99

Printed and bound in Great Britain by
Antony Rowe Ltd.

To Deanna Gutschow and my mother, Ethel Sloane

Contents

Preface

Themes of hospitality and inclusion figure greatly in the lives of Malays, and, indeed, nearly everyone I encountered during 18 months of research in Kuala Lumpur, Malaysia, between January 1993 and June 1994, proved to me that Malays live as they believe people everywhere should: they are generous, kind, and caring. Capitalist economic development does not inevitably result in the depersonalizing and social fractioning of people's lives. Much of the present analysis is devoted to showing that the opposite is true, at least in the many Malay lives I came to know in the modern conurbation of Kuala Lumpur.

Economic development and its effects have fully enmeshed with modern Malay life, and, in the minds of its protagonists, modernity has also borrowed much from traditional Malay culture. Yet the language of business in Malaysia – despite the government's efforts to create an economic language in *Bahasa Melayu*, the Malay language – is English, what my informants called the 'universal business language'. As such, business discussions and meetings in which I participated in Malaysia were conducted in English, or more accurately, in the seamless admixing of English – *Bahasa Inggeris* – and *Bahasa Melayu*, what some people felicitously call 'Minglish' (and some, 'Manglish'!) Much of the social life of Malay business people is also conducted in its up-to-the-minute vocabulary. In more domestic locations, however, such as my landlady's house, we often spoke *Bahasa Melayu*.

None the less, business and economics remain much-discussed subjects in all settings, public and private. The weekly television listings invariably included programmes featuring Malay entrepreneurs and Islamic teachers speaking about economics; nearly everyone I knew was interested in learning more from such experts. People discussed these programmes, both at home and in social or business settings. They listened to government ministers speak over and over about the crucial role of citizens in economic development. Young Malays, my informants' children, learned about entrepreneurship in school and talked about it at home. Indeed, the most remarkable aspect of my stay in Malaysia was that nearly everywhere I went, I met people knowledgeable and interested in the very subject I had come to research. It was strictly my good fortune – not canny ethnographic method – that senior executives of major conglomerates took time to share their understanding of Malay entrepreneurship, that the very word 'entrepreneurship' opened doors of both businesses and homes, and that people – variously placed in society – began to seek out (not just be sought by) the visiting anthropologist to discuss business ideas and projects.

This analysis is an attempt to understand the choices, images, and changes economic development has brought to the lives of Malays I knew in Kuala Lumpur. I hope that in portraying my informants' understanding of their role in moral and responsible economic development, I have done justice to their ideas and beliefs. To all of these enterprising, generous, and hospitable people, I express my gratitude.

I first learned the importance of networks in Malaysia before I arrived, when Polly Friedhoff, who keeps the alumni lists for St Antony's College, Oxford, printed out for me the names of the Malaysians who had once been members of my college. On the list was Amarjit Kaur, the historian of colonial Malaya. Dr Kaur, who, unbeknown to St Antony's, no longer lived in Malaysia, received my letter seeking Malaysian contacts after it had been forwarded to her in Australia. She passed my letter back to Malaysia, to Norani Othman, a sociologist and student of Islamic modernism. Norani did not hesitate to offer her supervision to a project that sought to understand the relationship between Islam and economic change in Malaysia. With Norani's assistance, my entry into Malay life was eased, almost cushioned. I cannot thank her enough.

I had the good fortune to be sponsored by the Department of Anthropology and Sociology, Universiti Kebangsaan Malaysia. Chairman Associate Professor Hairi Abdullah enthusiastically recommended my project for approval by the Unit Perancang Ekonomi (EPU), which, in turn, granted a research permit. Many faculty members at Universiti Kebangsaan Malaysia and at various government institutions showed interest in my work. I express my particular appreciation to several outstanding social scientists: Shamsul A.B., Halim Ali, Kadir Din, and Rustam Sani.

Through these people, I had the opportunity to meet Clive S. Kessler, whose insights into the culture, religion, and politics of Malaysia remain, in my assessment, unequalled in the anthropological literature. I would wish for any first-time fieldworker the concern, perspective, and attention he provided me during his trips to Kuala Lumpur from Australia; indeed, there is nothing in my understanding of Malay culture that does not somehow reflect a conversation I had with Clive. Equally powerful was the impress of several other anthropologists. Hildred Geertz first introduced me to the cultures of Southeast Asia at Princeton University. I structured my research along her guide-lines; no student could receive better instruction on what anthropologists do and how they think. Deborah Gewertz taught me anthropology at Amherst College; in doing so, she planted the seeds of her wisdom and creativity, many of which grew and bore fruit during my research. Finally, my supervisor at Oxford University, Bob Barnes, has had a significant influence on my work and remains a great resource, supporter, and friend.

Over the past few years, in America, Oxford, and Asia, a number of people have figured importantly, enriching my life and serving as my own network of affect and instrumentality. Elinor Pettit has always given me a place in her home and in her heart. Addison Pettit, Gavin Whitmore, Michael Franklin, Barbara Lee, Ellen Rubin, Trudy Turner, Carol Goldberg, Patrick Fiddler, Susan Mansfield, and Ed Campbell all helped me get to Oxford or helped me finish what I had started. In Oxford, I had a second home with Ewa and Roli Huggins, and the loving friendship of anthropologists Tina Stoecklin and Sandra Dudley. Owen White provided devoted emotional and intellectual support no matter where I was. In Hong Kong, Bobby Cheng was the first to hear many of my ideas about Malay business culture. Wolfgang Krahl, Ulrike Jobst, the Bouwmeesters, and Helene Tychsen were friends in Kuala Lumpur who enhanced my life with their kindness and concern. Later, as this book emerged from the dissertation upon which it was based, Au Yong Geok Lian, Kho Suan Giak, and Nor Azman bin Mahat made life in KL delightful.

Lastly, and most of all, my parents, my sister Kate, Jeff, and Adam have always believed in my work and supported its peregrinations, learning how to send their love across thousands of miles.

P.S.

PART I: GOOD WORKS

1 Introduction

I first arrived in Kuala Lumpur during Chinese New Year of 1993. The streets and highways of this modern city, lined with skyscrapers, housing estates, mosques, and shopping malls, were quiet. Stores and shops were closed, barricaded with metal gates, and padlocked. I had come to Malaysia, one of the world's fastest-growing economies, to study entrepreneurship and the effects of rapid development among the Malays; paradoxically, my first view of Kuala Lumpur – a prosperous city built on petroleum income, foreign investment, and an enormous state-led push towards industrial capitalism – showed none of the flourishing signs of modern life it had been built to contain. To arrive during Chinese New Year threw the constructions and fitments of Malaysia's accelerated modernity into high relief; empty of people, Kuala Lumpur looked like nothing more than a cunning architectural model – an orderly, functional *design*.

Wherever I looked, stores and businesses displayed signs scrawled in Chinese and English, announcing that the proprietors were observing their week-long holiday. I had read that the ethnic Malays, who make up a little more than half the population of Peninsular Malaysia,[1] had, in the past decade or so, rapidly, even breathtakingly, advanced their business interests and ownership – emerging as a class of entrepreneurs, still somewhat behind the ethnic Chinese, but very much a part of the modern enterprise sector.[2] In this motionless, ultra-modern city, I did not see evidence of what was claimed by the Malaysian government to have been significantly counterbalanced; among the preponderance of Chinese enterprises, there was only a tiny, almost fugitive handful of Malay restaurants – identifiable by the sign announcing *halal* or Muslim food – and shops selling Islamic literature. In the inevitable anthropological paradigm of arrival, I was fearful that what I had come to study, Malay entrepreneurship, was still what Malays call *belum* – not *yet* here, *surely* soon, but actually *not now*.

Just 20 years earlier, very little of what I saw – this all-encompassing modern conurbation with only traces of the colonial city remaining – and what I had read about economic development in Malaysia – the vast nurturing and rapid state-led modernizing of the Malays – had yet occurred. In a vertical and horizontal landscape of development which stretched as far as I could see, Kuala Lumpur and, as I had understood it, the lives of the Malays who lived there, were equally new, emergent, just now. In the quiescence into which I had arrived, those lives, and my interest, Malay entrepreneurship, were yet invisible. Over time, I would see how the effects and ambiguities of economic development and social change wound endlessly through this ready-made place, shaping the lives of the men and women – Malay entrepreneurs – who would become my friends and informants.

Indeed, when I left 18 months later, my first perception of the landscape of Kuala Lumpur had been transformed into what it was to my informants – a tangibly enterprising place, deeply personalized, full to the bursting-point with plans and ventures, everywhere bound up with cross-cutting and overlapping relationships and the shared meanings they reflected and produced. I was to learn that Kuala Lumpur was not built only upon petro-leum revenues and massive national and multinational investment, but also upon ramifying networks and alliances, ever-extending social, economic, and communal ties focused on obligation and action; paradoxically, that sociological set of behaviours which often is said to disappear in modern capitalism, but was here an essential definition of Malay modernity.

This analysis is primarily about the choices, images, and strategies development has brought to the lives of the Malays I knew, men and women who believed deeply in the development paradigm of modernity and responsibility their government exhorted, and fashioned meaning and validation out of the changes and opportunities which characterized their lives.

Lives in Kuala Lumpur are shaped not just by the forces and images of late-twentieth-century capitalist development, but by an expressly Islamic understanding of fate and human agency, one which leaves the end-point and rewards of all worldly action necessarily unknown, as these are deter-mined only by the will of Allah. The *source* of development, on the con-trary, can be easily pointed out – a particular moment over 20 years earlier. Indeed, as my informants characterize development, its precise starting-point was a day in May 1969, and its starting place was Kuala Lumpur – once a Chinese tin-trading city, later the British colonial capital – born of bloodshed between Malays and Chinese. The post-colonial *status quo* of ethnic complementarity,[3] what one analyst calls the 'funda-mental contradiction of Malaysian society – the concentration of economic wealth in the hands of the rich Chinese and monopoly of political power' by Malays (Horii 1991: 281) exploded into ethnic riots. The proximate cause appeared to be the result of ethno-political conflicts in the aftermath of the 1969 general elections. The deeper cause, however, was said to be a mounting, fulminating Malay dissatisfaction with their role in the modern economy, and their corollary perception that the Chinese had monopolized all economic activity in a nation which, the Malaysian Constitution stated, rightfully belonged to the indigenous Malays.[4]

May 1969 became emblematic of the urgent need to accelerate Malay economic development, and, indelibly connected to the idiom of ethnic conflict and redress, the New Economic Policy (NEP) was launched – a massive, 20-year plan to reduce economic inequity and ensure cohesion throughout the troubled nation. Proposing multiethnic policy aimed at overall poverty reduction, social restructuring, and the creation of what the government called 'national unity',[5] NEP actually took shape as a highly interventionist economic and affirmative action programme directed exclusively at Malays. It replaced the essentially *laissez-faire* economic framework established in Malaysia upon Independence (Jesudason 1989). NEP was (and is – while its original 20-year time-frame ran out in 1990, it has been reinstated indefinitely [see Chapter 4]) a set of policies and strategies that provided the state with the means to help the Malays, called *bumiputera* or 'sons of the soil',[6] to take greater control over the nation's economic resources, and to do so in the name of national stability and national development.

As envisaged by the policy leaders of NEP, economic equity *vis-à-vis* the Chinese would be reached when it could be demonstrated that Malays had reached 30 per cent ownership of and participation in all industrial and commercial activities.[7] To reach this goal, an enormous transformation and expansion of the economy was put in motion, leaving almost no institutional apparatus untouched. There was a huge increase in the number of 'quasi-public bodies and government agencies that were charged with providing special assistance programmes for Malays or that acted as surrogate institutions for the transfer of capital shares and ownership to Malays' (Means 1991: 26). The United Malays National Organization (UMNO),[8] the Malay hegemonic political party which had dominated the national front coalition which had ruled since Independence, and had long looked after the special constitutional privileges of the Malays, now also looked after Malay economic privileges, ever broadening its base of Malay political support for the government. Along the way, both the state and UMNO were to become massively involved in the corporate sector, and many of the Malay business elite, some of whom shall be met in the pages of this book, became closely tied to them. Over 20 years, Kuala Lumpur was transformed into a modern city, built to support the growing policy-led enterprise sector and the public and private interests of the mushrooming Malay middle class which had been educated to serve them.

But contradictions and paradoxes emerged in NEP. The strategies for poverty reduction, social restructuring, and 'national unity', intended to create a 'just society' (*Masyararakat Adil* – NEP's slogan) for all citizens, were defined not in terms of individual or equal opportunity or need, but in aggregate ethnic terms, Malays *vis-à-vis* non-Malays as a whole. As such, rather than attending to the substantial, multiethnic population of the nation's poor, or the Malay poor, NEP policy-makers tended to provide the greatest resources to those Malays who had already been socialized for mobility. The primary beneficiaries of NEP were the Malay civil servants who had themselves been favoured by earlier, colonial-era pro-Malay educational and professional opportunities and their children[9] – people who were already one or two generations of modernization ahead of Malays in the rural sector (Naipaul 1981), where poverty and economic 'backwardness' were, of course, much worse.

Over the past 20 years, the opportunities for these Malays have been vast. NEP made tremendous provision for educating Malays beyond the secondary level. Malay university students 'enjoyed favourable quotas for admission and received generous government stipends' (Means 1991: 26). Many were provided with the opportunity to study overseas. Quotas for industry and professional recruitment were established, requiring that Chinese and foreign businesses place Malay managers in strategic positions (Jesudason 1989). Alongside these strategies, a massive effort to create, train, and provide capital to Malay entrepreneurs was launched (Milne and Mauzy 1978) to ensure that Malays would have increasing ownership in the industrial and commercial sector.

As we will see from the many lives which comprise the present analysis, unlike other anthropological studies of the effects of NEP (Guinness 1992; Kamaruddin M. Said 1993; Ong 1987), mine does not examine the destinies and perceptions of those disadvantaged by NEP, but of those who were advantaged by the enormous contexts of change, of men and women who saw the world nearly full to the bursting point with promise. The present analysis is one of a handful that concentrates on the Malay culture of privilege (cf. A. Kahar Bador 1973; Kahn 1996; Mokhzani 1965; Scott 1968). Despite status differences among them, the thread that connected the lives of my informants was the empowering, fulfilling perception that they could, individually and collectively, explore the dimensions and parameters of economic development, and the conviction that they did so – as NEP itself had established by valorizing results in *aggregate* ethnic terms – on behalf of the entire Malay group.

As such, my study concentrates on the Malay 'haves', but does not challenge or critique the relations of power their lives assume, primarily seeking an understanding of my informants' assertion of their right to power and leadership. Put another way, unlike many students of Malaysia's economic development (Jomo K.S. 1989a,b, 1990; Mehmet 1986; Shamsul A.B. 1992a,b), I am not concerned with the ways in which state-based elites degrade the rest of humanity to assure their own hegemony, but rather, the ways in which they grade their own, often claiming to do so on behalf of others (cf. Cohen 1981). Beyond this, however, is the much more complicated perspective of the present analysis, which seeks to understand the perceptions of the Malay 'haves' not in aggregate terms, as NEP did, but in the highly nuanced terms of hierarchy that they, too, have accepted.

Quite simply, my interests in development in Malaysia were, like NEP itself, ethnically and elitely framed; I had come to Kuala Lumpur, this young, modern city, to learn more about the lifestyles, identities, and careers of the Malay men and women who were the primary beneficiaries of NEP. Born around the time of Malaysian Independence in 1957, these people were my own age, often as educated and as well-travelled as I, and certainly more financially secure – they had well-paying jobs, government-sponsored shares in *bumiputera* investment funds, and access to capital and resources through various NEP-era business-enrichment schemes. Many of them had read, I was to discover, the same books and magazines on business and management as I had, and were as interested in America's culture of entrepreneurship as I was in theirs. But much of the modern enterprising lifestyle which we shared was new to my informants: they had come from small towns all over Malaysia, almost exclusively children of the Malay civil-service generation which flourished in the post-Independence period, now living far from their parents and their roots.

Full participants in the nation's formidable economic growth, it was easy for my informants to point to NEP as the absolute beginning of Malay development, and, as we shall see, the beginning of the most forceful demonstration of modernity, Malay entrepreneurship.

THE 'PROBLEM' I SOUGHT AND THE 'PROBLEM' I BROUGHT

While 'entrepreneurship' was what I called, as anthropologists shouldering the burden of their first fieldwork do, my research 'problem', I arrived in one of the economically fastest-growing nations in the world's fastest-growing economic region, Southeast Asia, shouldering a set of complex self-reflexive 'problems' as well. As such, no less a point of departure for my research was a particular set of questions which had come from my own past, the motivation behind a move which had led me from a corporate career of my own in the entrepreneurial bastion of Wall Street, to ethnographic research on the other side of the world. Eight years of experience with managers, executives, 'idea people', sales people, traders, arbitrageurs, marketers, consultants – modern entrepreneurs and capitalists all – had led me to a troubling paradox. Success in the American culture of business I knew first-hand was least of all determined by those things which were said to comprise it: rational, economistic behaviours such as long-term planning, profit re-investment, impersonalism, and so on.

My understanding of economic culture in America's – indeed, the world's – most advanced capitalist location, peopled with autonomous heroes of the free market, was that it was a labyrinth of personalism and social ties, highly dependent on forms of patronage, favouritism, and access to political and social power, built upon vast reciprocal exchange networks of a highly social nature, and characterized by a short-term orientation – that is, a remarkable lack of purely (and sometimes of any) economistic behaviours. If Wall Street – that epicentre of economic rationality and entrepreneurial self-determination – could be characterized largely by social ties and social strategies remarkably like those of less-developed economies, which are said to be singularly comprised of relationships based on what Sen calls 'entitlements' (1981), and of behaviours which evidenced little of what Max Weber called 'rationalization' (1974), where, I wondered, *were* the parameters of so-called modern capitalism?

Moreover, if entrepreneurship in America was indeed what I came to understand it to be – a set of assumptions devoted to explaining an ideal, a great mythic cultural denial of what was most true about modern Western capitalism and economic change, masking the entrepreneur's dependence upon conditions largely determined by social life and social alliances, precisely those things which are said to be economically over-determined and stagnating in traditional societies[10] – what was entrepreneurship in modernizing locations elsewhere? As such, I suspected that observers had seen in newly capitalist economies the dysfunctional structures of 'traditional' society (patron/client, feudal, entitling, non-rational, personalistic, corrupt, short-term orientated, and so on), reproduced and re-emergent in non-Western economic development (Scott 1977; Rutten nd) but not in our own. I knew that the same criticisms could be applied to the Western entrepreneurs and capitalists I knew best (cf. Mills 1956; Granovetter 1992).

When I left Wall Street in 1991, its innovators were awash with excitement over a new entrepreneurial paradigm called 'venture capitalism', in which large institutions and financiers sought to invest, at great profit, in small, promising, 'unknown' high-tech firms which lacked capital. Both the small-ventures' owners and the big institutional financiers were evocatively described in marketing literature (which I was responsible for producing) as 'entrepreneurs', 'innovators', and 'visionaries'. The 'promising unknowns' – the small-venture owners – were, of course, already well connected to sources of major capital and influence, for these are the invisible requirements of entrepreneurial success in America, and factors which had brought them into the ambit of Wall Street investors. But both the big institutional investors and the small unknowns were identified as 'entrepreneurs', a perfect example of the way in which any definition of 'entrepreneurs', as Hart established (1975), generally means whatever we would like it to mean (but invariably presumes a kind of self-generative heroism). This definition is as common among analysts of entrepreneurs as it is among entrepreneurs themselves.

It was no surprise to me that once I became familiar with ideals and images of modern entrepreneurship among my Malay informants, the term 'venture capital' had already become common in everyday discourse, for indeed, much of the mythic culture of Western entrepreneurship – including its unmistakable language and remarkable assumptions – had been sequestered in the Malay theory of development.

Many of my informants, aside from being advantaged beneficiaries of Malay-only educational opportunity and investment-based enrichment programmes, were, in many cases, well connected to sources of major capital and influence (sometimes exceeding those which even Wall Street can provide), but the ideals and images of entrepreneurship they had elaborated muted, even erased, the on-going role of the state, institutions, and policy in their endeavours. Like their Western entrepreneurial counterparts, my informants valorized an ideal type – the heroic entrepreneur – who appeared to *create and generate power*, rather than merely access it. This ideal type – which had been constructed in my own culture of capitalism, allowing both huge Wall Street institutions and small high-tech firms to be thought of as 'entrepreneurial' – now transferred to the developing world, had taken on, as I was to learn in Malaysia, enormous local and cultural meaning. Moreover, in Malaysia, in addition to localizing and reinterpreting a Western entrepreneurial model, increasingly my informants also looked towards an entrepreneurial model obtained from Japan – the nation its Prime Minister admires the most – whose leaders had elaborated an entrepreneurial paradigm itself partially borrowed from the West (Yoshino 1992), surely what Geertz (1973), referring to layers of cultural ideas, famously called 'winks' upon 'winks' of meaning.

The 'problem' I brought to Malaysia was a kind of insider knowledge of the peculiarities and assumptions of one culture of entrepreneurship – a self-reflexive problem – which was complicated by the partly Western-reflected, partly Western-prefabricated image my informants had cast upon their culture of entrepreneurship. Paradoxically, much of my informants' formulation of *Malay* entrepreneurship and capitalism as they believed they practised it, was predicated on preserving in economic development the social arrangements and social relations they believed we had removed from our own, precisely those arrangements which I had seen operating in Western entrepreneurship and capitalism. The 'winks' went on and on.

What really was twentieth-century 'entrepreneurship', in Malaysia or anywhere, if not a series of explanations that validated destinies and arrangements already made? Social scientists and economists, as we shall now see, had not come up with a satisfying answer, despite a generation of massive development and analytic interest in entrepreneurship.

THE CONCEPT OF ENTREPRENEURSHIP IN DEVELOPMENT THEORY

As a cornerstone of NEP, Malaysia, along with other developing countries in the 1960s and 1970s, enthusiastically jumped on the 'entrepreneurial bandwagon'. Through 'entrepreneurship', the government sought to 'create a new class of small capitalists' leading to 'the formation of a middle class' (Chee Peng Lim *et al.* 1979: 9). Hundreds of training programs were given, millions of *ringgit*[11] in loans were handed out, and consultants from Western countries were hired to assist the *bumiputera* entrepreneur. Much of the language of NEP was the language of entrepreneurship: the government believed that by providing Malays with access to education, opportunity, resources, and capital, they would emerge as enterprising, business-minded, innovative, self-sufficient modern men and women – that is, as entrepreneurs.

Indeed, this was the international development paradigm of the time. In a report published by the Development Centre of the OECD, it was asserted that 'a model of economic behaviour, set by entrepreneurship, could contribute in a most important fashion to a country's development' (Derossi 1971: 86). This model of entrepreneurship had been codified for the West by the economist Schumpeter, whose ideas had gained popularity in America during the Depression. Economic growth, Schumpeter said, was the work of an innovating entrepreneur; entrepreneurship stimulated progress, producing dramatic upswings in profits, investment, and progress (1934). Schumpeter's actor-based economic theories had enormous impact on social scientists interested in development, who, in the 1960s and 1970s, picked up and elaborated his theory on the role and psychodynamics of the innovative individual in economic change.[12]

Anthropologists became interested in entrepreneurship in an attempt to explain processes of economic change (Carroll 1965; Firth 1967) and the crucial role of social actors in it (Barth 1963; 1967). Various socio-anthropological theories of entrepreneurship emerged: entrepreneurs were people who abandoned traditional forms of prestige in pursuit of new ones (Geertz 1963b), or people who pursued opportunity and profit in the new cash economy by manipulating traditional cultural factors and local meanings (Parkin 1972). Entrepreneurs became seen in Marxist terms as exploiters and accumulators, the agents of capitalism and destroyers of traditional exchange-based morality (Cook 1982; Cooper 1980), or as a handful of morally legitimate, rational business people who could be distinguished from corrupt state-level capitalist accumulators and exploiters (MacGaffey 1987). Problematically, the characteristics of the entrepreneur in all of these approaches associated ideal types and economic paradigms from our culture with determinants of change everywhere (Hart 1975). The anthropology of entrepreneurship became the study of how entrepreneurs fulfilled a largely pre-emptively defined role.[13]

Therein lies the real 'problem' of entrepreneurship and the 'problem' I sought to understand. Even though my informants, along with their government, were often profoundly inspired by the universal image of entrepreneurship, I was determined to move beyond this uniform construct, towards a reconceptualization of entrepreneurship in a highly specific social and cultural context, as a set of meanings which provided my informants with a sharp understanding of self and society in processes of change. Indeed, as I was ultimately able to see, their theory of entrepreneurship included a remarkable assertion of their cultural distinctiveness. Malay entrepreneurship may have entailed, like Western entrepreneurship, a great, mythic muting of power arrangements already made, but it was taking on a highly specific and increasingly confident articulation of Malay cultural identity as my informants defined their place in their own, and global, society.

LOCATING THE DOMAIN AND STRATEGIES OF THE MALAY ENTREPRENEUR

Despite my initial, panicky impression in that moment of arrival during Chinese New Year – giving rise to my fear that enterprise in Malaysia still remained in the hands of the Chinese – I was quickly confronted with a different reality altogether. Where, I had wondered on my first day in Malaysia, were the Malay entrepreneurs? According to people I was soon to meet, they were everywhere in the modern sector. As I began to talk to Malay men and women and to introduce myself or be introduced into social situations, people actually identified themselves and others to me as 'entrepreneurs', always using the English word.[14]

Entrepreneurship was, in Malay urban society, what NEP had intended it to be: a middle-class, even elite, phenomenon. There were Malay hawkers in Kuala Lumpur, but there had long been informal-sector Malay hawkers in Kuala Lumpur, mobilizing their own labour. Malay entrepreneurs, the people my informants pointed out to me, on the other hand, started big and were in public view. Indeed, entrepreneurship earns public, grand-scale attention in the Malay community; the government honours individuals who are deemed successful entrepreneurs, bestowing titles and honorifics, and magazines and the media report endlessly on the lifestyles and management secrets of Malay entrepreneurs (Abdul Maulud Yusof 1986). Entrepreneurs in Malay society, people who are organizing themselves and others into businesses, absolutely see themselves as part of the modern sector: In skyscrapers and elegant offices, in factories lining the industrial corridor from Kuala Lumpur to the famous Straits of Malacca, and in the prosperous neighbourhoods that have spun out from the city centre – these were the places I would meet the people my informants called entrepreneurs.

Soon, I was to learn that to one degree or another, every educated, middle-class and upper-middle-class Malay man and woman I met in Kuala Lumpur claimed or wished to demonstrate the highly valorized position of the entrepreneur in economic development. In this identity was proof that my informants had learned everything NEP had asked of the Malay citizenry. In Malay life, I would learn, entrepreneurship was least of all a set of business behaviours, it was an *identity*. Indeed, as we shall see in the pages of this analysis, the *businesses* which my informants established to demonstrate their entrepreneurship sometimes received the least attention of all. As such, sequestered in my informants' understanding of Malay entrepreneurship – what they construed as a never-ending set of lapidary behaviours intended to serve the needs of the nation and Allah – was, I was to learn, an enormous allowance for failure. Even the bankrupt among them could claim the social identity of the entrepreneur, and as we shall see vividly, often the entrepreneurial identity is more resilient and indomitable than the entrepreneurial *enterprise*, a paradox I found to be true on Wall Street as well.[15]

In the course of my fieldwork, in an attempt to understand both Malay entrepreneurship and the society of change which it had produced and which had produced it, I spoke to hundreds of entrepreneurial people who were participating in the modern economy in Kuala Lumpur or attempting to cast a wider net to economic and social niches in the rest of Malaysia, Southeast Asia, and the world. I spoke to people in their houses and their offices, factories, and country clubs. I spoke to male and female entrepreneurs – both participated with equal fervour in the modern economy. I spoke to parents and to children, students, and teenagers – every one of them wanting to be an entrepreneur one day; to recent university graduates (all wanting to be entrepreneurs); to professors and to professionals in big corporate businesses who were planning to go out 'on their own' or were already doing so on the side. I spoke to or met people in groups: women's and men's entrepreneurial societies, college alumni cohorts, executives' networking organizations established to capture greater entrepreneurial opportunities. With my informants, I attended workshops on Malay entrepreneurship, Malay entrepreneurs' clubs, entrepreneurship talks, entrepreneurial development societies, entrepreneurial award ceremonies, and huge conferences and trade shows sponsored by government ministries and agencies to develop local, regional, and global *bumiputera* entrepreneurship.

But Malay entrepreneurship and the changes it implied had affected other, less visible aspects of life, especially in relationships between men and women, children and parents, brothers and sisters, individuals and cohorts, even human beings and Allah. In an attempt to understand these dimensions and nuances of change, I started a working mothers' 'discussion group' to talk about modern women's roles, men, work, and children. Because Islam has shaped so much of modern identity in Malay life, I was extremely lucky to be invited into Islamic study groups and into long eschatological discussions with people who had intensified their concern with the religious teachings of their youth. Everywhere I found Malay men and women actively seeking to understand the role of Islam in contexts of social and economic change and, as we will see, in multiple contexts of contestation. I travelled frequently to the natal homes of my friends, going back in cars loaded down with gifts of food and luxuries, to the small towns where their parents still lived, for holidays, ritual celebrations, births, and deaths. There, I could speak to the families left behind, engaging them – and their modern adult children – in endlessly amusing and valuable talk about the 'old days'. I travelled even further afield with some of my informants: to Malaysia's new tourist islands where, as entrepreneurs, they sought business opportunities in tourism, and, as tourists, to the Philippines and Thailand, where my informants, like me, were eager to understand where Malaysia fitted in with the other cultures and economies of Southeast Asia. Everywhere we went, however, we talked mostly about that subject in which both they and I were deeply interested: business and entrepreneurship in modern life. There was nearly no context in which this subject ceased to hold interest or failed to elucidate a point or an idea about the modern world which my informants and I shared.

In time, I became increasingly interested in several particular ventures which seemed characteristic of the various kinds of entrepreneurship in which my informants were engaged. While many businesses I talked about with entrepreneurs were small, flexible ventures set up to capture quickly a perceived opportunity, or were businesses still in the ideational phase, I sharpened my focus on several new businesses – these were established businesses, a year or so old, well beyond the drawing-board stage, in the sense that they had already been capitalized, registered with the government, and so on. The enterprises I focused on had been formed with the injection of government or private capital, and consisted of several large manufacturing concerns, as well as enterprises which represented the non-industrial sector into which much *bumiputera* private capital is flowing: real estate, insurance, tourism, advertising, publishing, communication, and consultancies. (These, of course, were the Malay businesses I could not see when I arrived at Chinese New Year; indeed, the single-proprietor, street-level, old-fashioned retail trade remains in the hands of the Chinese. Malay entrepreneurs are dismissive of it.) Some of the men and women who engaged in these businesses became my closest entrepreneurial informants and friends; I ultimately became the tenant of one of them; and, some of them even became – more 'winks' upon 'winks' – 'clients' of my own self-styled 'entrepreneurship', as I will now explain.

THE ENTREPRENEURIAL STRATEGY AND IDENTITY OF THE ANTHROPOLOGIST

In each of these closely studied cases of entrepreneurship, my increased participation in the businesses and the lives of their participants was granted as an agreed-upon exchange for 'services' which I offered. I spent a great deal of time talking about and describing kinds of marketing, advertising, and 'corporate image' strategies to my informants, topics in which they were very sophisticated, but activities they were confused in executing. This ability to talk about business and marketing, not merely in general, but in specific detail, made me valuable – indeed, an entrepreneurial resource in Malay networks (see Chapter 5). Over the course of my year-and-a-half in Malaysia, I performed several actual 'jobs' for my informants, such as writing advertising copy and producing corporate brochures, thinking up logo designs, company names, and marketing campaigns, and inventing and formalizing business plans my informants used in hope of obtaining government or bank loans.

The international marketing 'language' of entrepreneurship and capitalism which appears in corporate brochures and advertising copy was one I had already mastered professionally on Wall Street; when my informants learned of my background and agreed to let me help them produce such things with them, they explicitly asked for me to write in what they called 'American style'. Indeed, I once found myself in the peculiar position of sending fax messages to New York, asking an old colleague to send me a supply of glossy brochures I had once written. My informants wished to see them, and, with my help, model theirs fully upon mine, momentarily bridging the two cultures of entrepreneurship.

Yet the ultimate ease of my successful and rapid entry into Malay entrepreneurial society was, I believe, determined by the sheer importance of the subject of entrepreneurship to my informants. I was, first and foremost, interested in the subject that interested them most. With my own background in business, I was not only good to talk to and a good resource; my appearance in their lives was also a validating sign of how far they had come in entrepreneurial development: *they saw themselves as good for me to talk to*. That an anthropologist from Oxford with a Wall Street background of her own would come to study how they were organizing themselves into entrepreneurial businesses was an on-going source of pride and interest to my friends and informants; one more sign that they had, indeed, become fully fledged entrepreneurs. This perception of my identity as an 'expert' and an 'analyst' of entrepreneurship opened many doors for me, until I had the privilege of belonging to and having value in the society I had come to study.

But this experience wound back upon itself in curious ways. At one level, I was engaged in 'entrepreneurship', dabbling in my own form of 'business' and validation, earning rights of participation and access through reciprocity. At another level, the way in which adopting a role as 'analyst' allowed me access into other sources of understanding and meaning in Malay culture, into far-reaching social and business networks, into personal events and public ones, into homes and corporate offices, was not very different from what all anthropologists do, themselves entrepreneurs of a kind – networking, building social alliances, earning status, bridging and transacting in multiple spheres of cultural exchange (cf. Stewart 1991). Indeed, this set of anthropological activities matches a definition for entrepreneurship which Barth first elaborated (1967). Another layered set of 'winks' seemed to emerge.

Finally, as this book will show, through 'winks' of ideas, identities, roles, and meanings, theirs and mine, I came, in time, to understand the highly social nature and theory of Malay entrepreneurship. My close involvement in and contribution to their entrepreneurial projects became crucial to understanding what was happening in the vast social networks of affect and information which characterize Malay entrepreneurial society and Malay society in general. In these overlapping and ever-ramifying social relations which I was drawn into, in the constant conversations and group debates about business and development, in the endless episodes of people and ventures intertwined with risk and profit, the image of a con-joined Malay society of modernity and its theory of cohesion and commu-nal obligation – what my informants said distinguished it from Western societies – became profoundly real to me, ultimately allowing me to repre-sent them in this analysis primarily as they represented themselves to me, as modern, moral, Muslim, and fully Malay.

My analysis attempts to show how a certain group of educated, cos-mopolitan, middle- and upper-middle-class Malays demonstrate the ways in which the late-twentieth-century experience of accelerated social and economic change has become meaningful and validating to them. The process by which moral obligation to others, hard work, and Islamic faith have become symbolized together in economic activities which are at once 'modern' and 'Malay', and are demonstrated by 'entrepreneurship', is the subject of Part I, which I present under the rubric of 'Good Works'. By exploring the theme of 'good works' in Malay life, I attempt to show how entrepreneurship has become the main vector of ethnic, religious, and moral worth and a test of virtue and modernity among the beneficiaries of NEP.

In Chapter 2, I explore the complex themes of Islamic duty and financial obligation which enframe Malay life in relationships with parents, spouses, cohorts, and the communal group. I establish that Malay social arrangements are bound, represented, and shaped by the expressly *material* performance of duty.

In Chapter 3, I explore the crucial, self-consciously 'modern' redefinitions of Islamic economic beliefs and meanings which have shaped the Malay understanding of entrepreneurship and human agency. Focusing upon several individual stories of eschatological and economic self-development, I examine the ways in which a Muslim world-view establishes balanced definitions of self-interest and group interest and clarifies the culture of social and moral entailments in which my informants operate.

In Chapter 4, I explore 'Malayness' through the descriptions of cultural uniqueness my informants – and their government – were elaborating for and preserving in modern Malay and Malaysian life. I focus on the ideals of Malay 'hospitality', 'openness', 'generosity', and 'egalitarianism' – the cornerstones of 'Malayness' in establishing ritual harmony, but also in confirming roles of power in a hierarchical society. I examine the belief my informants had that they were preserving – often through entrepreneurship – traditions and values from the Malay past through a futuristic government-supported programme for capitalist modernity called 'Vision 2020'. Invented by the Prime Minister, this paradigm established how traditional Malay Muslim virtues could serve the modern, civil needs of the citizenry of the multi-ethnic nation. Summing up, in Part I, we begin to see how entrepreneurship implied to my informants an Islamic development process which could reveal key, group-orientated moral and traditional behaviours – the material demonstration of 'good works' – until Malay entrepreneurs see themselves acting not just for themselves, but for all Malays and the Malaysian society.

Part II, presented under the rubric of 'Networks', is an attempt to elucidate how my informants sought to enact their understanding of Malay economic modernity and entrepreneurship – that is, how they infuse their altruistic image of 'good works' into economic and social action. In Chapter 5, I describe the way in which networks and relationships form in Kuala Lumpur society, often in the context of lavish banquets among members of the NEP cohort, but as frequently in the open, casual settings of night-time food stalls. I explore the ways in which social arrangements give eidetic form to the theory of shared and conjoined economic development ('good works') which my informants were elaborating as an entrepreneurial demonstration of 'Malayness' and their responsibilities to others; I describe, too, the ways in which social life can be manipulated in pursuit of economic results.

The next three chapters are case studies of entrepreneurial networking and the entrepreneurial objectives of three of the enterprises I knew best. Chapter 6 describes how alliances form among Malay entrepreneurs, often as a consequence of the way in which the government represents modern economic opportunity and enterprise to Malays. I explore the expectations my informants had of one another and of their ventures in pursuing such opportunities, and the often disappointing returns that their swiftly formed alliances brought.

Chapter 7 continues the discussion of the role of networking in social and economic life, examining the consequences of achieving a high profile for one female entrepreneur in Kuala Lumpur. I describe the positive effects of networking used for building alliances, but also the *negative* effects of networking – when gossip and rumours of sorcery are used by network participants to diminish the identity of an entrepreneur who is thought to be dangerously self-interested, indeed, not Islamic at all. I suggest that these consequences are often experienced by autonomous women in Malay entrepreneurial society, who induce a certain cultural ambivalence about the true source of their powers.

In Chapter 8, I examine an entrepreneurial venture which harnessed its very existence to the role of Malay networks, to the point at which 'networking' became the primary purpose – indeed, the product – of the enterprise itself. I relate these to other forms of Malay action which explicitly use social relations for economic ends, and how this strategy has become increasingly concatenated to the Malay theory of 'good works'.

In the Conclusion, I attempt to draw together my ideas about Malay entrepreneurship. I discuss the crucial role of entrepreneurship in establishing and legitimizing Malay identity and representing Malay ideals of morality, egalitarianism, harmony, and tradition in the contexts of rapid social and economic change. I show that through its seemingly endless incorporativeness, through the enmeshing of material and affective ties in networks, Malay entrepreneurship, to its actors, symbolizes diminished eliteness and Malay classlessness, and implies openness, shared power, and free access to opportunity. I describe what I learned from my informants as a *Malay* theory of entrepreneurship, one which locates Malay entrepreneurs in their local culture, validates the pro-Malay policies of NEP, and connects Malay development to a global culture of capitalism. Then, I elucidate *my* theory of Malay entrepreneurship. I describe the way in which entrepreneurship tends to confirm, determine the gender of, and politicize Malay eliteness, at the same time that it elides these consequences, closing out many of the entrepreneurs who will be met in the pages of this book, and, moreover, denies the crucial role of the state in creating and supporting its high-level entrepreneurs – some of whom also will be met here.

2 Obligation and Identity: Parents, Spouses, Siblings, and Malays

Rokiah and her business partner, Ishak – two ambitious Malay entrepreneurs – had been searching for an entrepreneurial venture for their new company when Arif, Rokiah's cousin, called her with exciting news.[1] 'We are going to make a lot of money', he announced. 'I have been developing a business I want you to share in. Please meet me tonight to discuss this project, but *you must keep it top secret!*'

Rokiah was inspired by his enthusiasm, and, after dinner, she and I went to meet Arif at the outdoor food stalls near his house – one of the many locations in Kuala Lumpur where people gather at night to drink tea, socialize, and discuss business. Rokiah was my closest friend, and often included me in her social and family life and business dealings; Arif already knew me well and had said I was welcome to come along. Perhaps I, too, could offer my help. We found Arif at one of the popular Muslim food stalls under the dim light of electric bulbs strung on wires through the trees, the sound and smell of cooking food surrounding us. Dramatically, Arif pushed his chair away from the rest of the evening crowd, and whispered conspiratorially, 'I have an idea which only a few people can know about, because it is so valuable. I want the two of you to hear it. Once it is produced, thousands of people will want it'. He waited while Rokiah and I moved our chairs closer to his. With quiet pride, he told us his entrepreneurial idea: 'I am inventing a children's board game, like Scrabble or Monopoly, which will teach children how to speak and write better English. We will sell it to every school and to every parent – there is no limit to how much money we can make because the idea practically sells itself. No Malay parents will want their children to be without it'. He told us that he had been secretly developing this game for several years, thinking of nothing else, even when he was at his job as a manager for another company. He sorrowfully admitted he had spent little time with his wife and family because of the hours spent thinking up this project and discussing it with a few trusted confidants, but soon his loved ones would be rewarded, with money and recognition, by his efforts.

19

Complimenting Rokiah on her own recent successful ventures, Arif said he now needed both her business acumen and capital, as well as her contacts in business and government circles, which he knew were good. In return for her help, he said, Rokiah could profit handsomely. Arif promised to give us all the precise details the next day, in Rokiah's office. She told him she always explored new business ventures with her business partner, Ishak, and asked if Arif would mind Ishak's presence. She portrayed Ishak as deeply interested in helping other Malays develop their businesses and full of good business ideas himself, thereby justifying his participation, which Arif readily accepted.

As we returned to her home, Rokiah told me she was pleased Arif had come to her for help, not just for money, and how he had demonstrated his respect for her business knowledge and contacts. Rokiah had an extensive network of friends and associates in the Malay business and political sectors. Already successful in a real-estate business, bright, educated, and ambitious, Rokiah was increasingly spoken of as a model Malay businesswoman. As a consequence, more and more people were seeking her out for information and alliance, a fact of which she was quite proud, and also honoured. The next morning, as we read the daily newspaper over breakfast in a local coffee shop, she discovered an article which said the Malaysian government was going to encourage greater use of English among Malay students, who were falling behind Chinese students in their English exam results.[2] She became very excited, and described the fortuitous timing of Arif's request for help as a sign from Allah. She believed that as she searched for meaningful entrepreneurial ventures for her business, she would be shown good ones and bad ones, and prayed that Allah would tell her the difference. This one, she thought, was already demonstrating itself to be a good idea. Could this be the opportunity Rokiah and her partner Ishak had been looking for?

Arif came as planned to Rokiah's office, and was introduced to Ishak. We went into the conference room for what Ishak called a 'brainstorming session'. Often I joined them in such meetings, when they discussed potential projects with other ambitious Malays in their social or business networks. Delineating their shared qualities, Arif began, 'Like you, I am an entrepreneur. Entrepreneurs must have an honest and deep desire to want something for themselves, and to want to help others. Like you, I have been improved by my education and economic development. Like you, Allah and the government have given me the knowledge and the chance to improve other Malays – this is our duty'. He mentioned the article which had appeared in the newspaper as additional proof of the validity and apt timing of his entrepreneurial mission.

'My idea', he continued, 'is to produce an educational game, similar to Scrabble. But it is much more than Scrabble, because instead of just creating words, players create whole sentences, learning grammar along the way'. He wrote terms rapidly on the chalk-board – 'word chips', 'game board', 'grammar manual', 'picture guide', and so on, explaining each component of his idea enthusiastically. 'Children will pull word chips out of a bag; each chip will have a word on it; the words can be placed on the board and made into sentences'. He told us that the game would not only teach words and grammar, but, because the players would 'barter' for chips, it would teach something equally crucial: children can learn *business* this way. 'Can you see', he explained, 'how it teaches competitiveness in an atmosphere of good will?' He pointed out, 'These are the same values the government wants to teach Malays. It teaches Malay children to earn, to learn, and to grow with others'. Then he described how the same government-valorized benefits would accrue to the Malay entrepreneurs who, along with him, invested in and produced the game. 'We will make so much money', he explained, because 'as a child's language ability grows, parents will have to buy more advanced "game phases". The money will flow in as the children get smarter and smarter'. Books and newsletters could be sold along with the game, eventually even computer-based games. The varieties of business opportunities opened up by this single venture could be limitless, he speculated, as Malay children became ever more sophisticated in their educational and technological needs. I could tell by watching Rokiah's and Ishak's faces that they felt Arif's idea was a convincing one.

Solemnly he said, 'I want the very first game that is manufactured to go right to Prime Minister Mahathir, and ...' he paused dramatically, 'I want to call it "EG2020" to stand for "Educational Game 2020"'. Rokiah and Ishak nodded enthusiastically, for this important-sounding name echoed a major plan for the social and economic development of Malaysia which the Prime Minister himself had recently introduced.[3] 'Then', he continued, 'with the Prime Minister's blessing, we'll have open access to every government minister and every educational facility in the country'.

These were familiar themes in the actual or planning-stage business ideas I had heard from many of my entrepreneurially ambitious Malay informants. Arif, like many Malays, expressed his business idea in terms of a sense of duty and dedication to other Malays and to their social and economic development. Themes of self- and group improvement, ethnicity, obligation, religiosity, and even a kind of soldierly patriotism wound through his narrative (cf. Biggart 1989). He made clear how much he had already sacrificed to reach this point, infusing into his work an even

deeper sense of urgency and commitment. Not only did the effort he
had already put into the game he called EG2020 reflect important modern
economic values which the government extolled and he himself had
already attained, but the game would also teach those same ideas to other
Malays – things like 'competitiveness' and 'business'. Beyond that, the
game would open doors to government offices – even the Prime Minister's
– and be recognized as a national resource for Malay change and economic development. EG2020 was, to him, a seamlessly perfect construction
of entrepreneurial means and ends – a formula he had devised for other
Malays to reproduce and gain from his experience, a formula to turn his
private interests into group gain.

Arif, like many of my informants, insisted that making money was only
part of what concerned a Malay entrepreneur; an equally important challenge was to improve others. Inviting his cousin Rokiah and then Ishak to
share in his venture, he made it clear that he wanted them to share in these
ideals and his profits, not just because he needed their money, but because
he perceived them to be equally committed to such values. Indeed, the
decorous emphasis he gave to asserting their shared interests and values
was not merely polite, it was a claim of significant cultural distinctiveness, of a shared world-view, as we shall soon see.

Fully convinced of its merit, the three of them quickly turned the discussion into what Ishak had hoped it would be, a strategic 'brainstorming'
session about who they could access in their multiplex networks for
support, how they could advance and pursue its multiple spin-off business
ventures. Perhaps, they said with excited laughter, we will become famous
as educational visionaries and Malay entrepreneurial leaders, for, as as
will become increasingly clear, they wished to be not merely private
profit-seekers but also exemplary public figures committed to a form of
public service.

Considering an idea for an entrepreneurial business which was introduced to Rokiah and Ishak, we have an initial sense of the social, economic, and moral dynamics of entrepreneurship and duty in the lives of the
Malay men and women I knew, people who saw themselves as agents of
change and modernity. Like most entrepreneurial ideas I tracked, EG2020
was to gather much participatory social steam as it went along, gaining
creative, strategic offers of help and suggestions from various interested
people who knew this government minister or that manufacturer, before
finally dying out from lack of commitment and capital. But before it did,
Arif, Rokiah, Ishak, and others who shared in the 'secret' venture were
convinced that through an enterprise given the futuristic, slogan-echoing

name EG2020, they could, somewhat oxymoronically, achieve profitable ends for both themselves and for all Malays.

ENTREPRENEURSHIP AS DUTY AND IDENTITY

A Malay man or woman seeking to demonstrate entrepreneurial capacity paints, as did Arif, a full, rich portrait of how entrepreneurship, however self-interested, serves, in actuality or symbolically, other Malays, often conveying in the image of individual success the multiplicity of success and opportunity for all. As we shall see, this valorized image of develop-ment took much of its power from the directives of the state, as well as from crucial Islamic ideals. But entrepreneurship is not merely about service and obligation, the terms in which my informants (and their gov-ernment) most often construed it; it is about self-validation and a key to the construction of modern Malay identity. It represents, to its protago-nists, a most crucial membership.

As entrepreneurs with important social and national goals pointed at the future, my informants sought to identify themselves with members of a select Malay status group[4] – often called *Melayu baru* or new Malays by government ministers and business leaders. 'New Malays' are represented as newly ambitious and newly professional – *korporat* Malays, united even with the most elite among them as members of a new social category, a morally attuned Muslim generation of leaders of a social, economic, and moral revolution, as concerned for the welfare of their whole ethnic group as they are for their own. Entrepreneurship among the *Melayu baru* blurs material self-interest and socially embedded affect until they are often indistinguishable from each other.[5] But similarly indistinguishable threads of moral and financial duty weave throughout Malay family life, Malay married life, and contemporary Malay society as a whole. As we will begin to see in this chapter, the emotional relationships framing Malay lives are everywhere constructed in terms of substantial material form, reflecting Malay attitudes towards money and its value in defining affec-tive relations. Malay relationships can (and in Malay perception should be) measured, documented, and remuneratively compared. While modern life and economic development promise great returns to entrepreneurially ambitious new Malays, great, too, is their sense of duty to somehow share the material benefits of development with others. One cannot take lightly such claims as Arif's, which demonstrated a doubled motive of material self-interest and the performance of a substantial duty.

ESTABLISHING OBLIGATION IN THE ARENA OF FAMILY DUTY

The performance of duty is referred to by Malays as *wajib* – obligatory in *adat* (Malay customary practices) and in Islam – and thus established by tremendous, indisputable social and moral force. No other arena is defined as clearly in Malay life by the terms of *wajib* or obligation than that of one's natal family. In demonstrating familial duty, Malays claim to manifest everything they wish to be, never autonomous and ever other-centred – performing endless, sacrificial action on behalf of another to whom measurable respect and devotion must be shown. While familial duty can theoretically be ignored, to do so is a moral crime, and Malay Muslims can state quite clearly what happens in hell to men and women who do not perform required duties on behalf of their parents.

Again and again, when asked about duties and responsibilities, my informants told me that the most crucial obligation was the one established at birth; the demanding reciprocal terms of this gift of life are inescapable for its value is immeasurable. The one relationship that is bound by what was *wajib* and honoured above all others, even before the relationship of self to God, is that of the child to the mother.[6] Indeed, in illustration of this, I was often told the story of the man who came to Muhammad and asked, 'O Messenger of Allah, who are the persons who have the greatest right on me with regards to kindness and attention?' The Prophet replied, 'Your mother'. 'Then who?' 'Your mother'. 'Then who?' 'Your mother'. 'Then who?' 'Your father'. Defined by the Prophet to an exponent of three, such supplication and recognition only begins to clarify the acute sense of duty Malays bestow upon mothers and, as will be seen later on, upon the blessings of origin in general. We can begin to understand the force of affect and control (Kondo 1990) mothers hold over adult children, for, as the story below demonstrates, those who have the ability to sustain life also have the instrumental, if not terrifying, power to take it away.

THE DEBT OWED TO MOTHERS: THE STORY OF *SI-TENGGANG*

Often when I asked my informants to tell me about their duties to their mothers, they mentioned the story of *Si-Tenggang*, an old folk tale that every Malay child is told. (It now appears in picture-book form.) The story is about a very poor woman and her son who have no rice to eat. The mother struggles to grow potatoes, and with these, is able to feed her son. When there is extra, she herself eats. But the boy, who is good and uncomplaining, just as Malay children should be, thrives on his meagre meals and grows up quite happily, becoming strong and handsome. When he is a man, he tells his mother he is going off to make a fortune ('A Malay entrepreneur!' my friend, Rokiah, said when she first told me the story). Many years pass, and he does make a fortune, with gold and treasures of all kinds, which he puts in a great palace that is built for him near the poor village where he grew up. One day, the mother learns that her son is living in the palace nearby, and she comes to see him, bringing his favourite food, potatoes. The son, seeing her, is angry, and shouts, 'She isn't my mother! I would never have a mother like her, dressed in rags and carrying a dish of potatoes!' He refuses to see her and she is led, weeping, out of the palace. The mother stumbles off in grief, not fully believing that this man is really her son. In prayer, she begs Allah to tell her if truly he is her son. 'If he is', she cries, 'then let him be turned into stone!' At that instant, the son turns to stone, to remain that way forever, a statue in his own palace.

According to the folk story, a mother's powers to bestow blessings and security are so great that she can raise a strong and capable son even when he has been given very little to eat (and, conversely, that her grief upon betrayal can destroy blessings and security). What is thus *wajib* – obligatory – in the nature of maternal–child relations, as my Malay informants understand it, implies that in return for being sustained so well – in effect, for being given the maternal gift of life itself – a child, upon reaching maturity, must accept the primary moral obligation of adulthood, that is, to return the gift (cf. Li 1989). Having fed and nurtured a child materially and immaterially, and, as Malays see it, at considerable sacrifice, a mother's appetite for recognition and supplication is deservedly profound. Malay Muslim tradition establishes the indisputability of her claim over grown children. Obviously it is not enough for a child to have earned riches and status; in fact, these, the story shows, become useless to a man who cannot even return to his mother the gifts he has been given. Malay entrepreneur or not, *Si-Tenggang* does not belong in the Malay world.

When my informants insisted their mothers had 'given everything' to them, it underscored the Malay belief that an all-consuming 'giving' is the measurable symbol of love (Banks 1983: 131). My informants' description of maternal 'giving' in traditional Malay childhood was surprising to my ears, as childlike behaviour, the learning of self-control over desire, is regulated primarily through maternal punishment, coercion, threats, and the often painful withdrawal of privileges. In the childhood memories of my informants, by the time they were schooling, their conduct was guided by rigid maternal expectations and the compendium of rules that equalled those in Islam: when to rise and when to sleep, how to eat rice, how to dress, how to bathe, how to sit, how to address others. Standards of conduct and rules of deportment were lessons well enforced and even foredoomed by the bamboo switch or *rotan* nearby, which their mothers readily and daily used. Prayer, school, play, Quran lessons, prayer, chores, studying, are represented as obligatory items on every Malay child's schedule and of which all my informants' lives were nearly identically, repetitively, and rhythmically comprised (Wazir Jahan Karim 1992), to the point at which adult Malays describe themselves as having had a nearly collective and interchangeable childhood, an idea which will be returned to later on. And while fathers were remembered for coming home every day from a government office for lunch, prayer, a short sleep, and perhaps an enquiry about the child's school-work, it was invariably the Malay mother who maintained what is remembered as the enormous control over the lessons of life, school, and Islam that every adult child remembers learning and for which he or she is obligated to express eternal and material gratitude.

THE MATERIAL PERFORMANCE OF DUTY

The men and women I came to know in Kuala Lumpur now generally live at a distance from their parents and the close 'familialized' community of their childhoods. Today, parents, grandparents, aunts, and uncles left behind are often marginalized by distance and difference from life in the city, and except for their role in providing meaning to holidays, life-cycle events like birth, death, and marriage, and in crises in their children's lives like divorce and separation, much of the reality of the interaction between adult children living far from home and parents is often relegated to and framed by financial arrangements.

To be a grown-up son or daughter far away in Kuala Lumpur does not imply any lessening of what is *wajib*, the obligations of deference and respect owed to parents, and, in fact, if the affective value placed on monetary representations of family duty is any indication, the sheer materiality of the debt that adult children owe to parents is becoming ever more costly. In the competitive environment of NEP, the demonstrable proof of the value of the bond between sons and mothers and daughters and mothers, no longer tied by contiguity, is cemented by economic value. NEP has fuelled the sense that a grown, economically successful, high-status adult child owes parents objects of increasingly greater monetary worth, often far beyond the actual material requirements of the parents' lives. Although the government under Prime Minister Mahathir generally represents the Malay obsession with status-based consumption as the result of a Western conspiracy, at the same time, the overwhelming focus of pro-Malay policies during the NEP period has been primarily on Malay ownership of assets. This cannot be dismissed as an important factor in the obvious Malay tendency to symbolize economic ascendency and status through the idiom of material goods (Jackson 1979), a material tendency which is already culturally framed by terms of familial duty. Enforced by the bonds of what is *wajib*, the sense of owing something – an ever greater debt that must be paid off with ever more valuable goods – holds significant power over the men and women I knew.

My landlady, Aziza, who owned a thriving travel agency, was a typical example of the way in which increasingly affluent Malays provide material support to their parents. She, like many of my informants, gave her parents a fixed monthly amount, but also, in bursts of affection and sacrifice, sent home unanticipated luxuries and treasures that her parents would have never purchased for themselves. Aziza took great pride in seeing herself as profoundly generous, supplying her mother and father with a seemingly endless flow of goods and modern luxury items, as did her siblings. Capitalizing on the dutiful emotions of childhood, Aziza's mother had requested that her adult children pay for the renovation of the parental home so she could easily and publicly demonstrate how much her children had achieved, an obligation the children were happy to satisfy. Aziza and her siblings demonstrated this successful identity in Kuala Lumpur; the parents, although far away from Kuala Lumpur, logically sought to benefit from their children's identity, too. When I last saw Aziza's parents' house before I left Malaysia, it was already substantially changed; the ubiquitous balustrades, blue roof, and a tiled patio had been added, and a huge cement wall with an enormous electronic gate surrounded the property, renovations which had been paid for by Aziza and her siblings.

While these dutiful demonstrations of both familial loyalty and success are readily and happily fulfilled, they also generate a certain amount of conflict, for the social and emotional costs of affluence, along with much greater expectations of what life should deliver, are quite high. Economic success may have empowered Malay men and women (and, vicariously, their parents) in ethnic and status-group terms, and sharply refined their abilities to perform material duty to others, but it has not done so without upsetting some of the traditional and domestic premises of their lives. This especially affects the relationship between married men and women and the obligatory duties they perform on behalf of each other, duties with different dimensions and implications than those performed on behalf of parents, as will be discussed below. The measurable role of money in the affective relationships between spouses is as great as it is between parents and adult children, but it appears also to be a source of much greater ambivalence.

THE CONFLICTING OBLIGATIONS OF CONSANGUINEOUS AND CONJUGAL DUTY

My first poignant experience of how money and what is *wajib* can require conflicting obligations to parents and spouses occurred when I joined my Malay friends – unmarried Asma and her married brother Din – driving from Kuala Lumpur to Ipoh. This was the small city in which they had grown up and where their parents still lived. It was the day before Hari Raya Haji, the Muslim holiday honouring pilgrims to Mecca. What made this journey 'home' complicated was that Din was spending the holiday in Ipoh with *his* parents; back in Kuala Lumpur, his wife and children were spending it at the home of *her* parents. Din was visiting his parents as if he were a single and childless man. He explained that his wife, Fauziah, a bank manager, 'doesn't get along with' his mother, 'so we had to come up with a "modern" arrangement to solve the problem. At holidays, she goes to her family, I go to mine'. In Ipoh, I asked Din's mother if she missed seeing Fauziah and the children. On the contrary, and much to my surprise, she told me that the daughter-in-law was no longer welcome in her home. Her lips white with rage, she told me why. She claimed that because Din had done so well in his business, Fauziah wanted more of his money for herself and therefore had tried to prevent Din's mother from getting more money from him. She claimed Fauziah was turning Din against her, blocking her access to him and the children. The mother-in-law and daughter-in-law had simply stopped speaking to each other. Din, guilty and troubled, was sending greater amounts of money to his mother to prove his affection to her, to a point where Fauziah reported he had 'impoverished' her and the children. There were dark reports in the family that the marriage would not last. While the 'modern' accommodation to the affinal conflict – Din and Fauziah visiting family separately – was unusual, the disjuncture in the conjugal relationship was more than common.

For men and women, far from their parental homes, the pull of loyalty and duty is still so intense that sometimes, as with Din and Fauziah, the conjugal tie seems weaker than the consanguineous tie (Carsten 1989). Women feel they compete with their in-laws for their husbands' attention and money and vice versa. When wives object to the intensity of the pull in-laws have on their husbands, they usually claim husbands give 'too much' money to them. When men claim to have no more money to give wives, they often state that they were 'obligated' to give money to their parents or that they have given more to wives than Muslim men are minimally required to, and consider the subject closed. These are clues to the complex religious and customary ideas which wind around the subjects of money, affect, and obligation in contemporary Malay marriage. The men and women I knew believed that marriage had provided solace, security, and comfort to their parents; today, they said that was not true. Both sides claimed that this had resulted from changing terms of conjugal obligation and duty, terms both material and instrumental. Both sides claimed this had consequences for their interests in money, entrepreneurship, and economic autonomy, as we will see. Perhaps most importantly for understanding the dimensions of affect in the married lives of Malays in the NEP generation, whatever the source (or resolution) of conflict in marriage, it was most often couched in financial terms.

CHANGING PATTERNS AND EXPECTATIONS IN MALAY MUSLIM MARRIAGES

In the past, a potential bridegroom's choices of whom to marry expressed ideas of a woman's social refinements and personal attributes – that she be soft-spoken, fair skinned, religious, and accomplished in home-making skills (Ong 1987). I first learned the somewhat outdated, commodifying language of valued female attributes when my landlady Aziza showed me an old photograph of her mother at the age of 14. She pointed out how fair her mother was, and said her '*puteh* [white] skin, soft hands, and her long hair and *halus* [refined] expression' were enough to start very strategic marriage negotiations between her mother's parents and the man who would become Aziza's father, who had a prestigious and promising job as a clerk in the state financial office. Aziza's mother was believed to be distantly descended from a Dutch relative, the source of her much-prized fairness and a valued social asset. For 'traditional people', Aziza said, this was an obvious and excellent match, with much to gain on both sides. In a society in which access to other people's networks often determined the success of one's own social and economic strategies, marriage – which established new alignments within and across hierarchically arranged communities – played an important role among the socially and politically ambitious (S. Husin Ali 1975, 1984; Wilder 1982). Status-based marriages were actively pursued among the pre-Independence era civil-service class (Khasnor Johan 1984), much in the same way as alliances with royal lines had been pursued before them (A. Kahar Bador 1973), and, as I will show in later chapters, just as business and networking alliances are today pursued feverishly among the Malay entrepreneurial group. In fact, it could be said that networking alliances today are believed to have the same potential rewards as a 'good match' did a generation ago.

Among the Malay men and women I knew in Kuala Lumpur, the nature of selecting a partner has changed from their parents' day. No longer are marriages arranged by parents.[7] Men and women who have benefited most from NEP education policies generally freely choose and endogamously marry each other. Potential spouses now meet at university or in corporate offices, or are introduced by mutual friends. The importance of a good match based on the modern commodifying language of educational and economic attributes is made clear to anyone who attends a wedding between two such products of NEP education policy. Guests are treated to a long, impressive recitation of the university and career achievements of both, when what Malays call a 'biodata', a *curriculum vitae*, is read loudly into a microphone during the *bersanding* or blessing of the marriage.

While Malay men and women are making their own choices about whom to marry within essentially non-negotiable modern status and ethnic norms, they also marry later than their own parents did, a source of some parental concern.[8] Men who remain single are reminded by their mothers to not put off too long the choice of a wife, and single women are warned to not be too choosy about a potential husband (Carsten 1989). Mothers – as well as the Islamic religious authorities in Kuala Lumpur, who see independent women living in cities and towns in terms of a potential moral crisis (Ong 1987) – are alarmed by the rising incidence of unmarried daughters. While demographic studies show that a rising age of marriage in Malaysia is associated with increased education, urbanization, and freedom in spouse selection (Jones 1994), there is a feeling among unmarried daughters – and also among the daughters themselves – that single women are doing something to prevent themselves from being married.

Many modern, independent Malay women are said to have increasingly loose morals, making it easy for men to remain unmarried, a view which some women share with their mothers and Muslim religious leaders. A well-connected Malay businesswoman whom I asked for introductions to other Malay women entrepreneurs warned me about 'false' women entrepreneurs, that 'new breed of single Malay women who do anything to get to the top', including exploiting men's sexual needs for their own financial ones. It is in men's nature to take advantage of women, but a perversion when women take sexual advantage of men, she claimed. The sexual and financial autonomy potentially available to Malay women in modern life holds a sharp contrast with what is said to be their traditional Islamic role. Let us look now at that ideal definition.

WAJIB AND MARITAL DUTY

In Islam, the relationship of what is *wajib* or obligatory between husband and wife is ruled by the principle of *bagi nafkah* (literally, the part distributed for sustenance), which obligates the Muslim husband to provide for the maintenance of his wife and children. This is a symbol of his identity as a Muslim and an adult male; it also underscores the Islamic belief that he is responsible for his wife materially and morally, a commitment symbolized in a marriage contract when he pays her the dowry or *mahr*. The dowry is a symbol of his ability to 'shoulder and discharge the economic responsibilities' of marriage (Raja Rohana Raja Mamat 1991: 59). He must – it is *wajib* and established by the Quran – provide for her basic needs, giving her and their offspring food, housing, and clothing (Li 1989); these things are her measurable rights as a wife.

In return, a Muslim woman must serve her husband's needs sexually, bear his children, obey him, respect him, and follow the laws of Islam. A marriage becomes, then, a kind of rational bargain between a man and his wife; he provides support, she owes him obedience and obeisance. The Malay Muslim wife must behave in accordance with her domestic role as 'queen of the house' where she, according to the Prophet, 'is answerable for the conduct of her duties' (Yusof Ismail 1994: 17). If she does not, the husband can claim that she is recalcitrant or *nusyuz*.

A recalcitrant wife is one who disobeys her husband's command to provide him with sexual access to her, refuses to pray or to fast, or leaves the house without his permission unless, as the Quran graphically puts it, the roof caves in on her. Recalcitrance on the part of the wife 'implies that she does not keep her side of the marriage bargain which is to obey her husband', crimes which include 'not cooking for him and visiting other people's houses including her own parents' without his permission' (Sharifah Zaleha Syed Hassan 1986: 192). A recalcitrant wife forfeits the rights she earns in marriage – that is, to receive his on-going maintenance and protection. Furthermore, it is said that a good wife does her marital duty with a smile, because she knows this duty is *wajib* in Allah's eyes, and to serve the husband is to serve Allah. One woman told me that a woman is always to remember that she is the grateful servant to the husband. 'Even if she has just gotten home from work as the director of a corporation, she must be his servant. She carries his coffee on a tray, all the while thinking, "*pahala* ... *pahala*" (good deeds counted up on Judgment Day) with each step, because it is her *kewajipan* (a duty)'. Even though my informant admitted performing this duty reluctantly, like a sullen servant and not with a smile, she knew she had no choice in the matter. Feelings do not particularly matter in marriage, she said grimly, and happiness comes ultimately from pleasing Allah, not one's husband. Time and again, I saw one of my vivacious, dynamic, outspoken female informants become stony-faced and submissive upon crossing the threshold of her house, a transformation in identity from autonomous entrepreneur to servile wife to which I never became fully acclimatized.

In Islamic Malaysia, marriage is explicitly not what Schneider (1980) found it to be in America, comprised of immaterial and diffuse notions of love. It is, on the contrary, as in Muslim marriages in general, an 'explicitly contractual affair' (Rosen 1984: 82) about expressly material things, a finite series of ideas, duties, or responsibilities which every Malay would be able to list. This material dimension was made clear to me when Salbiah, the very successful owner of a security business, told me how the very day she got a lucrative government contract she went to the *kadi* or judge to plea for a divorce and was summarily awarded one, because her husband had not worked since she began her business. 'I worked; he was the layabout', she told me. 'A husband buys the food, clothes you and the children, gives you a house. *He* was not the Muslim husband – *I* was'. To Salbiah and the *kadi*, a Muslim man ceases to be a husband when he neglects the financial obligations of marriage. (Women are also entitled to sexual fulfilment from their husbands and can theoretically seek a divorce on grounds of sexual dissatisfaction. To further prove her husband was not a man, Salbiah emphasized that he was sexually inadequate as well.) For many women, like Salbiah, as we shall soon see, the resolution of marriage conflicts – both financial and emotional – was to come from seeking wealth of their own, as well as the public status and identity which that activity could ideally confer. Before examining the various dimensions of modern Malay women's economic pursuits, however, we must look briefly at the subject of financial autonomy, which has been said to characterize Malay women's lives well before the policies of NEP educated some Malay women for high-level economic participation.

THE HANDLING OF MONEY AND THE STATUS OF MALAY WOMEN

The first modern analyses of the roles of Malay women were conducted by Rosemary Firth (1943) and Judith Djamour (1959). Both described a remarkable degree of social and economic independence among Malay women who, while still subject to a certain amount of control by the social order and Islam, were found to be largely self-directed in the realm of the market and household financial management. Among contemporary Malay communities as far apart as rural Langkawi in the north (Carsten 1989) and urban Singapore in the south (Li 1989), recent research has shown that Malay household expenditure and savings, as Firth and Djamour first noted, is still largely in the hands of women. Theories in feminist anthropology which examine the importance and value of women as evidenced by economic participation seek to elucidate a kind of structural balance and gender complementarity in traditional Southeast Asian societies. The Malaysian case holds much theoretical interest for analysts, who see Malay society as perhaps the first case study in feminist economics (Stivens 1992). Following a gender-balancing feminist framework,[9] some analysts explain that money, earned by Malay men who often work in competitive contexts, symbolizes self-interest and potential exploitation of others, and therefore has disruptive effects on Malay social norms and kin-based community interests. Malay women, more at the symbolic core of social exchange and affective relations than men, by handling money, diminish its socially discordant effects; that is, they 'socialize' it, imbuing it with their more egalitarian, communal spirit (Carsten 1989: 132; McAllister 1990).

These generalized views on the valued and mediating role of women in Malay social and economic relations contrast with the theoretical position of other contemporary researchers in the Southeast Asian context, who argue that women handle and manage money not because they symbolize important social norms or exist in balanced domains of value, but because they are socially lesser than men. Alexander (1994) showed that in Indonesia men, whose social identity is constructed on their practice of refined or *halus* behaviours, relegate rough, *kasar* behaviour – the indisputable mode of the marketplace – to women. As such, men simply stay away from money because it is socially discordant. Filtering it through women's hands does not make it less so; in fact, it roughens women. Because it is socially dangerous, men devalue cash as unclean, and assign the whole dirty business of domestic financial management to women (Stirrat 1989).

Both sides of the polemical debate about why and when women handle money in Southeast Asian societies must be held against the matter-of-fact reality of the connection among money, autonomy, and power in Malay life.[10] Money has long been a means for representing power and control in Malay society, ideas generated in the very nature of hierarchical relationships. Hierarchical dominance – not just symbolic balance – is also part of the Malay cultural inheritance, and is frequently and vividly represented between husband and wife, among consanguineous and affinal kin (S. Husin Ali 1975), and in the circles of economic and political influence generated in the Malay community (Bailey 1976; Mokhzani 1965; Roff 1967; Shamsul A.B. 1986a). Indeed, money does not merely frame affective relations or make them demonstrably real, as Malays believe; nor does it neatly balance them, as some ethnographers believe. *Because money is so closely identified with status and identity in Malay culture, it also establishes and confers power.*

I knew of no marriages among my Malay informants which reflected traditional patterns described by Firth, Djamour, or contemporary ones described by Li and Carsten in which men simply handed over all their money and wages to their wives. Furthermore, despite the widespread ethnographic evidence, I was puzzled to learn that there were no marriages in my informants' parents' generation in which this had been true. Men today, and, as my interviews showed, their civil-servant fathers before them, give a *portion* of their earnings to women, as established by the *wajib* terms of *bagi nafkah*. Women in my informants' mothers' generation also maintained their own private store of savings established by dowry, inheritance, or work, just as they do today.

Djamour noted that in situations where a Malay man made an irregular income, as a shopkeeper would, he tended to hand over his weekly receipts to his wife in full. But in cases where the man earned a regular wage (*makan gaji*), he kept it and doled out weekly fixed amounts to his wife, who rarely knew how much he actually made (1959: 42), a pattern which matches my findings among all the contemporary Malays I knew in Kuala Lumpur (and their parents). Djamour did not offer an explanation for this difference she discovered between wage-earners and non-wage-earners, which I maintain reveals unexplored status issues in her otherwise remarkable study, and underscores the possibility that evidence of financial independence among Malay women – or more specifically, a gender balance elucidated from it – may have been overgeneralized.

Money in Malay life does not just have cash value, an economic symbol, it has social value and therefore significant implications for the status and primacy of its possessor. Salaried men were civil servants who had

significant cultural importance and authority in the Malay community
Djamour studied in Singapore in the 1940s, just as *korporat* professionals
and entrepreneurs in Kuala Lumpur do today. For them, salaried money
was more than the source of daily survival and not the rice-barrel-scraping
household management burden that poorer or rural men relegated to their
wives, but an achieved symbol of power and autonomy in the Malay social
hierarchy (cf. Nagata 1975). A man would not likely then or today hand
over any excess to his wife, but would use it for his own social and economic ambitions and objectives, as a means of what Siegel calls the conversion of money into the symbolic 'idiom of status' (1986: 168). This
is precisely what the Malay men among my informants did with the
money they did not give to their wives; they used it to advance their own
autonomous interests, purchasing material goods and status items, paying
the high price of a country-club membership, or often investing in one or
another entrepreneurial business or venture. Successful women, it will be
shown, often used their own money for precisely the same status-
orientated purposes, but not without generating a certain social distrust. As
such, I suggest that the more status a man had (and has), the more he might
use his money to demonstrate power, including the power he holds over
the interests of others. Women, however, may not be free to do the same.

Having and handling money does not generally appear to provide the
Malay wives I knew with a satisfying sense of equality or power; more
often it is a source of increased conflict with their husbands, and an
increased ambivalence about their mutual roles.

WORKING WOMEN AND WOMEN'S WORK

Among my informants, the educated elite beneficiaries of NEP, the standards of moral censure since the rise of Islamic fundamentalism in the
early 1980s – a subject which will be returned to in Chapter 3 – have
weighed less heavily than they have upon factory women (Ong 1987),
impressionable university students (Zainah Anwar 1987), and clerks in
government offices (Muzzafar 1987). Malay professional women in my
circle of close informants did not feel much restraint in conducting business with men; they often moved freely among men, sharing meals and
socializing with them with relatively few limitations. Damage to a
woman's social reputation could frequently be averted by using certain
techniques like engaging in group activities rather than in mixed-sex pairs.
Rokiah benefited from my on-going interest in her business dealings
because, by inviting me along, she could avoid potential gossip when she

spent an evening socializing with businessmen and male friends at the local food stalls.

My female informants, English-educated beneficiaries of government-sponsored tertiary education, the daughters of civil-servant parents who stressed Malay advancement and socialized them for achievement, insisted that, like men, they had a certain ethnic, moral, and religious obligation to contribute to Malay economic development. While NEP established modern women's role outside the home by providing the daughters of the previous generation of government-policy beneficiaries with substantial, high-level educational and career opportunities,[11] perceived crises of industrialized modernity, however, threaten to redefine that role.

The near-obsession with 'backward' Malay childrearing skills in villages (Mahathir Mohamad 1970), common in the early days of NEP, has been transformed, in modern Kuala Lumpur, into moral panics about the vulnerability of urban Malay children to modern, Western dangers. Endless examples of Malay 'backsliding' appeared in my fieldnotes. The *lepak* (hanging out) crisis in 1993, in which Malay teenagers were observed in aimless, unsupervised, and unIslamic activity in Kuala Lumpur's shopping malls was succeeded (and exceeded) by the promiscuity crisis in 1994 involving adolescent Malay *boh sia* girls (Hokkien for 'no sound' because they reportedly 'said nothing' when picked up by men in Kuala Lumpur's dark streets to dispense sexual favours for money). Both were represented in the media as Western-influenced crises of Malay family values. Newspaper editors and government ministers placed the burden of responsibility on absent and increasingly unIslamic parents who were neglecting the duties of Malay parenthood. But as Islam itself relegates the primary parenting role to women, it was often working mothers who were most to blame for neglecting their duties.

Islamic officials have carefully pointed out that women work only at the discretion of men; for them, women's work is a privilege and certainly not a right. If a wife's work proves to harm the husband or children in any way, the husband, my male and female informants both agreed, can demand she stop immediately, as it is known that her primary role is preservation of the family. The majority of men and women I spoke to generally believe that ideally the wife's place is in the home, with the children, looking after her family's 'needs and wants'. But modern life is far from ideal. When I spoke to married couples together, they agreed that the best situation would be for the wife to stay home, but that the reality of domestic economics simply prevailed over that wish. All of my informants, except for the most wealthy, claimed that both parents had to work in order to maintain the material lifestyle that modernization required. All

Malay parents expressed concerns about school fees, extra lessons for their children, house renovations, and car payments, and claimed that women work by unfortunate necessity; at the same time, they worry about the increasing lack of supervision and control they have over their children. Despite the lack of time they spend in the home (often, time spent in the nightly food stalls, discussing entrepreneurship), men often blame any behaviour or school problem seen among their children upon their wives, and, in return, women blame it upon their overwhelming responsibilities which involve contributing to the household income *and* handling all domestic responsibilities.

In contrast to the theory of *bagi nafkah*, which states that the husband's duty to support his wife frees the wife from any financial obligation to support the husband or the household, working women now often contribute substantially to household expenses. In most families I knew, however, men and women did not pool their money; a joint checking account into which both put all their earnings is almost unheard of in Malay marriages. When a major expenditure is planned, such as furniture or a home renovation, some men and women negotiate whose money will be spent and in what proportion. For many women, these negotiations seem unfair. In dozens of conversations held in the *absence* of husbands, women I knew said they contribute too much to the household, and often wondered what their husbands do with all the money envisaged to be in men's private bank accounts, imagining men are sending most of their money to their mothers, or worse, supporting a girlfriend or even a second wife. Men claim their money is none of women's business. Women I knew said they deserved social and economic freedoms that men did not want to give them, and were suspicious and jealous of the freedoms men gave themselves. Men claimed women no longer understood or performed their uncomplaining, supplicating role as Islamic wives and were in no position to repudiate men's domestic demands, for whatever Muslim women do beyond the performance of wifely duties, whatever autonomous economic and entrepreneurial interests they may aspire to have, men said, it is at men's largesse.

Malay wives often want to work to ensure that they are not too dependent upon men who fulfil what is *wajib*, the minimal obligations of marriage, but who, in all likelihood, according to women, cannot be trusted or relied upon beyond that. Rather than a satisfying demonstration of their social value and autonomy evidenced by handling and earning their own money, today, some Malay women told me, their financial independence is a painful necessity, and that without it, they are foredoomed by the independence and power of men.

FEAR OF DIVORCE AND THE NEO-TRADITIONAL PARADOX OF POLYGAMY

The issue of not being a good Islamic wife, of being *nusyuz* or recalcitrant, is more complicated than a woman's moral fear of neglecting the *wajib* duties of Islamic wifery. A modern Malay wife perhaps has, as did many of my informants, a very real fear – greater than her mother ever did – of her husband divorcing her or taking a second wife. Divorce is easy for Muslim men, and, as will be shown below, polygamy, among the *nouveaux riches*, has become increasingly associated with male economic success.

We shall look first at divorce in Malay life. The Islamic Religious Department, Pusat Agama Islam, believes there has been a significant rise in the rate of Malay divorce, suggesting that divorce among Malays is a very recent, suddenly urgent problem, a problem of urbanity and modernization and Malay maladjustment to rapid change. An alarming report appeared in a Malay-language newspaper demonstrating a 100 per cent rise in divorce in Kuala Lumpur since 1991 (*Berita Harian*, 5 March 1993). The article stated that Western-style materialism, financial pressures, and a lack of basic Islamic education were to blame. Statistics prove otherwise. Various reports from the past show that nearly half of all Malay marriages ended in divorce, and one census shows a remarkable divorce rate of 92.7 per cent in 1940 in the Malayan state of Perlis (Azizah Kassim 1984). In the classic studies of traditional Malay communities, Malay marriages have always been described as unstable, and both analysts and Malay women alike have said that Malay women have always had considerable freedom to seek divorces from their husbands (Djamour 1959; Firth 1943), more evidence of their so-called independence from men.

Divorce is and always has been common among Malays, but it is actually *decreasing* among the well-educated. In the middle- and upper-middle-class neighbourhood of Petaling Jaya, near Kuala Lumpur, divorces were shown to be steadily declining in the early 1980s. Among the well-to-do Malays, it was established that women would generally tolerate an unhappy marriage or a husband's infidelity because they feared that with divorce their standard of living would drop markedly (Azizah Kassim 1984). Divorce is harder when more things – houses with mortgages, furniture, cars – are at stake (ibid.), as the settlement and maintenance provision of Islamic Family Law in Malaysia does not clearly provide for distribution of property or assets accumulated by the husband alone. Beyond that, the assessment of maintenance to be paid by a Muslim man is generally quite low. Moreover, a divorce awarded to a man who can prove his wife is *nusyuz* does not entail payment of any maintenance at all. As such, women I knew felt bound to their marriages for economic reasons, as they correctly believe that without their husbands the requirements for material abundance and the experience of affluence which help define their modern Malay identity will disappear. The only woman I knew in Malaysia who had actually sought a divorce was the woman entrepreneur described earlier who referred to herself as a 'Muslim husband'. She knew, of all the married women I interviewed, that she could sustain the material lifestyle which she was used to, because she herself had provided it.

Just as the financial expectations and requirements of modern life help sustain women in what they feel are unsatisfactory marriages, modern images of affluence – and their power to attract desirable, socially ambitious women – often lead men towards second wives. Malay women accept polygamy because it is economically advantageous to do so (Strange 1981), whereas divorce is clearly disadvantageous. Polygamy, relatively uncommon in traditional Malay communities and in the generation of my informants' parents, is newly legitimized and significantly on the rise among 'new Malays'. Many successful, ambitious, entrepreneurially active, modern Malay men, by establishing a new definition of the appropriate balance between traditional Islam and modernization, have found in polygamy a way to be both Muslim and modern in a changing world.

A polygamous man, according to Muslim law, must ensure that he can support his wives and children adequately and equitably, hence, a man who can afford several wives obviously demonstrates his substantial affluence. Many Malay men I spoke to claimed that with polygamy they could express both religiosity and the sincerity of their Islamic social responsibility. Men explained to me that the Prophet Muhammad married more than one wife, and, while taking another wife is not obligatory, *wajib*, it is always recommended to do as the Prophet did, and thus some feel they should choose to follow the example of the Prophet's *sunnah* (actions and revelations) through polygamy.[12] Furthermore, because of the widespread belief that men are adulterous by nature, Malay men claim and women concede that Islam *protects* women by sanctioning polygamy. Increasingly, the argument is made that, through polygamy, Islam provides for conditions of sexual morality rather than allowing, as do Western cultures, abuses of it, and as such, it is often held up as a demonstration of Muslim superiority in human relations (Muhammad Imran 1979).

The complex themes of entitlement and conflict between modern men and women that polygamy elicits are illustrated by the case of a young businessman I knew, Jamil. Jamil was married to a woman who had become a successful doctor. He had received a business degree from a local college and then obtained a job in the shipping office of a large company. Soon, like many young and ambitious Malay men, he quit that job to become an 'entrepreneur', and to explore independent ventures that might make him rich. His search for business ideas had led him to meet with other entrepreneurs, and he began going out late every night. If his wife expressed anger, he told her it was her *kewajipan* (a duty) to do what he said 'without questioning it; that is the Muslim law' and demanded her silence. Despite his on-going threats about her recalcitrance, he claimed she was going out at night with her friends, leaving the children alone with the maid. With a look of both pride and shame on his face, one day Jamil told me that instead of looking for business opportunities, he had started to go to night clubs where he claimed he had seduced three different women in one week. I asked him if it was right for him to expect his wife to act in the obligatory Muslim way when he did not. Jamil admitted that his unhappiness with his lack of entrepreneurial success and the pressure on him to be more successful than his wife made him act weakly, as a man sometimes does. 'When she does not perform tasks which are *wajib* and fulfil her role, I am unable to concentrate on my work. When she makes more money than I do, then I am lonely and unhappy, and I look for companionship'. Jamil agreed that his search for freedom from his wife and sexual solace from other women was an infraction of Muslim law but certainly was understandable and forgivable, given the greater crime of his wife's disobedience. His wife, by being *nusyuz*, paradoxically gave him tacit permission to stray, just as the potentially legitimizing force of polygamy and the innate sexuality of men gave him – and the women he said he slept with – vague permission to commit *zina* or adultery. Such loose Malay women, Jamil said, knew he *might* marry them, which is why he claimed they agreed to sleep with him.

THE ECONOMIC ZEAL OF MODERN MALAY WOMEN

If polygamy establishes the potential freedom of modern, educated, economically ambitious Malay men, it symbolizes a corresponding freedom for modern, educated, economically ambitious Malay women. Married women claim, often in moments of frustration or restraint placed upon them by husbands who limit their social and economic freedoms, that they wish their husbands would take on a second wife and simply disappear. Often, the fear of a husband taking on a second wife fades, replaced by feelings of self-determination in which women say they pursue entrepreneurial activity to prove they do not need their husbands to provide them with respect or status.

My jaded, married female informants sometimes wished for the benefits of marriage without the hindrances – this is how they often characterized polygamy. 'Being a "first wife" is better than divorce', one woman said, 'especially if you don't want your husband around but you want to keep his money. The Muslim law says you don't give anything up'. Unmarried women claim to want the bungalow and the material status symbols that to them are associated with being elite second wives. Polygamy, one woman told me, 'is a real option among modern women; it allows you to reach a higher level of wealth ... to have an arrangement in which you keep your independence, your job, and get a BMW, a better house, and better clothes than you could give yourself'. Gullick (1987) suggests that in the traditional Malay past, polygamy, always equated with male wealth and status, was also a marker of female independence – of assertive, respected women controlling property and people. These cultural concepts, in somewhat shifted contexts, may still be true today.

Thus, when some of her jaded, married friends told my nearly 40-year-old, entrepreneurially ambitious, unmarried friend Rokiah *not* to pray for a husband and others comforted her with the possibility that she still could easily be the second wife of a rich man instead of staying a spinster, they were expressing, on the one hand, views about the increasingly fractious sense of what marriage produces and on the other, the relation of a good marriage, especially a modern polygamous one, to economic success. Both views, however paradoxically, expressed the notion that it is not in *marriage* that most women will find satisfaction, but in economic validation and in the freedom to engage in unfettered economic activity. A good husband is one who, usually pursuing economic (or sexual) activities of his own, allows his wife freedom, or a polgynous husband, best envisaged as a Dato or even a Tan Sri (the Malaysian equivalent of Sir and Lord, honorifics bestowed respectively by the Sultan and the King) who can provide access to increasingly lucrative social and business opportunities. To many of my Malay female informants, only a naïve and innocent girl would dream of romance and love from a man; a practical woman with entrepreneurial ambition dreams of charity dinners and high-level business contacts, the rewards of networking at the very top of society. Among my female informants, the disappointment and disenchantment with modern marriage is easily overcome if the return is freedom to participate in the booming entrepreneurial economy.

The Malay Muslim definition of marriage as a material relationship may have deep roots in traditional Malay Muslim culture, but the image of modernity, religiosity, and the social value of financial independence in the NEP era has thrown into dramatic focus the issue of economics as the central theme of the domestic relations between modern, educated Malay men and women – just as it has between adult children and their parents. In Part II, we will return to the subject of women's economic power in contemporary Malay life and what happens when Malay women truly do become autonomous. The social consequences can be striking, as will become clearer later on.

I have suggested that entrepreneurship today has profound implications for modern identity and status in Malay society, and therefore is important, for somewhat different reasons, to men and women alike. But neither men nor women represent economic success in terms of status achievement. *Both men and women look towards entrepreneurship to validate and represent their modern sense of ethnic duty and obligation.* While domestic relations between married men and women may be fractious, social and economic life competitive and even ruthless, and consumption levels strategically demonstrable, through economic activity and participation men and women alike publicly claim to establish a deeply felt sense of kinship with and 'connectedness' to others in the Malay community, the theme with which I opened this chapter. Below, we will consider how my informants saw themselves in relation to others within the larger community of Malays, contrasting it first with a theory of Malay social relations which established community identity in the past.

SIBLINGS AND SOCIAL RELATIONS IN MALAY COMMUNITY LIFE

Many studies of Malay social relations in traditional communities rest on a kinship model, evidenced to researchers by the widespread supra-genealogical use of basic Malay consanguinal terms (Banks 1983). By using generational ('auntie', 'uncle') and sibling ('sister', 'brother') terms for non-kin, Malays are said to establish affective and behavioural norms for relationships throughout their entire community and beyond it, to the extent that some researchers believe Malay society as a whole is organized by an overriding moral principle of classificatory 'siblingship' (McKinley 1981).

Schneider (1980) pointed out, however, that kinship terms do not actually determine what the affective content of our real relationship to others will be, and despite claims Malays (and ethnographers) make that they treat 'everyone' like brothers and sisters, it often turns out that in real sibling groups they follow that principle least of all. In reality, there was often little affection among actual siblings in the families of many of my informants. Indeed, these relationships were often fraught with issues of financial competition, memories of past injustice, inequities in perceptions of parental love, and almost brutal jealousy. Moreover, this does not appear to be only a contemporary problem. My informants' parents made frequent references to past family crises within their own sibling groups, old stories about stolen land and misused capital which obviously still had such emotional power that they could not be told without a very contemporary feeling of anger. Anyone trying to map out family relations in Malay families would find, as I did, that real siblings are excluded from family histories as frequently as fictive ones are brought in.[13]

In the lives of my informants in Kuala Lumpur, sibling conflicts were sometimes on-going crises which hit at the very core of a man or woman's sense of identity and self-validation in the modern economy. An example of this is the entrepreneur we met at the beginning of this chapter, Arif. Arif's two brothers were extremely successful entrepreneurs with grand homes and imported cars, and, once, Arif revealed to me that he 'wanted to die' because his brothers 'lorded' their success over him. He insisted that his brothers had actually prevented him from succeeding because of their negative views of him, almost like a form of contagious magic. When Arif announced EG2020 to his cousin Rokiah and other people in his network, he made it clear that he would not include his brothers in his lucrative scheme, adding that he was no longer on speaking terms with them. McKinley noted that ties between brothers, who are expected to show age-ranked respect and deference to each other, are nearly always a source of tremendous tension (1975), and, as such, Malay brothers generally avoid economic relations of any kind,[14] while fraternal tension is mediated by brother–sister and sister–sister bonds (1981).

Yet, contrary to the harmony McKinley found in male–female sibling relations, conflict has seeped into these relations as well. If money and competitiveness was a source of tension between Malay brothers in the past, as it also often is in the present, between economically active brothers and sisters, financial arrangements are rapidly becoming a new arena of sibling disharmony and pressure. Some of my women informants had actually stopped speaking to their financially successful brothers whom they felt had not sent enough money home each month to their parents, echoing the marital theme that women inevitably feel they contribute more to domestic finances than their husbands. Sister–sister conflicts were also common among my more competitive informants. The sisters of Aisha, the women entrepreneur we will come to know well in Part II, complained that she had stopped sending money home because she was spending all her money on her own ambitions. Worse yet, there were rumours in the family that she had coercively sold some of her mother's land to capitalize her enterprise, an act, in the land-based terms of traditional Malay society, almost tantamount to matricide. As Malay women's roles become increasingly instrumental, their relationships with brothers and sisters, formerly only *affective*, are often profoundly altered, becoming, as was demonstrated in relations with their husbands, sources of conflict and cleavage.

If a principle of 'siblingship' is valid in contemporary Malay life – which I shall attempt to show it is, but in a less concrete and more ethnic-ized form – it does not, as McKinley suspected, reflect *real* sibling rela-tionships as much as it justifies and establishes affect in the pursuit of *social* and *instrumental* ones. Perhaps Malays did precisely the same thing when, in traditional settings, they used sibling terms for non-kin, for as other researchers have noted, it was precisely these deliberately constructed relationships which were used for negotiating and mediating in intra- and extra-village circles of political and economic influence (Bailey 1976; Wilder 1982). While they no longer use siblingship terms outside the family and village circle, Malays use feelings of *ethnic* 'connectedness' to establish valuable social and economic ties in the vast community of Kuala Lumpur and to confirm a sense of mutual obligation and entailment; this, as will be shown in Part II, is the very cornerstone of entrepreneurial activity. Indeed, the Malay 'kinship model', elucidated by field research in traditional communities, in which everyone, especially people in one's own generation, is symbolized as 'connected' in net-works, is increasingly recapitulated – if not intensified – as an emphatic moral and ideological symbol in the lives of modern, urban Malay entre-preneurs. When entrepreneurs such as Arif speak of a 'duty' to other Malays and expect other Malays, as he did Rokiah and Ishak, to feel a reciprocal duty to help him, he is providing heart-felt evidence of this ethnic connection.

Urban Malays may no longer represent themselves as classificatory siblings, yet demonstrate a belief that the Malay ethnic group is an imag-ined, extended family, an inevitable consequence of the symbolic con-struction of 'race' as an exaggerated form of kinship (Yoshino 1992). Indeed, many of my informants claimed that 'All Malays share the same blood'. What factors help to establish this modern Malay sense of wide-spread connectedness?

THE SOCIAL CONNECTEDNESS OF THE NEP GENERATION

A very small linguistic key unlocks evidence of a complex shift in social identity among the NEP generation. In their social and professional circles, my informants did not use the elder sibling–younger sibling terms of fictive 'siblingship' which, in the past, established social connectivity in Malay communities and maintained tacit hierarchy. Nor, perhaps more significantly, did they use the formal *Bahasa* terms of address which exemplify rigid social-rank positions among all but the most informal of speakers (S. Husin Ali 1975). Instead, they generally and consciously used the English words 'I' and 'you', even when speaking *Bahasa*. ('I *belanja* you' or 'I'll treat you' is an often-heard phrase among networking entrepreneurs in the nightly food stalls.) These are terms of social equality, used or sought even with the most important of people. For many of my informants, their use represented a deliberate trend toward 'modern relationships' among people in the NEP generation, who had first learned these terms in school.

An example of this 'modernity' was a friend of mine who worked in the Ministry of Education and boasted that she was on close terms with Deputy Prime Minister Anwar Ibrahim from the days when he was Minister of Education – she was 'I/you' with him, as she put it. When Ong (1987) heard factory women in Malaysia using 'I/you' terms she saw it as evidence of a Westernizing trend toward self-individuation and the erosion of a communalistic spirit among Malays. I had a different response to the same terms used among my informants. In my observation, the use of the familiar and English terms 'I/you' implied that the Malay men and women I knew were increasingly choosing to escape from or impugn the implications of unequal social relationships. 'Modern' Malay relationships, as Rokiah always breezily reminded me, are much more informal and simple than they were in the village. 'I/you' signals a new communal spirit among new Malays.

New Malays or members of the NEP community, like a cohort, have been conditioned by shared experiences – socialized for elite roles by civil-service parents; educated for modern lifestyles by a rigid, English-style educational experience which generally hand-picked privileged children for success and handicapped the rest; abruptly transformed by overseas or local university experiences; channelled into economic participation into one or another 'modern' course of study or diploma programme; and rewarded with sponsored opportunities for increased legitimacy and power, or at least promises of it, in the modern economic system. Despite these socially differentiating experiences, my informants increasingly represented themselves as highly bound by affective ties to the entire Malay ethnic group, eliding their obvious differences in status and power both from those Malays who have been left behind by development and from those who have been advantaged even more significantly than they.

My informants insisted they would always 'help another Malay' (or, more accurately, help *each other* out – *tolong-menolong*), underscoring their sense that economic modernization is a conjoined, dutiful activity, undertaken with and on behalf of the group. But belonging to a group has other important implications. Like the most elite members of the famous old-school-ties network described below, many of my informants proudly described themselves as able to access nearly every important Malay in Malaysia, a statement that implied they were connected and on nearly equal footing – 'I/you' – to even the most powerful Malay corporate and political leaders. This connectivity was also deeply suggested by their experience that wherever they went – from a food stall to a formal charity dinner – my informants inevitably met someone they already knew, what social psychologists call the 'small-world' phenomenon of urban life (which, of course, is really a class-based phenomenon), making the circle of affect seem very tight. These experiences have a profound impact on the importance of social networks in the lives of Malay entrepreneurs, as we shall soon see.

PARADIGMS OF NETWORKING: MCKK AS THE META-COHORT

No NEP-era beneficiaries in Malaysia are perhaps better known, more influential, and more emulated than the Malay College Kuala Kangsar, or MCKK, cohort, which Malays themselves call an 'old-boys' network'. The MCKK name has always connoted a special status as the colonial-era boarding school for sultans' sons; its distinction today is more a result of its elite alumni list, for the Malay College Old Boys Association (MCOBA) is virtually coterminous with the Malay corporate, entrepreneurial, and political elite.[15] It is the 1970s MCKK cohort, young men in their early forties, many now in positions of enormous corporate power, whom my most ambitious Malay informants sometimes feverishly pursued as the focus of particularly dramatic networking attempts at an entrepreneurial alliance. It is also these elite and politically connected men who have been selected as primary beneficiaries of the huge NEP-era privatization programmes in Malaysia (Gomez 1994), and as a result, in the increasingly elite construction of entrepreneurship, have become known as its leaders and paradigms. One of my informants from this group, Dato Hassan, called himself 'the Henry Ford and Rockefeller of Malaysia'. As paradigms of entrepreneurship, these millionaires believe that their particular interests both represent and serve the interests of all Malays. Dato Hassan's entrepreneurial ideology will be closely examined in Chapter 3. For now, it is important to note how deeply connected to other Malays these elite leaders see themselves and claim to be, and the cohesive affect this has on social relations in contemporary Malay society.

Partly a result of the typical and often traumatic English-style boarding-school experience upon which MCKK was modelled, MCKK men I spoke to perceive themselves to be joined like 'brothers' who have been through a rite of passage tantamount to a rebirth, symbolized by experiences of disintegration and synthesis. They describe not just an awareness of past shared experiences, but a moral duty to *continue* to share them. The key ideal that MCKK represents to entrepreneurially ambitious Malays is the widespread belief that MCKK men experience their *social* bond through generously shared *economic* opportunities. Thus, other networking groups I observed among my somewhat less-well-placed informants were consciously modelled after this feature of the MCKK cohort. Formal networking groups in the NEP cohort such as the women's entrepreneurial group Peniagawati and the men's entrepreneurial group PERSUMA thus openly established or manufactured social bonds of loyalty and group interest based on Malay ethnic and economic ambition.

My informants eagerly joined in such networking organizations for the express purpose of establishing social relationships with other Malays to whom they wished to be bound, expecting to benefit significantly and richly from such contacts, just like the MCKK 'old boys' did. The logical and obvious purpose of associating with other Malays in such social settings (cf. Biggart 1989 and Cohen 1981) is thus claimed by my informants to be for advancing the purposes of Malay 'entrepreneurship' and demonstrating moral bonds in achieving economic development.

What is the source of this enormous conviction that one Malay should and will always help another? Beyond the shared experiences and shared ambitions, what helps establish the sense of ethnic duty and connectedness claimed within the NEP cohort? Why are entrepreneurs in Malay economic life so devoted to the idea of mutual obligation and group loyalty? These questions require a careful analysis of both religious identity and the Malay sense of cultural inheritance, subjects of later chapters. Before that, however, we must address the ethnic concepts with which my informants painted the broad outlines of their cultural identity.

ESTABLISHING SYMBOLIC BOUNDARIES AROUND 'MALAYNESS'

A sense of 'Malayness' is created as much by Malays attempting to define and uphold was is perceived to be uniquely 'Malay', a subject which will be explored in a later chapter, as it is by defining (and casting out) what it is not, that is, that which exists *outside* the moral bounds of Malayness. 'Malayness' is not purely constructed out of a Muslim identity. On the contrary, Muslims in Malaysia who are not Malays – such as Indian, Arab, Filipino, Thai, Bangladeshi, and Indonesian Muslims – are often not perceived to be 'genuine Muslims', and as a consequence, are generally held outside the boundaries of Malay amity and affect.[16] Privately, such marginal Muslims are often the subject of scorn and distrust (Hussin Mutalib 1990). Amir, my friend, exemplified this notion perfectly. Looking carefully at the modestly covered heads of young waitresses in an Indian Muslim restaurant, he claimed to recognize them as street-corner prostitutes he had seen in the notorious Chow Kit district of Kuala Lumpur. Many of my other informants insisted that Indian Muslims drink and gamble, just like the Chinese, but give the appearance of piety only to bring in Malay customers. Hypocrites (*munafik*) are the worst Muslims, my informants would mutter at Indian Muslim merchants whom they suspected were trying to cheat them.

Another powerful example of this casting-out phenomenon among Malay Muslims occurred on a national level during my fieldwork when the government invited Bosnian refugees to seek shelter in Malaysia. Despite being brought to Malaysia in 1992 amidst great fanfare to symbolize the depth of pan-Islamic spirit of the Malays, the Bosnians were soon seen by many of my informants as very marginal Muslims, were secretly called *pacat* (leeches), and were increasingly blamed for unacceptable behaviour as guests in their hosts' country. Male Bosnian students were accused *sotto voce* of raping a Malay woman at the Islamic University, in a kind of reverse cathexis of the crimes being committed against Muslim women in Bosnia. Bosnian women were said to be seen in discos in Kuala Lumpur, dancing freely as no Muslim women should. In my household, Aziza carefully watched television coverage of the Bosnian war, but often only to remark that she never actually saw a mosque in pictures of Sarajevo. She doubted the Bosnians ever actually prayed; and soon a rumour travelled through various Kuala Lumpur networks that Allah was actually punishing the once-successful Bosnians with the war for being lapsed Muslims, a potent reminder that Malay Muslims should not forget the role of faith in their own economic development.

The huge influx to Malaysia of legal and illegal Indonesian and Bangladeshi workers,[17] many of them Muslims, justified by the state's claim of a labour shortage (Guinness 1992), has led to an increasing distrust of and even disgust for these Muslims as well, who are said to have imported to Malaysia social ills which Malays do not perceive to exist within their own boundaries: child and wife abuse, AIDS, drugs, and crime. Often, such 'outsiders' are brought by necessity into Malay homes as maids. While my female informants claimed to treat Indonesian maids well, 'like a sister' most said, and even used *kak–adek* (elder sister–younger sister) siblingship terms of address with them, maids none the less frequently run away from Malay homes, some reporting physical and emotional abuse. One Malay woman told me that in one year alone, three Indonesian maids had run away from her house. She insisted that she was never strict or hard on these women, yet they rarely had a day off. She explained, 'Given such freedom, they will run away, drink alcohol, become pregnant, steal from us, even steal our clothes and our cars'. Although the maids are Muslim, speak *Bahasa Indonesia*, nearly identical to *Bahasa Melayu*, and are called 'sister', they remain social outsiders, with social, sexual, and moral behaviours that are claimed to erode Malay norms.

Around such Muslim outsiders, Malays tighten the construction of Malay community. But despite their frequency, these demonstrations of social marginality within the Muslim community are insignificant in the lives of Malays I knew; by contrast, it is in relation to the Chinese – social and economic outsiders representing a threat of such brute force – that many Malays turn the screws of ethnic identification and connectedness ever more tightly.

ECONOMIC OUTSIDERS

One of the primary goals in the early NEP 'national unity' campaign (Tan Chee Beng 1984) was to separate the identification of race with geography or urban/rural space. In the 1970s, in the rapid Malay urbanization of Kuala Lumpur and its surroundings, the structural boundaries separating the races were indeed blurred. Quotas were established to ensure that new communities reflected a blended racial make-up.

Yet, over time, in the housing estates of Kuala Lumpur, despite efforts to integrate the various ethnic groups, people 'continue to reside in traditionally racially segregated areas in most parts of the city' (Mohd. Razali Agus 1992: 47). Taman Tun Dr Ismail, the community in which I lived, was generally thought of as a 'Malay' area. Much of Petaling Jaya is known as 'Chinese', with discrete pockets said to be 'mostly Malay'. But in suburbs which appear to be well integrated, there is very little social interaction across ethnic lines, and none in the night-time food stalls, which, partly as a consequence of Islamic food prohibitions, are isolated from one another – Malays at one end; Chinese, far away at the other. Moreover, many Chinese business people congregate in places where alcohol is available, such as pubs and lounges where Muslims would be loath to go. Private space is sharply demarcated as well. Although there were several Chinese families along our street, Malay families did not seek out connections with them. No conversation passed across the fence that marked off the shared boundary of a Chinese yard and a Malay yard.

Much has been written about the ethnic riot which exploded in Kuala Lumpur on 13 May 1969, its consequences in Malaysian constitutional history (see, for example, Clutterbuck 1985; Comber 1983; Means 1991), and how it was used to legitimize the economic interventions of NEP (Shamsul A.B. 1986a). It is not my intention here to review those events or those before it, such as colonial relations between the British and the Chinese, or the treatment of the Chinese since or during the Chinese Emergency, in which many Chinese were forcibly resettled into 'new villages' with the intent to isolate them, a practice which may have actually contributed to what Malays compete with them for most, their superior urbanity, connections, and economic modernity.[18] My intent is to show that the watershed symbol of 13 May 1969 established to most of my informants the sense that all Malays had been victimized by the Chinese, an idea that was already becoming deeply entrenched in policy strategy well before the violence broke out (Jesudason 1989). This haunting sense of having been victimized as a group is so profound that Malays who emerge as entrepreneurial successes matter-of-factly and ingenuously refer to their individual material accumulation and sectional interests as benefiting *all* Malays, a claim so often and so vigorously stated that it cannot be critiqued as a mere ruse.

My informants spoke of that famous date – during which most of them were barely teenagers and, of all of them, none was even living in Kuala Lumpur – as a moment in which all Malays realized together that they had been living in a kind of innocence, like children in a *kampung* (village) idyll, and yet deeply at risk. One woman told me:

We never thought about the difference between Chinese and Malay in the *kampung*. We thought they were our friends but we were just like children, so trusting. We didn't know what we know now. But suddenly, in 1969, we learned we were behind. You began to have the feeling they would take something away from you. Maybe they already had. Malays then were too stupid to know. We didn't really know what had happened in Kuala Lumpur, but what you heard was that the Chinese were attacking Malays. We thought they would come to get us next.

While the Chinese are constantly accused, in private, of continuing to victimize, cheat, and exploit the less advanced Malay economic actor, they are, on the other hand, admired as a source of ideas for establishing the modern Malay entrepreneurial identity. The overseas Chinese are believed throughout Southeast Asia to be somehow temperamentally, organizationally, or culturally better suited for business (Mackie 1976) and better at economic self-development because of their 'frugality, self-reliance, venturesomeness, and skill' (Skinner 1963: 98). Many of my Malay informants had incorporated a kind of Weberian social-science view of Chinese business success and claimed that Muslims had mistakenly believed that Islam eschews accumulation, whereas Confucianism extols it. As I will explain in Chapter 3, many Malays have attempted to rethink the relationship between Islam and wealth in such a way that making money is represented as what Allah wishes for them; and if not, having it is certainly better than giving it to the Chinese.

The Chinese, my informants widely believed, closed Malays out of their Chinese networks for hundreds of years. Now, my informants claimed, Malays must do the same. Malays spoke about 'Chinese secret societies' and 'kin associations' with envy and distrust, claiming that these bonds of loyalty, true to the death, were what had made the Chinese rich in Malaysia. Malays, they said, must establish such loyalty among themselves. The enormous interest in creating associations and organizations among Malays I knew was thus part of a conscious effort to be more like the Chinese, to use affective relations in instrumental ways much more than they felt they had in the past.

To exemplify the exclusionary 'ethnopreneurial' power of new Malay economic activity, I shall return briefly to the story of Arif's entrepreneurial idea, EG2020. This will illustrate an example of how my friends Rokiah and Ishak resisted including a Chinese businessman in their plans for this enterprise. After that, we will be better able finally to evaluate the power of Malay entrepreneurship's inclusionary ideology.

PLANNING THE VENTURE, EG2020

After Arif announced the important name 'EG2020' for his product, he revealed, somewhat apologetically, that his financial partner was a Chinese. Rokiah and Ishak shook their heads. Rokiah in the past had told me how disappointed she was in Malay entrepreneurs who, following an unfortunate historical example, partnered with Chinese[19] and often ended up being exploited by them. But it should be a *bumiputera* (Malay-only) company, they both insisted. It has to be a *bumiputera* company. They began to enumerate the reasons why for Arif, who quickly wrote them down. Perhaps they could get 'research and development loans', 'import and export benefits', 'pioneer status', 'venture capital', and lower taxation on royalties for EG2020, using the financial words which have become commonplace in Malay entrepreneurial business conversations. 'Who knows how the laws might change even further to benefit *bumiputera* companies in ways we don't now know?' Ishak pointed out. But Arif was uncomfortable. 'He is my investor and he has helped me', he insisted, 'How can I close him out like that?'

Rokiah and Ishak began to discuss the complex structure of an organization which could minimally include the Chinese man. The 'holding company',[20] comprised of Rokiah, Ishak, and Arif, would be a *bumiputera* company. The 'research and development' company would be a *bumiputera* entity. The marketing and trading company would be a separate entity, a partnership between Arif and his Chinese friend, and therefore a non-*bumiputera* company. Rokiah pointed out that everyone gains something this way: Arif gets to be a partner with his Chinese investor, in one company, which will be carefully overseen by the partnership of Rokiah, Ishak, and Arif in the other. Ishak further emphasized the benefits: if loans need to be obtained, the R&D or the holding company will get them. If the government needs to be approached to get help with the launching or publicity or to make the product available to the Education Ministry, it will be a *bumiputera* company. For marketing the product all around Malaysia, it will be good to have a Chinese involved, and, he continued, perhaps it can even be marketed as a Chinese-made product in Chinese networks extending to Singapore or Taiwan, bringing in money that can further support their Malay cause. Most of all, they emphasized, such an organization would better serve the objective that Arif himself most believed in, that Malays should benefit the most. Arif ultimately concurred that such an arrangement was indeed best for them and the Malays he wanted to help.

'Anyhow', Rokiah asserted, 'this game is going to make us Malays better than Chinese. That's the reason we want to support it'.

THE POWER OF INCLUSION THROUGH ENTREPRENEURSHIP

Earlier in this chapter, I suggested that the key to understanding Malay entrepreneurship is an understanding of how particularistic, autonomous, status-focused, individual interests among people differently placed in a modern economic system have come to be represented as claims of duty to enhance the interests of the group. I suggested that this problem could not be approached without a discussion of how deeply Malays see themselves as affectively bound, dutiful, real and symbolic kin, mutually entailed by obligations, and threatened by outsiders. Submerged in the optimistic image of social equality envisioned in 'I/you' are the darkly powerful NEP-era implications of an ethnic 'us/them' conflict.

In this chapter, I have attempted to show that for Malays I knew, what is *wajib*, the dutiful performance of a material obligation – what is owed to parents and spouses – is one of the complex and confining ideals of obligation which are represented as being truly 'Malay'. In performing familial duty, Malays claim to manifest everything they believe themselves to be, submissive, other-centred, and altruistic, an identity which is today often demonstrated by returning parental love with material goods, as these expressions provide for parents the vivid symbols of their adult children's success. I examined the complex and often ambivalent notions of duty and the power of money that bind married Malay men and women to one another, as well as how these terms of dependence and control increasingly alienate the sexes and exaggerate individual concerns for entrepreneurial independence. I suggested and will return to the idea that while Malay women may have long been alloted certain economic and social freedoms, as the more elite among them are today, they are – and are likely to have always been – limited by religious and social norms from achieving true autonomy.

However fractious, even internecine, many marital and some sibling relationships in Malay society are, the current fostering and idealizing of ethnic bonds is a particularly potent cultural concept among the NEP beneficiaries, who represent themselves as especially cohesive. As entrepreneurs with important social and national goals pointed at the future, my informants identified themselves as members of a select Malay group – *Melayu baru* – perceiving themselves to be united even with the most elite among them as members of a new social category, a morally attuned Muslim generation of leaders, as concerned for the welfare of their whole ethnic group as they are for their own. As such, they are newly aware of and draw attention to their responsibility to others, to the government which conferred the blessings of modernity upon them and to the roots of tradition and family which sustained them. My Malay informants, like Arif, Rokiah, and Ishak, if not in reality, were ideologically united by a deeply felt sense that they represented a generation building themselves and all Malays. Among them, entrepreneurship was the key to both an individual identity and a group identity; it provided inclusion to both the status group of entrepreneurial Malay leaders in which they claimed membership and the Malay ethnic group they wished to serve.

But inclusion to the entrepreneurial status group served more than to provide a reference for a modern Malay identity. I suggested that entrepreneurial 'networking' is deliberately woven of strands of obligation, affect, and anticipated returns, in which many Malays attempt to use social and affective relations for economic ends (cf. Biggart 1989). Duty to the larger Malay 'family' is thus increasingly symbolized by network-based economic action among the NEP cohort – portrayed as the indigenous, rightful owners of the Malaysian economy – Malay 'brothers and sisters' acting in harmony, not merely self-interest.

Ethnic concerns, as well as religious values, have established a heightened sense that Malays are 'connected' to and must serve one another, a concept repeated so frequently by my informants that it became a kind of refrain in my interviews. I attempted to show that by accentuating the boundaries between themselves and the Chinese and outsiders in general, modern Malays have responded with an exaggerated image of themselves as members of an extended communal group. Selected by NEP to show themselves as capable of modernization, Malays I knew perceived themselves to have responded bravely and boldly, as if in a call to battle, like soldiers and servants. With this ideology, my informants tend to symbolize their own interests as those of the whole of society, until they represent themselves almost figuratively, synecdochically, as if they individually were *standing for* the whole. To demonstrate this, I provided a glimpse into an entrepreneurial venture, Arif's educational game, which suggests the sense of duty and group action which is woven into the entrepreneurial identity along with dreams of financial success and social recognition.

Economic 'dutifulness', then, today, helps to establish both the literal and symbolic terms of obligation to others, from family and conjugal roles to group and nation, and confirms a sense of connectedness and commitment among the beneficiaries of NEP, who use entrepreneurship, as did

Arif, Rokiah, and Ishak with EG2020, as a social and economic construction of means and ends, a formula to turn private interests into group gain. In the next chapter, we will consider how my Malay informants further constructed an ideal of a brotherhood through a modern re-examination of Islamic religious doctrine concerning fate, equity, duty, and wealth, and extended the dutiful notion that wealth for Malays was not merely an entitlement, but a higher form of service.

3 The Islamic View of Entrepreneurship: Modernity and its Rewards

To one degree or another, all of my informants were struggling with the problematic issues of the apparent contradiction between self- and group interest and between this- and other-worldly concerns. These issues underlined another contradiction which economic change had thrown into high relief: the difference between the Malay past and the Malay present, and all the complex moral responsibilities which modernity and development entail. Bolstered by the deepening sense that they represented a new group of Malay Muslim leaders (*Melayu baru*), my informants had begun to look back on a Malay past which was vaguely embarrassing to them, for they believed Malays once – and indeed, until quite recently – had profoundly misunderstood Allah's intentions for men and women on earth concerning material wealth. Partly because of a misunderstanding, they reasoned, Malays had fallen far behind the more practical Chinese in their own land. When Allah asked for men and women to show humility and simplicity, he surely did not intend Muslims to live in the impoverished and backward *kampung* or village.

Yet in my informants' ideas about economic behaviour, different 'pasts' came into varied focus: not just the naïve *kampung* past for which all Malays feel they share responsibility, but also the retrogressive, anachronistic society envisaged by fundamentalist Muslims; as well as the recent NEP past, rife with patronage, which is equated with Malay elitism and feudalism. All of these 'pasts' will be examined in this chapter, for in critiquing these various 'pasts', my informants were able to establish their vision of Islamic economic modernity. Indeed, they emphasized the way in which modern economic action, especially what they called entrepreneurship, was primarily directed towards the faithful service of Allah and other human beings, modern and progressive behaviour representing timeless Islamic virtues.

To argue that religious ideas influence economic activity is well-trodden ground in Southeast Asia; this, of course, was the objective of Geertz's famous study of pious Muslims in Indonesia (1956; 1963b), which was mapped along the lines of Weber's study of Calvinists in seventeenth-century Europe. My theoretical intent in this chapter is not to prove or disprove the Weberian debate about specific religious mentalities which cause or inhibit capitalism. The classic Weberian frame requires a theoretical position that economic action is the unintended consequence of belief, as opposed to possibilities entangled in concrete historical processes, a discussion worthy of a much longer treatment than is possible here. In this chapter I shall take a different approach, examining the ways in which my informants themselves pointed to both economic action and its rewards as part of the intended virtues and consequences of their belief.

A 'VIRTUOSO' – THE ZEAL OF DATO HASSAN

In an attempt to describe the complex nature of the entrepreneurial Malay Muslim religious identity, I turn to the example of an informant of mine, Dato Hassan, who instructed me on how entrepreneurship and its rewards brought him to a deeper knowledge of Islam. It was greatly fortunate that Dato Hassan agreed to meet with me to discuss what he called 'Malay Muslim entrepreneurial culture' over the months I lived in Malaysia, for he was among the most successful and best-known young men in the NEP cohort, described by many of his peers as one of a new breed, a *real* entrepreneur. As a major figure in the Malay entrepreneurial economy, itself primarily focused on the privatization of state- and UMNO-owned businesses, he operated within the daily reach of senior politicians and economic strategists.[1] Yet, unlike the earlier generation of *bumiputera* businessmen whom he described as mere 'puppets' of political and aristocratic patronage, he believed he was a product of the will of Allah entwined with hard work and human effort. As such he had earned the right, in his own words, to be a puppet master, a corporate *dalang*, one who knows the moves and determines outcomes.[2] He made it clear that this position was well deserved, and that his enframement of Malay entrepreneurship should be the one I represent as the sole direction to which others in Malaysia were moving. Holding him in the highest esteem, all of my other informants would have agreed with this. Indeed, as will become clear, I have chosen Dato Hassan to speak on the relationship between his faith and duty as a leader because he represented to me – and to many of my informants – what Weber called a 'virtuoso' (1974). The term has an important double meaning (Biggart 1989), describing both one's exemplary skill and ability, and one's 'virtue' in serving both God and human beings.[3]

Dato Hassan was deeply interested in my experience of corporate life from the years I had worked on Wall Street. He wanted to demonstrate points of universal congruence between his entrepreneurial culture and mine; but he also wanted to teach me what was unique about Malay Muslim entrepreneurial culture. He often contrasted the culture of entrepreneurship on Wall Street – to him, peopled with notorious figures like Michael Milken and Ivan Boesky, convicted criminals representing the excesses and greed of American business – with the moral, ethical culture of entrepreneurship he was helping to create for Malaysia. He sought to demonstrate to me that in *his* equally sophisticated corporate domain, entrepreneurship was directed as much towards the advancement of others as it was to one's self. This other-directedness (cf. Scott 1968) was, to him, a consequence of the Muslim *roh* or spirit, which opened itself to others. Indeed, it was because of his *roh* that he was willing to spend time tutoring me, time, he emphasized, which another less caring or non-Muslim corporate leader would spend pursuing profit. Indeed, as I sat in his elaborately decorated office – and in many others like it – I could not disagree; my own corporate experience had taught me that the senior executives of American corporations are often nearly unapproachable. Malay executives are, in contrast, highly approachable.

But this 'personal approach' to corporate life which many Malays, in unison with their political leaders, increasingly extol has complex consequences. As will become clearer in Part II, the social relations of Malay entrepreneurship, played out in webs of influence and alliance as 'networking', rest heavily upon one's ability to establish personal ties with instrumental people. As one of the key figures in the massive conversion of state-owned companies to private corporations, Dato Hassan, the chairman of a huge conglomerate, was therefore not merely an entrepreneurial protagonist of a drama that was unfolding in the corporate and political corridors of power in Kuala Lumpur, but also the unwitting protagonist of dramas in the lives of much more average entrepreneurial actors than he. He was feverishly (and usually disappointingly) pursued by some of my other informants in the hope that he would participate in or sponsor their ventures, as it was believed, and rightly so, that Dato Hassan controlled and had access to extraordinary resources in the Malay political and economic domain. To have Dato Hassan in one's network was surely to succeed, for his multiple business interests could provide endless opportunities to other entrepreneurs. To many of my informants, he was thus both a powerful symbol (like Weber's virtuoso) and an object of entrepreneurship; he had established an entrepreneurial high profile that sharply defined the Malay dream of success – and he clearly had the means to establish others as entrepreneurial successes in their own right. Quite simply, people wanted to be like him; they also wanted him to *help* them.

My informants who pursued Dato Hassan through multiple links in their social networks were not merely Machiavellian, for they believed firmly, for reasons which I began to establish in the previous chapter, that one Malay should and would help another. (The degree to which such figures as Dato Hassan will help them, however, is a subject of a later chapter.) Yet Dato Hassan, too, proclaimed that the job of a successful entrepreneur was ultimately to be altruistic, to serve Allah and the *ummah* or community of believers well; this, of course, is the second meaning of 'virtuoso'. Just being a good Muslim was no longer enough, he taught me; one needed to be a good Muslim businessman to fully serve Allah and society.

Often I met with Dato Hassan in his corporate office. Like many Malay business people, he displayed trophies and awards and photographs of himself with important political and royal figures. His prayer rug was rolled up neatly in the corner; pictures of his family were arranged on his huge desk, which faced an oil painting of a Malay *kampung* by a famous artist. Dato Hassan's autobiography was not unlike his office, containing images and symbols of heightened meaning and self-reflection, experiences gathered from his familiarity with Eastern and Western cultures. He presented his personal history to me somewhat like a Malay fable, with moments of clarity and cunning neatly worked in, and an ending that cannily presupposed the events determining it. But it was also a religious story, an Islamic parable, in which themes of fate interacted with the force of human will, demonstrating how, after progressing through several stages of knowledge, a man comes to understand the wisdom of Allah.

Dato Hassan told me of his shamefully wasted youth, for it contrasted deeply with his identity as a wise, grown man who had flirted with sin before learning Allah's lessons. As a young man, he revealed, he had willfully engaged in *haram* or forbidden behaviours like drinking and gambling. But worse than pleasurable infractions against the word of Allah, he said, were his crimes of self-importance and selfishness. Such sins, committed against fellow men, cannot be forgiven by Allah on Judgment Day. These included his attitude towards privilege. Indeed, when he was chosen to attend the elite Malay College Kuala Kangsar (MCKK), he became vain, convinced that he was superior to other Malays. Worse, as an educated *bumiputera*, he believed he would never have to work hard for his wealth. As had other NEP-era Malays before him, he expected to be given an easy route, a guarantee of success. He had squandered his university days in Australia with carefree days and nights in pubs, knowing all along that many rewards awaited him upon his return to Malaysia.

Back in Malaysia, he also rode the wave of *bumiputera* privilege. His first job was at a multinational company scrambling to meet NEP policy requirements by hiring Malay managers; they asked nothing of him but his presence and he gave little in return.[4] Then, he worked for a series of Malay-owned firms, which he described as NEP-era bastions of political patronage and corruption. He became rich, but learned nothing about the virtues of disciplined work. But Allah's plans for a man may be different from those a man has for himself, Dato Hassan reminded me. Slowly, something deep inside him began to change. Rustily, he begin to pray. Soon, discarded lessons from the teachings of Islam began to weigh heavily upon him. Searching for answers, he sought out religious instruction with learned teachers. He performed the *haj*, the most sacred pilgrimage to Mecca. He described himself as 'lit up inside', as if a fire were burning in his heart. Allah was asking him to change, to 'burst' through the barrier of Malay passivity and entitlement upon which many *bumiputera* had come to rely.

And with this, tremendous transformations occurred in his life, new awareness and new insights. Suddenly, everything began to fall into place. Fate began to open doors for him, bringing him into the ambit of powerful men with important ideas. Allah – not privilege – was giving him ever greater opportunities. He learned much along the way – about arbitrage and reverse take-overs, power plays and international finance. He now understood the reasons why he had been provided with a sophisticated, Western education with its emphasis on technical knowledge. Obviously what he called 'new age' Malays could not live in the financial or technological 'dark ages', a highly nuanced phrase he used often and which will be returned to below. But these were the least of the lessons he needed to learn. He sought to understand the nature of wealth – why some people are rich and others poor. He sought to understand the responsibilities that wealth brought. He prayed and grew, he said, *until he understood.*

Dato Hassan believed he had finally come to a point of epiphany in which he fathomed man's dutiful relationship to Allah. Success was not an end in itself. Men must work hard to understand the purpose of Allah's choices for them and meet Allah's expectations with ever greater effort. What better means to show Allah his humble virtues did a man have than his worldly actions, his work? As we shall see, to Dato Hassan, as to many of my informants, awakening to a dutiful relationship to Allah was to be expressed best through the paradigm of modern entrepreneurship, purposeful action in the material world. In it, he would place his true Muslim *roh* or spirit and his business acumen at the disposal of Allah and others.

EMERGING FROM THE PAST – ISLAMIC LESSONS AND
ALLAH'S WILL

Much of Dato Hassan's narrative was a personal interpretation of the nature of fate and its relationship to the power of human effort, ideas which had taken on great force among many of my economically ambitious informants. My informants were in unanimous agreement that until recently, Malays had misconstrued the Islamic notions of fate and reward. From this perspective, they critiqued the Malay *kampung* past, as well those Malays who still lived according to its economic rules.

It is generally believed by Muslims that *takdir* or fate – what is willed by the divine decree of Allah – cannot be changed. But the old-fashioned, naïve *kampung* Malay, my informants told me, believes that *rezeki* – one's livelihood or allocation of wealth, what Malays call 'luck' – is fated and fixed by Allah. To seek to change it would therefore be to question Allah's wisdom. Malays in the past thus threw up their hands and waited patiently for Allah to send their daily allotment and fill their bowls with rice. Because Allah saw fit to provide Malays with abundant food in the *kampung*, they believed that they were blessed with great wealth, great *rezeki*; they believed their sole goal in life was to thank and praise Allah for his obvious demonstration of love for Malays. As such, life in the *kampung* did not change. This widely held view among my informants mirrors earlier, scholarly analyses of Malay 'fatalistic' economic attitudes (Parkinson 1968; Swift 1963; Wilder 1968), which are usually contrasted with the much more sophisticated and practical money-handling skills of the overseas Chinese (Freedman 1959; Hyman 1975). These theories have slipped into the common discourse of men and women I knew, and even my informants' parents are critical of the economic naïvety they believed characterized Malays of their own generation. Had it not been for the events of 1969, resulting in NEP, forcing reality upon Malays, most of us, my informants said, would never have emerged from the *kampung*.

Despite two decades of enforced development through NEP, the fear that Malays will still let everything rest in the hands of Allah – what my informants called a *mentaliti kampung* – remains powerful. It has such contemporary urgency in the ideology of Malay modernity and economic development that it was the primary subject of Prime Minister Mahathir's 1993 Hari Raya television message to Malay Muslims. The Prime Minister warned Malays against economic passivity. Laziness and poverty, he claimed, are equal sins, both humiliating Muslim men and women in Allah's eyes. Poor people, he insisted, are those who make no effort to change themselves or take responsibility for their fate; they look backward instead of to the future. Poor, backward Malays, he said, have misunderstood Islam. As I listened to the speech along with my friend Rokiah, her parents, and her siblings, they all nodded in silent agreement.

My informants reminded me frequently that in order to understand the Islamic notion of human action, I must understand that *takdir* – fate – mostly determines when and where a human being will live and die, for obviously, Allah owns life and can take it back when he wishes. Beyond that, people are largely on their own, for it is their own *ikhtiar* (free will) that determines what happens in life. It is primarily in the various shades of meaning of *ikhtiar* that my informants spoke of a dawning realization of how they were different from Malays in the *kampung*.

When Allah gave Dato Hassan opportunity after opportunity, and reward after reward, handing him wealth and privilege when he was not yet worthy of it, it was, Dato Hassan understood, a vivid sign of how Allah operates the strings of *takdir*, telling him that he must grow and change. But it was Dato Hassan's own choice to take on those challenges to demonstrate his worth. Worthiness entails effort, work, prayer, thought, questioning – all the things human beings must engage in to exercise Allah's gift of *ikhtiar*. Sitting passively in the *kampung* was evidence of how little Malays in the past had understood Allah's gifts. Nearly everyone I spoke to offered me the same vivid image: *kampung* Malays waited for coconuts to fall from the tree. 'Work' in the *kampung* simply entailed opening them up.

Thus, as my informants often stated with a kind of self-deprecating laugh, Malays previously had all of these Islamic understandings backwards. They thought that being humble to the will of Allah required a docile, passive acceptance of life as given. The sudden recognition of the necessity to exercise free will, and to engage in complex choices about how to live, progress, and demonstrate worthiness for the rewards Allah saw fit to give them was represented by contemporary Malays in the NEP cohort as a kind of collective *voilà*. Malays who did not understand this formulation deserved to remain in the *kampung*. There is, then, an increasing sense that *kampung* Malays – poor, rural folk and urban squatters living on the fringes of cities – are not good Muslims.

Ikhtiar – the individual's own free choice to show effort in life – has become a key ingredient of modern Malay economic identity and to many, the explanation for the difference between Malay poverty and wealth, backwardness and development, *kampung* past and Kuala Lumpur present, even sin and virtue.

EFFORT AND THE PROMISE OF REWARDS

Prime Minister Mahathir believes, as he stated in his holiday speech on laziness to the nodding assent of my informants, that people who work hard towards progress are *usually* rewarded more than those who do not. While this leaves the ultimate decision about who will be rich and who will be poor in the agency of Allah, my informants generally stated that Allah does not *like* poverty, for with it adheres a taint of laziness, passivity, and irresponsibility that allows time for sin. It is now generally agreed upon that Malays must work hard to honour Allah's abundant worldly gifts, which include the enormous advances provided to them during NEP. The Prime Minister frequently warns Malays against the 'subsidy mentality' which he feels they have often demonstrated during NEP, themes which have resonated in his ideology for many years (Mahathir Mohamad 1970; 1991a). Through such sources as political speeches and Islamic conferences reported in the media, a new formulation of the purpose of wealth – and the gifts of modern life – have begun to be widely accepted among modern Malays. As a headline in the national newspaper boldly announced, in Islam, 'Attainment of material wealth is now encouraged' (*New Straits Times*, 4 June 1993).

Malays I knew agreed that they would not now be rewarded, as Malays in the *kampung* had felt confident they already were, for sitting back and accepting Allah's gifts, but for action and progress. Human beings, it was believed among my informants, should thus be guided by the awareness that material rewards *may* be given in amounts that evaluate their on-going performance in this world, whereas immaterial rewards – those granted on Judgment Day – will absolutely measure it in the next. As such, there was clear evidence that the *pursuit* of wealth, in Islamically approved ways, can be seen as one of the virtues which make up the modern Islamic moral identity.

As I grappled with the ideas of free choice, rewards, and Allah's will, so too did my informants. These are not easy issues, for they involve a modern revision of Malays' past Islamic understandings, as well as complex evaluations of the moral intent of one's own behaviours. The painful, self-examining awareness that Allah might reward others more than oneself, might give evidence of his approval in this world and not only in the next, became clear to me close to the end of my stay in Kuala Lumpur, when my friend Rokiah, in an uncharacteristic display of helpless emotion, burst suddenly into bitter tears. Again and again, she spoke of her badness, of her sins. 'I think Allah does not love me!' she cried out. I begged her to tell me why. 'Because others have so much', she wept, 'and

I have so little'. She demonstrated the obvious evidence of Allah's disdain: 'I lost money on the stock-market when others became rich. I try and try to find new businesses, and people only take money from me. My work is hard and the money comes slowly. Allah is clearly punishing me!' Quietly, in a voice heavy with the burden of guilt, she began to list her sins: 'I don't pray. I didn't finish my fast last year and now it is time to fast again. I've played the gambling machine at my club and I bought a lottery ticket. I don't do anything that Allah asks'.

This was the beginning of a crisis for Rokiah, in which she examined her *ikhtiar* – free choices – and found herself lacking in all respects. Rokiah confessed that she had neglected all of the covenants (*uqud*) of her faith, her obligation to Allah, her obligation to her soul, and, worst of all, her obligation to her fellow human beings. Pursuits in life, she realized with dawning shame, could not be directed at greedily asking for more for herself, and she was guilty of that, a sin worse than not praying, not fasting, and gambling. Although she had not actually stolen money or earned it through Islamically prohibited means, she saw in her self-proclaimed greedy pursuits crimes that nearly equalled those. Rokiah knew that her service was not just limited to the five pillars of Islam – belief in Allah as the one true God, prayer, fasting, payment of charity, and pilgrimage – but by expressing her whole life in terms of worship and devotion and commitment to others. She knew she had sorely failed at both demonstrations of faith. Painfully, sickeningly, she realized she was already being judged.

When the doctrine of salvation, or inner-worldly asceticism, what Weber described as the ideology of the Calvinist businessman, became identified with the gospel of wealth, where proof of God's blessings were proven by success in this world, it amounted to, as Berger stated, 'a vulgar … [and] immense misunderstanding of the Calvinist view of salvation' (1987: 100). Does Islam, as it is represented by my informants confronting modern rewards, provide the easy means for a similar misunderstanding? Some of my informants, despite knowing doctrinally that Allah does not necessarily favour his chosen ones with rewards in this life, increasingly looked for (and found) material proof of divine approval prior to Judgment Day, just as the Calvinists were said to.

Indeed, my informant Zakri, an aggressive and ambitious owner of an architectural business, claimed that ever since he had gone on the *haj*, where he asked for Allah's help in his business, 'He has given me everything – wealth, customers, and contracts from very big clients'. Precisely the same sentiment was echoed by my informants Aisha and Rahim, owners of the Marchland factory, about whom we will learn more in a later chapter. They were convinced that it was their *haj* that made their business begin to take off. Money, like a huge loan from the government, promises of contracts, and good contacts with massive, UMNO-supported businesses, simply began, after their trip to Mecca, 'to fall' into their paths. 'Go to Mecca', Aisha urged her friends one day, among whom was Rokiah, 'there, you will learn Allah's plans for your business'. But Rokiah was somewhat sceptical about Aisha's claim. She said that one does not go to Mecca to *get* blessings, but to *give* them – the testimony of faith and oneness with Allah.

Rokiah was, eschatologically speaking, correct to question claims that demonstrated a simple correlation between practice and reward. She had been taught since girlhood that one's actions, reflected by the Islamic conception of *ikhtiar*, must be directed by *niat*, the proper 'intention' of serving Allah. Material rewards are only one of the possible rewards of devotional work; they cannot be expected, nor can they be the sole *niat* of one's effort, which Rokiah fearfully recognized, in her case, had actually been in the pursuit of only self-serving ends. She thought perhaps the pilgrimages made by her friends Aisha and Rahim might have made them better Muslims, which, in turn, established that they might earn bigger rewards. She thought perhaps that their business, Marchland, was somehow fashioned in a way which was more reflective of their Islamic virtues than were her own self-described greedy business ventures.

Central to Rokiah's guilt was the Quranic ideal that a Muslim must serve Allah by the constant reaffirmation of moral bonds to others in society, a nuance which is sharply highlighted in Dato Hassan's narrative, one which was, in his mind, given substance through economic activity – and one which underlined, as we shall soon see, the Malay understanding of 'networking'. One whose intention in dealing with others in the material world is truly moral is *ikhlas*, what Malays translate as 'sincere', a term which also carries with it a sense of guiltlessness, of an 'unburdened state of mind' (Kessler 1978: 223), a state reached by knowing and ensuring that one's moral intent is directed properly towards Allah's wishes and expectations for human beings. Although Rokiah had not engaged in forbidden acts according to the laws of Islam, she none the less felt she had sinned. She was greedy and therefore immoral, not other-directed and Allah-directed.[5] If she *had* been sincere, if she had respected all the covenants of Islam, most especially in her moral relations to fellow humans, wealth and success might have come to her more easily. Obviously, Aisha and Rahim had been more sincere in all of their actions – towards Allah and towards others.

In the days that followed Rokiah's crisis, she slowly began to judge herself less harshly. She recalled the kindness she had shown others in her everyday actions – loaning money when it was unlikely to be returned, hiring as an office boy a young man who had used drugs whom no one else would employ, turning away corrupt financial deals and offers of kickbacks in her business to search for more legitimate opportunities. She remembered as well the essence of free choice and Islamic service to Allah, that life is merely a pursuit of lessons in self-improvement and progress in anticipation of Judgment Day.

Just as Dato Hassan's transformation (and greater wealth) came when he realized that success was not an end in itself and that a dutiful relationship with Allah required morally responsible, sincere action in the material world, Rokiah concluded that she should redouble her efforts at self-development. Soon, she was again confident that her rewards might be measured by the enormous and often sincere effort with which she tried to run her business and improve it – and others – through various entrepreneurial ventures and network alliances. Duty to others and to Allah seemed increasingly framed by the theme of progress and morality elaborated in modern economic action. Indeed, entrepreneurship, because of its unique ability to be put in the service of others, because it required progress of the self through discipline and a sharp awareness of intent and confirmed that some Malays had indeed emerged from the *kampung*, increasingly seemed to characterize best the obligations and virtues of faith in modern life. To one degree or another, all of my informants, even those like Zakri, Rahim, and Aisha, who saw a simpler relationship between faith and material rewards than did Dato Hassan and Rokiah, genuinely believed that modern, individual economic action could best harness the demands that Allah had made of them. For some, performing it was a genuinely felt mission of good; for others, it meant they *were* good and deserving of rewards. In either case, it was in modern economic action – differentiating them from passive *kampung* Malays past and present, who did not engage in purposeful economic activity – my informants insisted, *that they were actually discovering more of their Malay and Muslim selves.*

The intense interest in entrepreneurship and development among my informants is construed in terms of modern religious ideology, but it did not become invested with such singular importance outside the influence of contestation and confrontation or political interests and alignments in Malay life. My informants' complex negotiation of belief and the entrepreneurial identity was made all the more crucial in the NEP period because of the problematic presence of Islamic intensification in the form

of fundamentalism. Fundamentalist Islam is the second 'past' – the highly
nuanced 'dark ages' which emerged in Dato Hassan's narrative.

DAKWAH AND THE FORCES OF SOCIAL CHANGE

Since the mid-1970s, Islam in Malaysia has been profoundly influenced by
the *dakwah* (literally, 'to respond to a call'; generally in Malaysia *dakwah*
means 'fundamentalism') movement, which swept primarily through the
young, recently urbanized Malay population, the first generation to be
markedly affected by the changes brought about by NEP. Most accounts
of this Islamic activism describe it as a 'predictable Malay response to
global and Malaysian issues of change and development' (Wazir Jahan
Karim 1992: 179), registering most deeply among the population intended
to be the vanguard of development. Other researchers found in *dakwah*
not just a reaction to a rapid social change, but a response to the ethnic
dichotomization of urban society created by NEP racialization (Muzzafar
1987), which Nagata characterized as 'a nativistic reaffirmation of
Malayness in a new form' (1984: 234). Hussin Mutalib (1990) described
the phenomenon as part of an on-going dialectic between the forces of
ethnicity and religion in contemporary Malay consciousness, which were
resolved by bringing together in indissoluble form the identification of
Malay with Muslim, a way to legitimate and safeguard Malay NEP interests against claims of other ethnic or religious groups in Malaysia. Other
approaches build on Kessler's argument which actually pre-dates both
NEP and the *dakwah* movement, in which he interpreted the trend towards
Islamically informed political movements in the Malaysian state of
Kelantan as a manifestation of class conflict (1978). As such, many
researchers argue that Islamic revival in Malaysia is either a justification
of or a subversive response to increasing inequality of class and gender
dominance and power in the industrializing nation (see, for example, Ong
1990; Peletz 1993; Shamsul A.B. 1986a; Wazir Jahan Karim 1992).

Whatever its multiple causes during the NEP period, *dakwah* often took
the form of a sharp critique of both Westernized modernity and materialism, two things which NEP was said to have established in Malays
(Hussin Mutalib 1990). But it also critiqued tradition. Indeed, although
many researchers describe the *dakwah* movement as 'revivalist' (Nagata
1984; Wazir Jahan Karim 1992), while in its more extreme forms it was
obviously anti-modern, it was not pro-tradition, because it rejected and
therefore did not 'revive' Malay cultural forms, it was instead, as Norani
Othman (1994) most appropriately calls it, neo-traditional. It tended to

focus on replacing in Malay Islam and culture those customs and rules which were believed to be pristinely Islamic, *ab origine*. In pursuit of a simple lifestyle based on the Prophet's *sunnah* or revelations, many members of *dakwah* organizations thus sharply marked themselves off from the rest of modern, Western, and Malay culture. They adopted clothing styles from Arab culture (men in Arab headgear [*serban*] and robes [*juba*], women in veils [*telekung*] or even full *purdah*-style covering), attended religious classes and retreats, and separated men from women in social and religious contexts (Wazir Jahan Karim 1992).

As the *dakwah* movement attempted to cleanse Malaysian Islam of what was perceived to be its animist or Hindu elements, much of *dakwah* actually became anti-Malay (Nagata 1984). Attention was drawn to the pantheistic immorality of *wayang kulit* (the shadow play) and the anti-Islamic spiritualism of *silat* (traditional Malay fighting). Traditional Malay customs, such as the *bersanding* ceremony in a Malay wedding, were suddenly declared to be alien, Hindu traditions. Traditional Malay dances were said to encourage illicit sexual relations between men and women and were banned. More and more women donned the veil (cf. Peletz 1996). Western and modern influences of any kind were believed by many Malays to be decadent, endangering the morals and values of Muslims by encouraging independence and selfish materialism.

While it is generally thought that *dakwah*, or at least Islamic intensification, generated its own momentum among all Muslims in Malaysia during the 1970s and 1980s, this view is too simplistic. Much of the increasingly public presence of Islam in Malaysia over the past two decades resulted not so much from the forces of *dakwah* acting upon Malays as from the increasing politicization of Islam. Threatened by the claims that the dominant Malay political party was too Westernized, sinful, and materialistic, UMNO, under the leadership of Prime Minister Mahathir, responded with its own form of competitive Islamization 'to counter any swing of the Malay-Muslim vote' to the increasingly strident Malaysian Islamic Party, PAS (Parti Islam Se Malaysia, the opposition party) (Hussin Mutalib 1990: 100).

In the 1970s and 1980s, under pressure to demonstrate his party's depth of religious integrity, Mahathir, first as Education Minister, then as Prime Minister, dramatically increased Malaysia's local and international Muslim activities and voiced strident anti-Western rhetoric. Domestically, he sought to absorb under state sponsorship key Islamic values, which ranged from establishing the International Islamic University in Kuala Lumpur to introducing Islamic banking, insurance, and pawnbroking. By the late 1970s, there was an intensification of Islamic media programming, the *azan* or call to prayer was broadcast on radio and television, political figures were photographed in the studied, solemnifying performance of Muslim prayers at official functions. Large state-aligned corporations built Arab-inspired buildings such as the Dayabumi building, and added Arabic or Islamic elements in hotels and architectural ornamentation. The 'national culture' of Malaysia, intended to somehow incorporate all three races, became aggressively Islamic. So too did the state's concern with its Muslim citizens' degree of Islamic compliance.

Various procedures were put into place to 'govern the matrimonial intentions and conduct of Muslim citizens, putting them under more bureaucratic assessment and scrutiny' (Norani Othman 1994: 136), ranging from increased arrests for *khalwat* (men and women in close prox- imity) to 'a special interview of prospective brides ... intended to ascertain their religious knowledge' as wives and mothers (ibid.). The effects of Islam on the perception of the roles of men and women has already been mentioned in Chapter 2, but now we can better understand the complex sources of dissonance and ambivalence as gender-role behaviour in modern settings came under close scrutiny (cf. Peletz 1996). Very little of modern life in Malaysia was, and still is, unaffected in one way or another by the constant juxtaposition of rival claims to piety and on-going claims of moral superiority among the various Islamic political forces. Islamic activism and politicization brought massive change to the lives of all Malaysians, and forced many Malays to question their own cultural – as well as personal – representation of faith and practice.

THE TRANSFORMED SELF OR THE TRANSFORMED SOCIETY

Most of my informants, who represented themselves as modern and mod- erate Muslims, had generally eluded some of the *dakwah* movement's more rigid social and behavioural controls.[6] Yet ever earnest to learn, develop, and change in their attempts to reach moral perfection, progress, and take account of their own shortcomings as Muslims – and, as will be discussed below, business people – the men and women I knew reported gratefully that they had learned a great deal more about Islam during the period of religious revival in Malaysia. Rather than openly criticize *dakwah* or its tendency towards social control, my informants, fearful of being accused of anti-Islamic behaviour,[7] appear to have responded to Islamization with a stepped-up, contrasting expression of their own reli- giosity, a parallel to the response made by political leaders in UMNO to the surge of power in the Islamic Party.[8] No one among my informants claimed to have been unaffected by the intense Islamic intensification in Malaysia; indeed, they offered optimistically, they had been much improved and transformed. For this they thanked the *dakwah* Malays. My fieldnotes were filled with account after account of recent religious transformations, when, like Dato Hassan, one informant after another told me how poignant, how vivid the presence of Allah now was in his or her life, how empty life had been before, how rich it now was. Sometimes tears came to the eyes of the speaker, when no words could describe the genuine devotional emotion which retelling the experience aroused.

Through the intensely felt, highly personal, and individualistic nature of these religious accounts, or perhaps because of the very contrast to those *dakwah* Malays to whom they claimed gratitude, my informants carefully distinguished their demonstration of faith with that of the highly visible, highly conformist fundamentalist Malays. These ideas about the visibility of faith, and moreover, how to demonstrate faith, became the modest terms of their contestation. True faith, people told me, could not be seen by anyone but Allah, and they frequently pointed this out In everyday contexts. As such, when we walked to a business meeting past a mosque to which Muslim men were arriving in streams for sabbath prayers, my friend Ishak spontaneously told me that praying in the mosque was certainly more visible, but it did not imply that men who did not pray in the mosque were neglecting their prayers. He proceeded to describe for me in detail the ways in which his whole life had become reorganized by the rediscovery of prayer, making his invisible faith ever more visible to me.

Other contrasts were made. Looking at a group of fully veiled women, some of my informants occasionally ventured a critique of *dakwah* that described it as 'merely a costume', for how could you tell a person's true faith simply by how he or she dressed? Indeed, Aisha, the manufacturing entrepreneur already mentioned, reported to a group of friends how she had been 'fooled' by a dishonest *dakwah* group into providing goods from her factory on credit, only to learn that they were really hypocritical 'thieves' who had donned the clothing of religious men to imply their honesty and cheat other Malays. People may be fooled by clothes, she said, but Allah is not. 'Allah looks on the inside to judge us', one of the women listening asserted, laughingly pointing to her blue jeans and T-shirt as if to demonstrate that she needed no such costume. In contrast, Salbiah, the aggressive entrepreneur mentioned in Chapter 2, who had gone to Mecca, wore her head covered, but insisted to her friends that it was not to conform to *dakwah* standards, but to demonstrate her own, private relationship to Allah.

Contrasts went beyond the concern for obvious and visible representations of piety. Unlike *dakwah* groups, which my informants believed
might make illegitimate and hypocritical claims of purity, my informants
reported, with a sense of satisfaction, that, like all of Allah's creatures,
they themselves were far from perfect. Indeed, many of my informants
openly admitted that immorality had once tempted and even swayed them.
As it was in Dato Hassan's story, a *leitmotiv* in most of the transformation
narratives which my informants shared with me was the revelation that
they had gone through a period of sinfulness and irresponsibility. This
included anything from engaging in drinking, gambling, and sexual
encounters to wearing miniskirts, long hair, going to a disco, or disobeying
their parents – all of which were described as unIslamic in nature. But,
common to these assertions, as we glimpsed in Dato Hassan's transformation narrative, was the belief that suddenly they had seen their own shortcomings and realized they had been nearly 'lost'. The meaning of Islam
had then manifested itself sharply in their lives, and, like a *coup de foudre*,
struck deep in their hearts and minds.

My informants represented their transformative revivals as interiorized
and private epiphanies in which the Islamic teachings of their youth –
which they had followed half-heartedly and indifferently – returned, now
blossoming and bearing the fruit of real belief, instructing them on the
nature of their sociological and eschatological responsibilities. While they
suspected that *dakwah* organizations had rigidly tightened controls upon
individuals through group pressure, my informants reported having
learned genuine self-control, to them a more valid Islamic lesson. This
transformation, although enormous and life-changing, was not, my informants said, anything like *dakwah* because it remade the self primarily in
ways that were obvious only to Allah. 'Look, look at me', one man said,
throwing his arms out wide to include his elegant, glass-walled office and
draw attention to his elegant double-breasted suit, 'how can you tell that
I'm a servant of Allah; how can you tell that I am not?'

Yet, like the *dakwah* groups, my informants insisted they had remade
their modern lives: making time for prayer in a busy work-day, developing
a deep concern about non-Western sources of morality and the well-being
of others in the *ummah*, and searching for ways to improve their own and
their children's Islamic education. I was invited, time and again, to peek
into a prayer room which had recently been built in the offices of many of
my informants, or to attend an Islamic discussion group which had been
established among a group of business associates. My informants lined
their children before me to have them answer any of my questions about
Islam, learned answers which my informants themselves could never have

provided at that age. But unlike the *dakwah* groups, who, they believed, had turned away from modern reality, my informants saw themselves as boldly confronting modernity.

Dato Hassan, whose elite position allowed him greater outspokenness than most of my informants, was openly angry at the forces and consequences of *dakwah*. He claimed that it was like the Malay feudal culture, for it replaced one kind of submission with another, as passive Muslims followed charismatic *dakwah* leaders. He claimed its followers did not think for themselves, but took the easy way out. To him, *dakwah* groups did not understand how to help Malays seize opportunities for progress; in fact, he said, *dakwah* was hurting Malays by closing them off from the modern world and scaring away foreigners.[9] They would produce in Malaysia a 'dark age' which would isolate Muslims, he feared. The true spirit of Islam was, Dato Hassan claimed, evidenced by a man maintaining an open mind, learning to grow and change, using modern technology and ideas, but none the less allowing himself to be led and influenced only by Allah. To be a true Muslim, like the Prophet, Malay Muslims had to increase, not decrease, their exposure to the world, while at the same time helping to improve it.

ISLAMIC ECONOMICS IN MALAYSIA? HOW VIRTUE BECOMES SYMBOLIZED

In current Islamic literature, there are two widely accepted definitions of the demonstration of ethics in Islamic economics. The first approach is an institutional one, the creating of systems of Islamic banking, Islamic pawnbroking, Islamic investment trusts, and so on (Jomo K.S. 1993), in which the contractual financial terms do not go against the economic teachings of the Prophet concerning such issues as the charging of *riba* or interest.[10] The second widely accepted definition is an individual one, which focuses on propagating Islamic values in one's everyday business dealings. Using the basic norms from the Quran and *sunnah*, all actions Muslims engage in can be socially responsible and just. The economic actor is thus free to produce and trade for a profit, but must not engage in exploitative or risky activities. They must not invest in *haram* activities (like gambling casinos or liquor manufacturing), must be moderate in consumption, must give money to others once they have enough for their own family, and must contribute to the social good. These practices would then comprise an Islamic 'economic system' ensured by individual intent (M. Umer Chapra 1992), not institutional structures.

While I was living in Kuala Lumpur, both definitions were explored by my informants and the state alike. Creating Islamic institutions as part of the menu of modern financial choices that Malaysia had to offer could be construed as one more political battle between the forces of neo-traditionalism and Mahathir-style Islamic modernity which has arisen during the past two decades. Islamization of the economy was increasingly represented by UMNO-aligned political leaders as Malaysia's contribution to the modern Muslim world, whereas the supporters of *dakwah* would return Malaysia's economy to the past. In the midst of it, my informants often thought about their ethical relationship to the money of which they seemed to be making more and more, and how it did or did not demonstrate Islamic virtues.

Thus, during the huge upswing on the Kuala Lumpur Stock Exchange in the last quarter of 1993, talk in the night-time food stalls I frequented with my informants sometimes centred on the problem of whether money earned on the market was *halal* or *haram* (permissible or forbidden by Islam). The stock-market was paying huge returns to Malay investors, and the government appeared to be actively encouraging it. Therefore was it not institutionally approved by the government? Even so, those in the *haram* camp said that stock trading was gambling, for earnings made from it came without work, which is a sin in Allah's eyes. (This was an unpopular attitude among the stall-goers, most of whom were there for stock tips and ideas.) One night, a friend of mine pointed out rather guiltily that people in Malaysia always talk about '*playing* the shares' (*main saham*) – to him, proof that they knew that speculative investing was not a form of work, even though he admitted he was one of the bigger 'players' himself. Another friend reminded us that work in the eyes of Allah was anything that produced *peluh* (sweat) and added, 'Certainly we've been sweating out these daily highs and lows enough!' His joke was received with general laughter. But he went on to say that investing in the stock-market was indeed *halal* because stock choices should be made based on careful research of the corporation's fundamental business values, which was undeniably hard work. Any profit made by the investor was therefore earned. Everyone present agreed that this made great sense, although the religious media remained filled with dire warnings from *dakwah* leaders who insisted that stock-trading was unIslamic, and that its creation of easy wealth allowed Muslims both the time and the means for sin.

Modern questions like these, as well as questions about the obligatory contribution of *zakat* (literally, 'purifier') or charity – or what one informant, a wealthy man, who worried about how much of his massive wealth he should give away and to whom, referred to with irony as 'his money problem' – came up often in my conversations with Malay men and women who worried about traditional responsibilities and modern identity. An example of how confusing was the seemingly simple obligation to purify oneself by giving charity occurred repeatedly in my circle, where Rokiah and her friend Norah were engaged in a never-ending disagreement about whether or not the money each of them sent home to their mothers every month was *zakat*. Rokiah insisted that any money sent to people in need, given in the spirit of generosity with no expectation of return, was *zakat*. The expensive suit of clothes she bought her brother before he flew to the United States for university was *zakat*. Hiring her boyfriend's brother to work in her office after he was released from a drug-rehabilitation camp was *zakat*. '*Zakat* means you help others, and we all know charity begins at home', she insisted. But Norah was adamant. *Zakat* was absolutely not that. It was the annual payment of 2.5 per cent of personal and corporate profits which all Muslims (based on income) were obligated to pay to the *Baitulmal* (Islamic Treasury), which went to the poor who had no houses or jobs. She said, money you gave to your parents would only count as *zakat* if they did not have houses or pensions. Rokiah, who did not give money to the *Baitulmal*, insisted that charity was a simple matter of sincerity of intention. Any money given with the sincere intention to help others less fortunate than yourself is *zakat*. They never were to agree on this point.

As such, many of my informants felt that modern life was too complicated to know exactly how to handle ethically every kind of financial situation; 'You just have to mean well and pray for moral guidance', Ishak often said. As an example of the power of this viewpoint, one of my informants, the Malay owner of a large brokerage house, told me that he explained to any of his anxious Muslim customers that the stock-market, because it concerns the development of Malays and all Malaysia, is therefore expressly Islamic and its *niat* or intention is surely for the common good. While much of modern economic activity both at the institutional level and individual level might not be demonstrably and strictly Islamic in the sense of Quranic doctrine, its intent, people said, is much to the benefit of the *ummah*.

The logic of this perspective was crucial to the formulation of entrepreneurship and modern Islamic identity. Thus, when Dato Hassan contrasted his Malay Muslim entrepreneurial culture with my Wall Street culture, he made it expressly clear that his – while equal in sophistication to mine – was not focused on mere self-advancement, but on the advancement of others as well. When Rokiah suffered her crisis over the nature of intent and the promise of rewards, she resolved it through vows of her personal commitment to national progress and altruism, by reaffirming the sincerity of her *niat*. The ways in which other informants expressed this mission through entrepreneurship will be explored in much greater detail in Part II. For now, it is important to understand how the obligation of altruism – putting the needs of society before, or at least alongside, their own, advancing the *ummah* or the nation, and sometimes even the world, through their sincerely expressed effort at self- and social improvement – was claimed by many of my informants as the very rationale for entrepreneurship itself. To many of my informants, *an entrepreneur was the public symbol of a modern, moral, Islamic economic and social actor*.

Therefore, Dato Hassan – one of Malaysia's most celebrated, virtuoso Malay entrepreneurs – and Amir – the low-paid clerk in Rokiah's office who dreamed of becoming a famous entrepreneur and concocted elaborate networking schemes in hopes of realizing it – shared the same valorized view of entrepreneurship (and both called themselves entrepreneurs). To Dato Hassan and Amir, entrepreneurship had itself taken on the gloss of Islamic goodness. Indeed, enacting it symbolized the norms of the Quran and the *sunnah*, and even reminded them of the behaviours of the Prophet Muhammad himself.

Amir thus told me how being an entrepreneur was 'a wonderful way to understand the real nature of Islam and the Prophet'. First, he elaborated, his eyes bright with a sense of purpose, 'an entrepreneur wants to succeed to the limits of his ability – that is what Allah wants for him, too. Second, an entrepreneur can never succeed only on his own. He needs to be a gatherer of resources and a manager of people and of opportunities, and therefore he must be humane, must realize his own limitations and bring others along with him – friends and employees, to whom he teaches excellence and offers growth'. Amir told me that because he supervised the work of Rokiah's more junior clerks, he felt a deep sense of responsibility to 'uplift' them by helping them become more disciplined and professional. He saw every interaction with them from the stand-point of a wise teacher and leader. Amir did not have the corporate experience that some of my other informants did, but his words matched theirs – the Islamic leader, an entrepreneur, just like the Prophet, 'motivates' and 'incentivizes' others to learn new things, to progress.

'Next, the real entrepreneur will remember that it is only Allah's will that made him rich, and then he will want to help others, as Allah helped him. That is why the true entrepreneur will start a company or a corporation, primarily to help others enter business. Never selfish, he will welcome others into his good fortune by opening the doors wide'. Amir, like many of my informants, told me this is why he disdained the small

Chinese entrepreneur, who ran a business solely for his own and his family's needs. To him, Malay entrepreneurship is bigger, more inclusive. It must provide moral direction and economic opportunity to others, even if they are not Muslims. This is exactly the kind of ideal community that the Prophet established in Medina, he said, using Islamic principles to establish Islam's golden age. As Amir spoke of his dreams of entrepreneurship, of being a leader who followed Allah's lessons, he explained his belief that Malays like him, seeking greater self-perfection, would increasingly use Islamic principles, such as 'fairness, justice, and balance', to establish and perfect Malaysia's *korporat* golden age. Dato Hassan, as we shall see later on, believed in this future as well.

Amir and Dato Hassan were at remote ends of the entrepreneurial spectrum: the former could only dream of how he would behave if he had power and opportunity while the latter had already achieved the Malay entrepreneurial dream of success. Both of them, however, shared the same genuine belief that, by joining economic action to Islamic principles, they could both enjoy material and immaterial rewards and contribute dramatically to the social good. This modern Islamic economic identity was clearly then neither 'too Western' nor 'too materialistic', nor, assuredly, was it anything like backward-looking *dakwah*. It was progressive yet doctrinal, for it served the *ummah*. It was, many people believed, a truly Islamic identity in modern life.

THE SINFUL ECONOMIC PAST: THE EQUATING OF FEUDALISM WITH ELITE *BUMIPUTERA*-ISM

I have already explained how my informants used the *kampung* past (and poor, 'lazy' Malays still marginalized in *kampungs*) for an economic and eschatological critique and how they established a definition of their Islamic modernity by virtue of the contrast to the anachronism – and rival claims to piety – they saw in politically powerful *dakwah* groups. A third past they spoke about was the recent, early NEP-era past, largely peopled by the antecedent generation of ex-civil-servant Malay 'entrepreneurs' who, my informants admitted, had taken advantage of policy and patronage for their own personal development, ignoring the social responsibility implicit in entrepreneurship. My informants were haunted by claims that, until quite recently, Malays did not earn the privileges they had been granted by NEP.

The Malay economic 'pasts', the *kampung* one and the patronage-granting one, were described by my informants in remarkably similar ways. In both, Malays were 'economically backward', 'stupid', 'lazy', 'used to the easy life', 'living off the fat of the land', and so on. In the *kampung* past, Malays suffered from a fatalism which engendered passivity and complacency. In the recent past, however, when opportunistic Malays took sinful advantage of relations of power and political patronage in the cash-laden, subsidy economy of the early days of NEP, their behaviour represented what many of my informants saw as the vestiges of Malay 'feudalism'. My informants pointed to the traditional culture of the Malay sultans, and the feudal culture of misused power and complacency it established, identifying in it the same behaviours which were evidenced by the early NEP-era entrepreneurs (cf. Milne and Mauzy 1978).

Many Malays say, with embarrassment, that in the early days of NEP, enormous mistakes and abuses of power were made in attempts to uplift and improve the situation of the Malays; as a whole, however, they are unwilling to talk in historical detail about this time or to point to the villains.[11] They believe some of these mistakes were made by leaders and politicians who simply did not know any better; other Malays who fell under the spell of greed and power were truly corrupt. Dato Hassan, as he elaborated in his narrative, had flirted dangerously with greed and passivity when, in the early days of his career, he rode the easy wave of NEP privilege. Increasingly, '*bumiputera*-ism', the early NEP-era elite mentality which established that wealth and economic opportunities are either deserved or easily acquired through political or royal patronage, is anathema to those Malays who describe their entrepreneurial rewards as the result of effort, responsibility, and modern business techniques which have been learned through hard work alone. Modern, economically active Malays see an abrupt end to *bumiputera*-ism, to the end of feudal power relations and easy wealth, and to the end of elitist complacency.

In the powerfully descriptive language of my informants, *bumiputera* culture was 'passive', 'pampered', 'insincere', 'lazy', and 'weak'. Malays who demonstrated such behaviours were 'feudal', 'blindly loyal', and 'servile' to anyone who had power to help them – kings, feudal lords, colonial masters, corrupt political leaders, patrons, and sultans. They covered their decayed emotions with a false face of pleasantness and the false, decorous words of etiquette, revealing their true feelings only anonymously, through such cowardly acts as sending anonymous 'poison pen' letters or even through the practice of black magic.

Such behaviours were evidenced in the pre-colonial feudal period, the colonial period, and especially in the early days of NEP, when well-positioned *bumiputera* exploited their status or relationship to political and aristocratic power for wealth. As a whole, such elite Malays were variously described as '*bumi* shufflers', 'free-riders on the *bumi* ticket', 'civil-service *bumis*', 'the old kind of *bumis*', or the 'old guard', and by a particularly vivid expression that was in vogue for several months, '*bumis* like the fat Fiji kings' who grow fatter and fatter on the backs of others. Such Malays exhibited no real business knowledge, and instead, had 'a short-term orientation', 'sought easy and quick fortunes', and 'were status orientated' instead of development orientated, just like the sycophants who had served the Malay sultans in the feudal period. Many people I spoke to condemned all the false, feudalistic values of the recent NEP past and contrasted them to nascent Malay Muslim entrepreneurial culture in an almost endlessly repeated comparative phrase: 'know-who' instead of 'know-how'.

In the new terms of Malay entrepreneurial culture of which my informants were the proponents, 'know-how' had become invested with nearly the same morally validating force as the Quranically prescribed concept of intention or *niat*. 'Know-how' meant knowledge, planning, responsibility, and effort – essentially, exemplary skill, the first of Weber's meanings for the term 'virtuosi'. It meant modern business knowledge, lessons learned in the 'school of hard knocks'. It meant understanding and using management techniques, high technology, and networking, both locally and across national boundaries. Nothing could be more different from the *kampung* past, from the society envisaged by *dakwah*, or from the feudal past than, in a word, 'know-how'.

Just one of many conversations I had about 'know-how' in modern life is recorded in full below, to give a sense of how deeply the sense of its claim to moral difference had been incorporated into the virtuoso rhetoric of contemporary entrepreneurship. The speaker was a self-described entrepreneur with important political connections to the Mahathir government.

The new Malay entrepreneur builds himself, then he builds others. He trains, recruits, tests, motivates, and rewards his employees with incentives. If he finds *kampung*-minded Malays who are lazy and undisciplined, he coaches and guides them to become more modern. He is interested in the long term, in a return on his investment, not a 'quick kill'. He is a good and sincere Muslim. He does not want *bumi* concessions or *bumi* handouts. He wants nothing to come for free. He believes in managing for success, managing his managers, open communication, technology, and feedback and input. The *bumi* or feudal boss, however, spends his day on the golf course. He makes a phone call and gets a contract from his patron. He makes a pay-off, accepts a bribe. This is not entrepreneurship! The new Malay has know-how ... and the days of know-who are simply over.

The force, pervasiveness, and uniformity of the language my informants used to explain the changes which they were implementing in Malay economic life was striking. Just as business information travels rapidly through Malay social networks, as will be described in Part II, business language does as well. Over the course of my stay in Kuala Lumpur I came to learn the words of entrepreneurial culture that echoed not just in the offices and halls of huge corporations, but in conversations overheard in night-time food stalls. My informants, from would-be entrepreneurs like Rokiah's clerk Amir and ordinary entrepreneurs to Dato Hassan and other newly ascendant corporate leaders like the speaker above, avidly read business magazines, listened to the speeches of economic policy-makers, and watched television programmes on business issues and masterful entrepreneurship. Using the government-valorized and Islamically validated language of entrepreneurship, they discussed business, tried to practise it, and, in all possible contexts, sought to demonstrate their entrepreneurial capacity and its relation to their Islamic identity. How and why this was so will continue to concern us in later chapters, but for now, I wish to draw attention to the discourse of change implied by the language of business in the lives of my informants, and how they employed its legitimizing idiom to identify with Mahathir-style national economic progress.

I became aware of how deeply the 'know-how' language of business had infused into the daily life of my informants when Rokiah and her partner Ishak first attempted to structure their varied entrepreneurial ventures into a management consultancy, overseeing such projects as Arif's entrepreneurial idea EG2020. They assigned each other complex corporate responsibilities (director of research and development, director of high-technology implementation) for divisions of the nascent company they envisaged. I spent several days writing up their ideas into a business plan and diagramming the organization. They spoke of a future in which they saw themselves as powerful and well-recognized Islamic entrepreneurs – what I have called 'virtuosi' – and when they were, their corporate organization would already be in place, structured in line with the high-technology goals of modern economic development envisaged by the government, as will become clearer in Chapter 4.

Korporat entrepreneurial 'know-how' was, to Rokiah and Ishak, a large part of *ikhtiar* and the demonstration of sincerity and responsibility. They demonstrated it by speaking its language in their networks and plans. With it, rewards would be sincerely earned, morally deserved. To many of my informants, learning, exploring, and showing an earnest and heartfelt desire to change and grow – crucial Islamic values – were simultaneously being condensed into the language of entrepreneurial and corporate values to establish Malay economic legitimacy, and beyond this, modern Islamic responsibility. With this, and only with this, did my informants claim to be deserving of rewards, to have earned the privileges and position of leadership (the second of Weber's meanings for the word 'virtuosi'). Indeed, the demonstration of the new terms of Malay Muslim economic validation and the dangers of unearned privilege had become all the more necessary for the new generation of ambitious Malay entrepreneurs as I arrived in Malaysia in January 1993. As it was with the surge of fundamentalism, this was a pivotal period in the legitimation of the modern Malay entrepreneurial identity.

THE CRISIS BETWEEN WHAT IS GRANTED AND WHAT IS EARNED: THE MALAY SULTANS

In the first months of 1993, the Malaysian nation was embroiled in a constitutional crisis concerning the legal immunity of the traditional royalty, the nine hereditary Islamic rulers or sultans of the Malay states. The background to the situation was set out long before, in provisions of the Malaysian Constitution. It is generally stated by historians that a racial 'bargain' was made in the 1957 Constitution: the Chinese would accept Malay political and cultural hegemony as the 'price to be paid ... for full participation in the Federation' (Milne and Mauzy 1978: 38). The Malays were thus granted substantial constitutional rights, including the position of the Malay traditional rulers, the declaration of Islam as the state religion under the protection of the sultans, the designation of *Bahasa Melayu* as the national language, and any 'Malay privileges', which could include providing jobs, scholarships, and licences, determined necessary by the *agung* or king (Mohd. Salleh bin Abas 1986).

Article 153 of the Constitution, which these elements comprise, can be construed as the legal foundation for the systematic intensification of the 'special position' of the Malays in the period after the race riot of 1969 and the justification of laws which spun out from it – including NEP and the amendment to the Sedition Act of 1948 which made it a crime to question the provisions of Article 153, marking what many see as the beginning of a culture of authoritarianism in Malaysia (Crouch 1992). The *agung* and his royal brethren, the sultans, were thus granted a role which was both

powerfully instrumental and evocative – they were to be the supreme protectors of Islam in their states and were to 'safeguard the special position of
the Malays' – and they were themselves untouchable, protected by full
legal immunity guaranteeing their 'sovereignty, prerogatives, powers and
jurisdiction' from any claim against them (Mohd. Salleh bin Abas 1986: 3).
The institution of rulership was invested with everything that comprised
'Malayness', embodying, symbolizing, and commanding Malay hegemony
with enormous religious, emotional, and cultural force (Kessler 1992). The
official, post-colonial framing of Malay political dominance was preserved
not merely by legal power, but anchored by the even more uncontestable
power of a purportedly historical royal tradition.

In 1983, Mahathir, the first commoner Prime Minister to lead Malaysia,
failed in the attempt to remove some of the privileges granted to the *agung*
as head of state. Nine years later, in 1992, a man reported that the Sultan
of Johore had hit him. He could not prosecute because, as Article 153
established, the nine sultans were 'above the law', immune from any legal
proceedings. Prime Minister Mahathir, by then the author of political and
economic policy that had led to his current, nearly unassailable popularity
(Khoo Kay Jin 1992; Khoo Boo Teik 1995), perceived himself sufficiently
empowered to take on the issue of the sultans once again. This time, he
armed himself well.

The Prime Minister pointed to the sultans' royal perquisites and privileges to demonstrate that they were excessive, self-interested, and contrary
to the values of a modern developing nation. He demanded that the
sultans' immunity be lifted, a decree which, as the Constitution confirms,
would require their assent. The sultans unanimously refused. In the weeks
that followed, the newspapers were filled with revelations of the sultans'
excesses, not only of luxurious, ostentatious lifestyles at the expense of the
public, but also of rape, even murder, committed by members of the royal
families and court. Malaysians, but especially Malays, were forced to consider that their traditional protectors had betrayed them, while, in contrast,
their modern political leaders were fighting boldly on their behalf.

By mid-January 1993, the Parliament had passed several amendments
which curbed the power of the rulers, to which finally, in March, the
sultans peevishly consented; their legal immunity was removed.
Newspaper stories described political leaders associated with the Prime
Minister as triumphant, claiming to have cleared the final obstacle to full-
scale progress and modernity among Malays and for all Malaysia. In his
speeches, Prime Minister Mahathir declared that the nation was now free
for all Malaysians to stand equal under the law, a great democratic
achievement for the citizenry and the *rakyat* (common people). The drama

had additional resonance for Prime Minister Mahathir, who was, in contrast, whipping up public interest among the *rakyat* with his persuasive and evocative social and economic development campaign, 'Vision 2020', which emphasized Malaysians' redoubled efforts at self-development and simple, traditional values and ideals like 'caring' and 'sharing'. This framed, as will be discussed in Chapter 4, a very different definition of Malay traditionalism, vaguely Islamic and egalitarian in form, in contrast to the elite-based, anti-modern, rulers-versus-ruled definition represented by the sultans.

All of this took place in my first few weeks in Malaysia, when, with only newspaper reports to follow, I feared I was missing the dramatic conversational coverage that good informants could provide. The few Malays I knew brushed away my attempts to ask questions. When, by the time of Prime Minister Mahathir's victorious *dénouement*, I knew enough people to broach the subject of what had happened, my informants' comments were surprisingly flat in comparison to the high drama of their political leaders' rhetoric. 'It was inevitable' or 'it had to come to pass', most people said, and then indifferently shrugged off the subject. Very quickly, even while the amendments were still being negotiated, it had somehow become old news. Were people reluctant, I wondered, to discuss the events because of the shame and embarrassment the lurid revelations caused? Were they reluctant to discuss it because of the reported unwillingness Malays have to criticize their leaders or any other Malays openly, which, as I have already stated, was to be confirmed again and again in my research? Or, still too new to Malaysia, had I indeed 'missed' the event, and all the feelings of conflict and ambivalence it must have engendered?

In many ways, I was to learn, all of these questions could be answered in the affirmative. It *was* acutely embarrassing to Malays that the traditional symbols of Malay Muslim ascendency had been stripped bare, even globally exposed, for the events were well covered in the international press. That embarrassment was made clear to me over the course of the next year and a half, when many of my informants did refer to what had happened, but only obliquely, in the context of hearing about similar scandals in the British royal family or in the Clinton presidency, affirming, as if with a deep sense of relief, that 'these kinds of things happen everywhere'. And, whatever anxiety about unseemly disloyalty to their traditional leaders the drama might have created among my informants was resolved, I was to understand later, by a kind of elective muteness, a typically Malay reserve born in the belief that a designated leader, in this case Prime Minister Mahathir, was speaking boldly for the common, but hushed, interests of the whole group.[12]

It was Rokiah who provided, quite late in my stay in Kuala Lumpur, the most powerful condensation of ideas about what had happened in the 'modern-versus-traditional' drama of the sultans. She and I had been discussing the rather innocent subject of how Malays 'launch' a business by inviting an important Dato or Tan Sri or government minister to officiate, so that the event is enforced with an impressive formality. Only a year or so ago, she said, sultans or tengkus (princes) invariably launched Malay businesses. Rokiah revealed, full of pride and a sense of validation, 'You know, *Melayu baru* – new-style business people like me and the others you've met – never had anything much to do with the sultans and all those terrible events that happened'. She went on to tell me that, indeed, kingship, that institution which was constitutionally framed to guarantee Malay Muslim dominance, was not even a Malay tradition, it was a 'Hindu tradition' that Malays – as Muslims – did not actually believe in. In Islam, she reminded me, no man stands above another and all are equal under Allah. The sultanate was therefore actually unIslamic.

Rokiah continued, 'Mahathir had long been planning this change. He knew that Malays like us were afraid of speaking out against the sultans for fear of sounding anti-Malay and encouraging the Chinese to advance against us. *We* knew he would change this. He waited for just the right time, and then, he simply fixed the problem'. The *problem*, she claimed, was not really or primarily a constitutional issue or even a moral one about beatings, rape, and murder, the way the newspapers had reported it. The problem – behind the scenes, known to the 'new Malays' alone – was about business, she said. The real crime of the sultans, Rokiah revealed, was that they had taken all of the significant business opportunities in their states – contracts to build roads, office buildings, resorts, factories, and oil rigs. But even worse than that was the effect this feudal monopoly had on ambitious, but unfortunately lazy, feudal Malays. 'When the sultans took all the business opportunities', she admitted, 'the corrupt Malay entrepreneurs looking for easy success ran around asking each other, "who do you know in the palace, and can you talk to him for me?"' Such people were hoping for a 'letter from the sultan,' just like in the old feudal days, when strings got pulled.[13] People boasted about and exploited even the slightest connection to a palace official and used it to try to get business. Bribes were paid and 'Ali-Baba' fortunes were made subcontracting jobs to the Chinese.[14] No one did 'real business', she said, 'because no one worked for it and no one wanted anything but the easy route'. Rokiah concluded sadly that this is what had tainted early NEP-era entrepreneurship among Malays, when sultans and entrepreneurs colluded greedily in an economy flush with opportunity, exploitable policy, and feudal mentalities. This was to be the most detailed information about NEP-era corruption I was to hear in Malaysia.

What was being contested, then, for Rokiah, represented publicly by the somewhat manufactured issue of sultanic immunity, was *who* – traditional sultans and their elite NEP-era sinecures or modern, sincere Malay Muslim business people – would rightfully hold economic power and who would rightfully claim the rewards of development. Put another way, the constitutional crisis of the sultanate was a conflict between 'false' Malay entrepreneurs demonstrating feudal 'know-who' and 'real' entrepreneurs demonstrating modern 'know-how' and Islamic virtue. This had long been brewing, she revealed. As real entrepreneurs arose, the *Melayu baru*, who knew that business belonged only in the hands of those who worked meritocratically for it, the ascribed and illegitimate holders of wealth – the sultans and the sycophants – could be torn down. She believed, as did most of my informants, that the feudal system of entrepreneurship was a regrettable but necessary 'stage' of economic development for Malays, one which had now ended. Rokiah portrayed the events of 1993 as a *coup d'entrepreneur* – a kind of well-planned political conspiracy of Malay economic legitimacy under the wise leadership of Prime Minister Mahathir who was himself a prime example of the Malay Muslim practice of 'know-how' meritocracy, commoner roots, and Islamic virtue – perhaps the most qualified virtuoso of all.

The Malay Muslim entrepreneurial identity which many of my informants had established was built on a demonstration of a sharp contrast to backward, elite, irresponsible, and unIslamic behaviours, such as merely 'riding the *bumi* ticket'. Business success today, to the new generation of Malays, would result from the techniques of modern, universal business management and hard work. New Malays would stake claims to material rewards that were rightfully earned, not merely granted through patronage or position. I realized that my informants who had seemed indifferent to the constitutional crisis had indeed been critiquing the sultans, for it was in contrast to sentiments of their illegitimacy, their old-style, 'know-who', NEP-era perquisites, even their unIslamic behaviours, that the concepts of a self-described, meritocratic Malay Muslim entrepreneurial culture were being worked out.

DATO HASSAN CONTEMPLATES THE FUTURE

Once, Dato Hassan invited me to lunch at the prestigious Selangor Club in Kuala Lumpur, where, years before, British colonial officers had played polo and drunk gin. Now it is a mark of entrepreneurial success to be able to afford its steep membership fees. As we sat in the coffee shop eating stall-style food which Dato Hassan said reminded him of his '*kampung* past', he said, 'Now, I ask myself – what should a man who has many million *ringgit* in the bank do for the next twenty years? I came into this world naked; I'll leave it naked, judged for my deeds on behalf of others'. He mused on various possibilities, describing a humble idea to open a small restaurant serving traditional and simple Malay food, 'like this', waving his hand at the food-vendors' stalls. Again and again he talked about 'humility' and 'simplicity' as the feelings he wanted to demonstrate. 'What I really want to do is put business deals together, to be a venture capitalist, like your Michael Milken did, but not dishonestly. I don't want more excitement or money, I want to show my humility by *giving* more, adding to the progress of the nation'.

He explained to me that he felt he had reached a point in his life where he needed to transform himself again: 'In Islam, we believe that at 40 a man is fully mature. I am now 45. I am a millionaire many times over. Now is the time to fully return most of what I have been given. Not my money – this I have earned honestly and may keep. I must find a way to help my people even more'. His voice became sharp with excitement. 'Everything I learned I can pass on to others. You see, once I was just a simple *kampung* boy. Now it is my turn to do more good for others. Some Malays, the *bumis*, the sultans, and the old civil servants always want more…. I want to give; I want *less*'.

I close this chapter where I began it, with Dato Hassan reflecting on the Islamic nature of modern entrepreneurship and his sincere wish to re-enact the simple values of life through his increasingly high-level corporate strategies for Malays and Malaysia. By exploring his entrepreneurial ethic and others, I have attempted to analyze a modern theory of Islamic entrepreneurial morality. My informants used this ideology to critique the past and explain the present. With it, they idealized the entrepreneur as a social leader and moral paragon, the virtuoso who will lead Malays to the future and demonstrate his or her own pursuit of salvation through worldly action.

Entrepreneurship concerns more than issues of faith in Malay life; it also resolves issues of political power and social primacy in an era of contestation. Its virtues were highly valorized by the political and corporate leaders to whom my informants listened and were closely aligned. I have thus suggested that entrepreneurship – seen as Malay economic intensification coloured by religious belief – provides an ideology which in many ways can be seen to have resolved some of the pressing, highly problematic, and contentious questions raised by Islamic fundamentalism. Like the *dakwah* groups my informants contrasted themselves to, entrepreneurship could publicly demonstrate a version of Islamic virtue in a changing world. Beyond this, my informants' version of entrepreneurship, in contrast to 'feudal' society, could demonstrate modern, democratic, and meritocratic virtues with which they could criticize their aristocratic leaders and could yet, like them, become wealthy – but deservedly so.

It was clear to my informants that the era of feudal patronage and ascribed rewards had come to an abrupt and welcome end, symbolized by putting the sultans back in their palaces and out of business. They elided or perhaps did not see that the system of elite entailments that established such entrepreneurs as Dato Hassan and tied UMNO leaders to corporate life had much in common with the system which they claimed had been abandoned. Somehow these were behaviours unrecognizable as familiar examples of patronage, but were now readily identified as the practical specifics of modern economic life, of know-how, of merely 'doing business'. In a later chapter, we will see how many of the people I knew, ordinary Malay entrepreneurs engaged in complex and ramifying relationships in search of economic access and social and religious validation, were actually being closed out of 'doing business' in the exalted arena of Malay Muslim entrepreneurial and virtuoso corporate culture that Dato Hassan represented and controlled.

Dato Hassan's entrepreneurial ideology had produced the power of self-justification, explaining not only what he and the less exalted, but equally ambitious, members of the NEP cohort had perhaps most sought to understand – why they should be rewarded unequally for their efforts – but also, as will become clearer in the next chapter, giving self-congratulatory and solipsistical primacy to the culture they themselves had created. The widespread belief among my informants that modern entrepreneurial behaviours will also re-enact or provide access to humble and simple *kampung* values, the past to which Dato Hassan now wished to return – community, ritual, justice, and egalitarianism – is the subject of the next chapter.

4 The *Kampung* and the Global Village

It might seem paradoxical that in devaluing the Malay *economic* past, increasingly – in the corridors of corporate power, in evocative images portrayed by government and the media, and in the ideology of modern Malay men and women now living far from the villages and small towns of their childhoods – the framing of a highly valued Malay *social* past is taking form. While the *kampung* encompassed no past economic behaviours that could be utilized in the present, and Malay feudal society had no social behaviours applicable to modern life, the *kampung*, now exalted as a kind of idyllic community, has, to my informants and their political leaders, instructive power in conducting modern relationships. Its norms and values are believed to be superior to those of Western societies to which modern Malays increasingly compare themselves; moreover, in its imparadisement we can find indigenous theories of 'Malayness' itself.

The men and women I knew, who construed themselves as 'new Malays', are moving ever farther from the small-town pasts of their childhoods. At the same time, as we shall see, the past is memorialized as being perhaps more humble and Utopian than their childhood experiences often actually were, pushing the 'past' back to the more dreamily evoked *kampung* of their parents' and grandparents', and perhaps not their own, childhoods. As my informants became increasingly distant from the real *kampung* of today – populated more often than not with marginalized rural Malays who have been left out of NEP development or squatters come to Kuala Lumpur with hopes of retrieving some share of it – their image of an idealized *kampung* grew ever sharper. The real *kampung*, as we learned in the previous chapter, is occupied by backward and passive Malays.

BEING '*KAMPUNG*' – A MODERN MALAY IDENTITY

As seen at the end of the last chapter, Dato Hassan revealed his core identity – and the one to which he intended to return – as 'just a *kampung* boy'. At first, I was much surprised by his description. His parents had long been urbanized, among the middle-class civil-service strata, essentially the 'new Malays' of their time. Dato Hassan, like many of my informants, despite an urban childhood, despite being programmed for success by ambitious, modernized parents who knew well the value of an English-style education and rigid academic discipline, despite all the socially differentiating experiences he had had as a result of NEP educational and economic opportunity, evoked an identity that returned him squarely to a rural village past.

But as the phrase '*kampung* boy' settled in my mind, I realized I had heard it often. Nearly every successful Malay entrepreneur that I spoke to, like Dato Hassan and the highly regarded Tan Sri Azman Hashim,[1] of whom we will learn more below, described himself as 'just a *kampung* boy'. This identity was not merely claimed by the entrepreneurial virtuosi of Malay society, but by the much more average entrepreneurial aspirants I knew. I began to realize that this claim had less to do with my informants' past experiences than it did with a crucial definition of their modern identity. Indeed, my informants frequently endeavoured to show me how their modern behaviours evidenced a solid continuity with the simplicity and humility of Malays in the past. Rokiah, for example, frequently and earnestly sought to explain to me how '*kampung*' she still was. She said that while the 'outside appearance' may change drastically, such as wearing Western clothes, and aspiring, by means of entrepreneurship, to high economic status and a modern *korporat* identity, her inside self – in terms of beliefs and values – had stayed essentially traditional. Westernized material existence is merely a veneer to my informants, rather like the 'costume' they claimed *dakwah* followers wore. But not only was the core self still firmly in place, but its traditional norms and behaviours were, Rokiah felt, alive in modern activities, contributing much to her pursuits and directing the social and moral content of modern relationships. This constellation of ideas had much to do with her perception of how to behave 'Malay' in modern life, and in turn, of how to behave as an entrepreneur, as we will see later on.

The Malay men and women I knew believed there were *kampung* values in Malay culture – sharing, fairness, equality, and balance – bred in the bone, that could not be tossed off, no matter how much any individual stood out in the context of modernity. They pointed out how these values could be demonstrated in modern entrepreneurial activities, when Malays pitched in to help one another by sharing business ideas and engaging in allied ventures. Indeed, what they called business 'networking' recalled to them the spirit of *gotong-royong* (shared labour) which they said characterizes life in the *kampung*.[2] As such, being a *kampung* Malay has taken on a newly valued eidetic form in urban Malaysia. There has been a revival of traditional *kampung* interests, such as *kampung*-style singing and male–female dancing, even a revival of a *décolleté* dress style for women – *baju kebaya* – which would have been thought highly indecent just a few years ago.[3] Significantly, the cultural return of forms of 'Malayness' marks, to many of my informants, the end of criticism and restrictions on Malay customs that Arab-centric *dakwah* consciousness enforced even among the more moderate Malays. Moreover, as we shall soon see, the *kampung*-based definition of 'Malayness' my informants were elaborating increasingly denied the culture of aristocracy and ascribed privilege represented by the sultanic and feudal past, as successful and ambitious Malays – common *kampung* boys and girls – insisted they had started from the same humble roots as those less successful than they.

A key theme was emerging in the ideology of modern, NEP-cohort Malays: material evidence of class, ethnicity, and social status was becoming increasingly irrelevant in determining social relations, because Malays, my informants said, always treat everyone equally – as they remember doing in the *kampung*. 'Inside' everyone was still 'just a *kampung*' person, open, genuine, and simple. In order fully to comprehend how my often affluent and always ambitious informants claimed a simple *kampung* identity, we must first look at how many Malays believe they enact those norms, beginning first with the powerful evidence of traditional, *kampung*-style 'Malayness' they asked me to notice most of all, their culturally framed, ritual selves. Through that festive definition of 'Malayness', many modern Malays even saw the end of ethnic – and economic – conflict in their nation.

'CULTURE' IN A *PESTA* NATION

For anyone living in Kuala Lumpur, the calendar year is experienced as serial demonstrations of Malay, Chinese, and Indian 'culture', each group taking a fair turn at showing off its holiday spirit, primarily represented by elaborate decorations and displays in commercial and public spaces. My landlady, Aziza, eagerly visited Kuala Lumpur's many shopping malls in December to gaze at the Christmas decorations which fill up the public space. Santa Claus is replaced by the vivid red and gold flags symbolizing Chinese New Year; these, depending on the timing of fasting month,[4] are followed or preceded by the exceedingly elaborate decorations for the Muslim Hari Raya season, when symbols of Malay neo-traditionalism explode into the urban setting in the form of decorative *kampung* houses and *kampung* culture on display in the lobbies of big hotels, the convention centre, and shopping malls (cf. Kahn 1992).

As a consequence of NEP-enforced economic policy, the assistant Minister of Culture told me Malaysia now has a *budaya rojak dan sukacita*, or a 'mixed' and happy culture, that could primarily be experienced through its various *pesta* or festivals. This concept echoes one which is often heard in speeches made by Prime Minister Mahathir, who describes Malaysia as a welcoming nation of spirited *pesta* offering warm hospitality to everyone, both locally and world-wide. My informants insisted that today everyone, Malay, Chinese, and Indian alike, all comfortably partook of and genuinely enjoyed one another's *pesta* culture – a fact no one would have been comfortable with just a few years before, when the issue of Arab-centric Islamization of the state and national culture was so acute.

Now, my informants, moderate and self-consciously 'modern' Muslims, felt that their own colourful 'culture' was a harmless way of expressing valued local cultural and social norms, one that did not, as the *dakwah* groups had insisted in the recent past, threaten or deviate from Muslim religiosity but merely showed its particular Malay form. Moreover, the new spirit of *pesta* culture is so relaxed that it even allows a cultural synthesis:[5] people pointed out to me the 'mixing' of various ethnic *pesta* traditions like Malays putting gifts of *duit raya* (holiday money) in little paper packets just like the Chinese do, and the Chinese serving and sharing special cookies on their holidays just like Malays do, as evidence that all Malaysians, regardless of ethnicity or religion, once again lived in a state of harmony and tolerance. My informants claimed that in the *kampung* of their childhoods, Malay–Chinese differences had been unimportant; everyone lived happily and comfortably together. Now, they said – as a result of economic equality – ethnicity and religion, Malaysian landmines of contestation in the 1970s and 1980s, had again become inconsequential. But so, too, had the definition of 'culture'. As one analyst put it, Malaysian ethnic culture had 'tapered off into a pot-pourri of outward manifestations of almost non-controversial items that promoted attire, food, and ... songs' (Oo Yu Hock 1991: 55). Moreover, the supposedly 'national' or civil claims about *pesta* norms became quintessentially Malay-based. Far more important than shopping-mall displays of that diverse *pesta* culture of admixtured ethnic harmony was its identification with a key *Malay* social and ritual value.

Indeed, when my informants proudly pointed out Chinese and Indian *pesta* decorations taking their turn with Malay culture, they saw in it a public and civil inheritance of a Malay traditional norm – a spirit of hospitality and openness, remembered from the *kampung* and now updated to modern life. Later in this chapter we will explore more fully the *kampung* inheritance to civil society, but now, we will explore its pervasive rearticulation in what my informants pointed to as their customary and 'traditional' ritual selves – that special Malay manifestation which allows the nation to live in harmony.

'BEING MALAY' IN RITUAL LIFE

According to my informants, Malay cultural values are at their most potent during the Muslim festival of Hari Raya, when a month of fasting (Ramadan or *puasa*) ends in Aidilfitri, an emotional ritual in which Muslims ask for forgiveness from people they may have harmed during the preceding 12 months. As a whole, this lengthy holiday becomes a discrete season, displacing normal, everyday life. Hari Raya is doubly celebrated by urban Malays as a feverish demonstration of what they see as *kampung*-like hospitality represented by the symbol of the 'open house' or *rumah terbuka* – and as a ritual of simplicity and renewal, expressed by the powerful symbol of 'returning home' or *balik kampung.*

The two years I participated with my Malay informants in the events held during the long Hari Raya season of fasting and forgiveness were core experiences in my field research, and not just because they were the stuff of great anthropological interest, exciting ritual suspensions of workaday life to which Malays look forward all year (Kessler 1978). In fact, I was *encouraged* to see these holidays as cornerstones of my research, for, as my informants increasingly sought to assist me in my understanding of Malay culture, they urged me to see the ritual events and experiences of Hari Raya – of a month-long build-up and its month-long conclusion – as the essential evidence of that which was 'really Malay'. Within these events are all the cultural things my informants readily identified as 'traditional' and '*kampung*'. Indeed, often in the midst of a discussion about Malay entrepreneurship, Islam, family life, or modernity, my informants would break away from their narrative to remind me that 'everything' I sought an answer to was evident in Hari Raya, where I could see for myself what being Malay meant.

The religious context of *puasa* or fasting is to suppress feelings of *nafsu*, or desire,[6] for food, sex, and water, in order better to understand the true nature of the self in humbled relation to Allah. Fasting, as my informants also pointed out, assures the spiritual equality of all Muslims, for rich and poor alike must resist the pangs of hunger (ibid.). Beyond this, fasting's conclusion in Hari Raya Aidilfitri, when Muslims ask forgiveness from one another and seek to atone for their transgressions, is an intensely humbling expression of the self in relation to others. Theoretically, then, the purpose of Hari Raya is to commemorate and reproduce Islamic reserve.

But *puasa* month itself is anything but solemn; indeed, nearly frantic, it disavows reserve, and does so in an explicitly Malay way. During *puasa*, Kuala Lumpur's main streets and suburban shopping areas are converted to nightly markets selling traditional *kampung* food favourites to thousands of Malay patrons who greet one another with warm holiday wishes. My informants sold, bought, and gave away thousands of Hari Raya *kuih* (sweets) and elaborate gift hampers to business associates and contacts. Fasting then feasting, they sought out and proffered invitations for huge all-you-can-eat breaking-fast and post-Aidilfitri feasts at hotels or their homes. They expansively told everyone they knew to 'drop by' during the holiday season, often redecorating the house to accommodate such entertaining. Hari Raya today is a festival which publicly and unabashedly concentrates on Malay sociability, established primarily in the context of food. The first point of departure for understanding modern *kampung* 'Malayness' is to see how Hari Raya urban culture was figuratively and literally consumed by my informants.

COMMENSALITY AND COMMENSURATENESS

Malay festivals – rambling, hospitable rituals staged in the domain of the ever-welcoming Malay home (and, as frequently today, the hotel banquet hall) – are primarily about eating and hosting: the Malay feast or *kenduri*. Cohen calls 'eating and drinking together … for achieving communion … a universally practised symbolic institution, a "language" in its own right', rituals of commensality which create, develop, and enhance communal relationships (1981: 211). Like *slametan* feasting in Indonesia, which mitigates hierarchy and conflict in the public sphere (Schweizer 1989), it has long been recognized that the *kenduri* tradition of Malay culture seeks to symbolize the commensal values of generosity and harmony among the entire *kampung* community (McAllister 1990; Wilson 1986). The Hari Raya feast in traditional Malay life meant that theoretically, one, as a host, would open the house to all, feed them *rendang* (spiced meat) with rice packets of *ketupat*, and give away *duit raya* (gifts of money) to children, neighbours, and beggars alike – a celebration which mediates and momentarily renders irrelevant all social differences, which, it will be recalled, is the very point of Hari Raya. In contemporary Malaysian life, as we shall see, this symbol of Malay hospitality – the open house – often takes on a very special significance.

The roots of this socially incorporative *rumah terbuka* tradition that 'opens the house' to visitors are perhaps found in the Islamic injunction that on holidays, men should go from house to house to join in prayers (see Zainal Abidin b. Ahmad [Zaba] 1949), an important embracing symbol of the *ummah*. But today, the official government view, as well as that of my informants, is that an 'open house' is a 'uniquely Malaysian tradition', what Prime Minister Mahathir rhapsodized as 'a celebration of harmony, a key element in the nation's quest' for economic development (*Star*, 27 March 1993). In his Hari Raya speech in 1994 (in counterpoint to his speech in 1993, which, as we saw in the previous chapter, warned Malays about *kampung* economic passivity), Prime Minister Mahathir reminded Malays to remember their *kampung* roots and 'generous nature by having open houses and inviting their friends and neighbours to join in the celebrations' (*New Straits Times*, 27 March 1994). Indeed, it is well known that the Prime Minister and top Malay political leaders have open houses on Hari Raya to which all are welcome, and images of them expansively greeting and feeding guests appear prominently in the media. (The photograph which appeared on the 1994 Hari Raya Aidilfitri edition of all Malaysian newspapers of the Prime Minister welcoming some Chinese Malaysian citizens to his open house evidently was intended to underline the perception that as one of just many festivals or *pesta* in the multicultural nation, Hari Raya could be interpreted as the prototypical 'Malaysian' holiday, a kind of generic holiday about harmony and sharing.)[7]

In theory, in the *kampung* past and urban present, and today in the exclusive community of Damansara Heights where Malay government ministers live, 'everyone' is welcome to the Malay *kampung*-style *rumah terbuka*. Everyone in the small city of Alor Setar, where Rokiah's parents still live, was invited to the palatial homes of Prime Minister Mahathir's entrepreneurially well-placed nieces and nephews during Hari Raya, but as Rokiah, her sisters, and I wandered through them, all we talked about in hushed voices was how expensive the furniture and the decorations must have been. As such, open houses and open hospitality – a traditional *kampung* virtue which many Malays want to demonstrate in modern life – actually appear to encapsulate and reproduce complex images of status, hierarchy, and power.

But this, too, may be a subversive fact of real *kampung* life, where, in all likelihood, such power strategies were also evidenced in 'harmonious' and 'communal' relations, a fact which is little reflected, if not openly disavowed in the memories of most of my informants. Several researchers have touched on the notion that traditional *kenduri* such as weddings were

highly calculative and competitive social events in which it was understood that if important people visit your feast, the implication was obvious
that you will be invited to theirs (Banks 1983; Firth 1943; S. Husin Ali
1975), and that Malay 'hospitality' culture is often a dialectical form of
largesse and tribute-paying (cf. Bailey 1976). As such, under the generally
accepted anthropological maxim that, as Mauss (1989) famously noted,
hospitality is, in fact, a potent form of social control, one takes on the role
of 'host' or 'guest' during contemporary Malay festivities – as one likely
did in traditional Malay festivities – with the knowledge that much more is
being symbolized in rituals of commensality than simple reciprocity and
communal sharing among equals. Involved in these, quite obviously, are
transactions of status as well.[8] In order to fully understand the discursive
themes of 'hospitality' implied by the Hari Raya ritual of 'open house'
that so dramatically evidences, to my informants and their government,
'being *kampung*' in urban contexts, we must look briefly inside the Malay
house. In that most traditional locus of hospitality is also a vivid display of
hierarchy, power, and status.

HOMES, HOSPITALITY, AND THE CANON OF DISPLAY

Driving through even the poorest *kampung*, my Malay informants would
often point out how the colourful curtains in the windows of the wooden
houses were poignant evidence that even Malays who have very little in
the way of material wealth care deeply about beauty and the welcoming,
hospitable feeling that such details in a home give. Malays are convinced
that concern for the domestic sphere is a quintessential trait of their
culture, in contrast to the Chinese, who they claim can live contentedly in
dirty houses, a stereotype with a long history (Rabushka 1973). Malays
state that Islam requires them to keep the house pleasant and welcoming at
all times, and to encourage the spontaneous appearance and resulting generous treatment of all guests, a norm found in other Islamic cultures as
well (Kanafani 1993; Rosen 1984). As such, there is a decorous, stylish,
almost exhibitionistic aspect to Malay 'hospitality' culture – which, aside
from an extensive knowledge of rules of etiquette (Khoo Kay Kim 1991),
also includes the formal presenting or displaying items of hospitality. In
Malay life, hospitality is not just a behavioural norm, it has a visual aspect
as well.

   While one cannot miss observing this tendency in modern Malay
homes, it appears to have a long history. Indeed, the celebration of hospitality possessions was remembered from my informants' childhoods, and

from their parents' childhoods, when their mothers exhibited items used during Hari Raya and *kenduri* in glass-fronted cabinets, in what Packard, in another context, called a 'showcase of culture' (1959) and Veblen called the canon of display (1957). Hospitality items, still on prominent display in my informants' parents' houses, were status symbols, collections and objects imported from England, like china plates, Pyrex dishes, and serving trays (cf. Mokhzani 1965).

There is strong evidence that Malays have long used the house and its furnishings as a key to social-status differentiation, as described in Khasnor Johan's (1984) study of the prestigious, British-orientated Malay Administrative Service officers. Gullick (1987) mentions the elaborate decor of homes of Malay political elites in the nineteenth and early twentieth centuries, and A. Kahor Bador (1973) describes the way in which these tastes were invariably copied in the homes and consumption choices of socially lesser Malays. In the 1940s, Djamour (1959) found urban Malays in Singapore to be similarly proud of their homes and identified home-ownership and styles of décor with status. Moreover, this was not just an urban or elite civil-service-class phenomenon, for, as Banks noted in rural Kedah, the size of the house represented social status (1983). This fact was confirmed by some of my informants, who said that each time their fathers' rank in the civil service increased, another room or more 'space' was added to the house (just as my informants today, as their own economic status increased, often provided luxurious renovations to their parents' homes, as discussed in Chapter 2).

My informants tended not to see that such images of material wealth were evidence of social differentiation and power in the communities in which they were raised, alternatively claiming that 'everyone' – civil servant and *padi* farmer alike – had the same meagre possessions or that no one had any at all (cf. Nagata 1975). Indeed, no matter how many times I pointed to extensive collections of brass or glass objects collected by my informants' parents in the 1950s, or learned about the early purchase of an automobile or a trip to Mecca, it was denied that any informant's family lived very differently from its poorest neighbours. The hospitality and open-house tradition of Malay community and ritual life evidently produced precisely what it was intended to produce: a disavowal of social difference.[9]

In the dozens and dozens of modern Malay homes I visited in Kuala Lumpur, where I was welcomed, served, honoured, and catered to, what people possessed for entertaining others was still very much on display. While owning and displaying objects of beauty and hospitality to increase the pleasure of one's guest is commonly understood to be a distinguishing

Malay and Muslim cultural value, today a guest in Kuala Lumpur is not merely *served* in luxury, but sits ceremoniously *amidst* it on intricately carved and upholstered Italian or Victorian-style furniture. My informants generally decorated the main room of their homes with heavy curtains, brocade fabrics, Persian carpets, silk or plastic flowers in enormous vases, crystal chandeliers, and a particular kind of ubiquitous ornamental china from Italy called *capodimonte*, moulded into flowers and fruit, a decorative canon of increasing elaborateness.

Moreover, many of my informants, explicitly referring to the Malay Muslim traditional cultural concern that their homes be ever more beauteous and 'welcoming' to guests, were also on a home-upgrading rage. In my primarily Malay community of cement terraced houses, every third or fourth house was in a state of dramatic renovation, individuated from the rest of the houses to the point of near architectural incoherence with elaborate touches, including pillars and columns, Spanish-style verandas, and English-style gardens which sometimes included an electric fountain or a goldfish pond. As described in Chapter 2, this upgrading was popular in the small cities and towns where my informants' parents lived as well, renovations provided by successful sons and daughters in Kuala Lumpur. During the course of my research, several of my informants gave an elaborate *kenduri* or a Hari Raya open house to celebrate the completion of their home renovation, often inviting everyone they knew with the typically Malay statement that everyone was welcome to share the pleasures of their home and hospitality, just like in the *kampung*.

Malay ritual hospitality is comprised of open transactions which supposedly mute social-status discrepancies; yet, as we will see, my informants also exploited such ritual openness and its symbol of low social distance for its entrepreneurial value. Through it, my well-placed informants could negotiate paths to individual pursuits in what appeared to be highly communal settings. For them, during Hari Raya, a *kampung* commensal norm at a nearly endless series of *rumah terbuka* does come increasingly to life, and at such eidetically 'traditional' and 'open' events, where representations of difference are indeed disavowed, many Malays seek to facilitate modern economic action.

MODERN OPEN HOUSES AS '*KAMPUNG*' AND NETWORKING EVENTS

Among my informants, being a guest or a host at high-status 'open houses' in Kuala Lumpur has become both a highly competitive and socially validating event. Through a traditional ritual – the Hari Raya open house – and its implication of commensurateness and 'openness' in the socially differentiated urban context, my informants could use *puasa* and post-Aidilfitri festivities to establish, cultivate, and validate exclusive network relationships, aimed at increasing their participation in the elite entrepreneurial economy.

In the month of fasting and the weeks after Aidilfitri, I, like the Malay men and women I knew who were interested in establishing and confirming business contacts in Kuala Lumpur, could theoretically attend one important fast-breaking or 'open house' function or another nearly every single night for almost two months. Some of the biggest social events in Kuala Lumpur are held during this time, elegant breaking-of-fast dinners at big hotels, at Tabungan Haji (the massive, NEP-landmark building housing the Muslim Pilgrimage Fund offices), at UMNO headquarters at the Putra World Trade Centre, at private homes like Dato Hassan's, where hundreds of people attended by special invitation, and at corporate dinners sponsored by huge *bumiputera*-managed businesses. People who themselves have received invitations often freely invite select friends and contacts to accompany them to these impressive events. Often these invitations are extended at the last minute, with an encouraging *marilah!* (let's go!), for to serve as a 'host' and symbolize open 'hospitality' in modern life, one need not be the actual sponsor of an event, but merely provide access to it. Just as in the *kampung*, where the door to the house was open to everyone, the same rule is applicable in Kuala Lumpur life. The etiquette of Malay hospitality guarantees this. A few examples of modern 'open-house' hospitality from among the Malay men and women I knew best should suffice to demonstrate its ramifications.

My informant Rahim had contacts at several huge Malaysian corporations, and, as a result, was invited to many prestigious corporate Hari Raya dinners and open houses. Through her own efforts, his wife Aisha was well-placed in various women's entrepreneurial organizations, and was invited to many top Hari Raya events held by its leaders. During the Hari Raya season, both Aisha and Rahim extended various invitations to their friends, including Rokiah and Ishak, allowing the latter to attend various important functions to which they themselves had not been invited. Thus, while Rokiah claimed to not really like Aisha, for reasons which will be revealed in Chapter 7, she always accepted Aisha's invitations. Despite her personal feelings about Aisha, Rokiah was, for a time, eager to be seen with her in the sociable season of Hari Raya, and she justified this to me by saying Hari Raya was a time to forget any differences people have had, 'just like in the *kampung*'.

In return for their hospitality, Rokiah invited Aisha and Rahim to events to which she had been invited. Although neither Aisha nor Rahim were involved in UMNO-party activities, Rokiah was one of the up-and-coming female leaders in its local political circles, and she reciprocated Aisha and Rahim's invitations by including them in the lavish open houses sponsored by her UMNO contacts. Ishak, Rokiah's business partner, having once been employed as a relatively high-level civil servant, had good contacts in government ministries and was often invited to open houses at the homes of various important bureaucrats. To these, he brought Rokiah and various friends and contacts to whom he promised introductions to 'top government figures'. In turn, these people proffered invitations to their events. I tagged along to nearly all of them, reaching, quite early in my fieldwork, the startling conclusion that through such networking, ultra-modern Kuala Lumpur could truly be seen as an open meta-village, a feeling I shared with my informants.

For the men and women I knew who were attempting to establish business contacts through networking, the subject of Part II, maintaining a high profile by appearing at such events was crucial for, more than anything else, what was discussed at these dinners was business, one's own and others'. At one such affair I listened to some informants at one table discuss: who was getting the contract to print the tickets for the new stadium and was likely to need help from other business people; how to tender for the contract to deliver the baseball caps and T-shirts to the spectacularly promoted international Malaysian air show to be held the following year (discussed in Chapter 6); what privileged government knowledge was required to develop a tourist attraction in a remote town (and a group of would-be entrepreneurs at the table excitedly hypothesized how they could join forces to capture the opportunity). At another table, Aisha and Rahim revealed 'off the record' that they had just received a several-hundred-thousand-*ringgit* order for curtains and bedspreads from an international hotel chain and might need to buy fabric from textile dealers. Immediately, some of their listeners offered to provide introductions to Malay textile dealers at an open house they invited Aisha and Rahim to attend the very next night.

In modern Kuala Lumpur social life, to its modern economic actors, this festive inclusiveness – in which economic ideas and business leads are expansively discussed, produced, and putatively shared – was a sign of what my informants genuinely meant when they tried to describe to me what it meant to be 'truly Malay'. At such events, they demonstrated what the Hari Raya festival was always about: a spirit of *kampung* community generosity and openness. They looked around a full hotel dining room or invited acquaintances to their newly resplendent homes and described their behaviour in an engaging, lively, welcoming, and food- and idea-sharing atmosphere primarily focused upon the pursuit of social and economic opportunity as 'being *kampung*'.

But perhaps an even more crucial *kampung* norm than urban 'openness' and 'hospitality' characterized the moral and modern cultural identity of my informants. A second key Malay norm was symbolized by a spiritual and ritual return to rural simplicity, humility, and equality. As we shall see, the material symbols of this 'return' were counterpoised to those of described above. They involved the shedding of urban modernity and economic development, reminding my informants – through a very different set of images than those of hotel banquets and open houses and the low social distance of status-based 'hospitality' – of essentially the same moral discourse: to look upon one another as true equals.

THE ROMANCE AND MORAL PULL OF THE *KAMPUNG*

As the month of Hari Raya fasting and feasting draws to its conclusion, the fever of festival has reached everywhere in Kuala Lumpur life – banks and stores give out small money envelopes for the purpose of holding the cash gifts of *duit raya*, radio stations play special non-stop holiday music, which, in 1993, included a new upbeat disco version of a beloved Hari Raya song made famous by Saloma, the wife of the Malays' favourite actor-singer P. Ramlee, and a song about a working-class man who has just received his Hari Raya bonus,[10] who shouts 'YAHOO' and dreams about now being able to take on a second wife.

Then, what people think about is *balik kampung*, returning to their parental homes for Hari Raya Aidilfitri, the festival of forgiveness. *Balik kampung* is a powerful, traditional symbol of village return, even if, as in the case of some of my informants, their parents' home was a new terraced house in the suburbs of Kuala Lumpur or in smaller cities like Alor Setar where Rokiah's parents lived. Wherever home was, it became, in the minds of my informants and the images portrayed by the media, a *kampung*, made into a distinctly Malay traditional place by the burden of feeding and hosting an endless number of relatives and friends, by the cooking pots on gas and charcoal rings out back, by everyone sleeping in what they call '*kampung*-style' on the floor on woven mats or three to a bed. When one returns to this '*kampung*', children wander in and out, visitors pass through, food is eaten catch-as-catch-can, a nap is taken amidst the din of conversation, in the beloved and random spirit of both excitement and exhaustion that Hari Raya establishes. When my informants told me that 'everything' I needed to know to understand what being 'Malay' really meant would become clear to me during Hari Raya, it was deeply symbolized by this ambience.

Balik kampung becomes – for my informants, fresh from the pursuit of economic and social opportunity in Kuala Lumpur – an explicitly traditional event, in which one consciously abandons all modern talk of business and goes back to simpler times. Indeed, as the entrepreneur Rahim once told me as he headed back to his parents' home, it would be inappropriate to talk about the Marchland company's newly found business success in the *kampung*, where doing so would imply he had somehow outgrown it. Moreover, the people I knew reported that the month of socializing and networking had worn them down, and they eagerly looked forward to *balik kampung*, where, for a brief time, life was perceived to be relaxed. The polar contrast between fast-paced, modern, urban life and simple *kampung* life could be bridged during this return, and while my informants attested to 'being *kampung*' in Kuala Lumpur, *balik kampung* was, people told me, where they collectively remembered who they 'really' were, beneath the costume of modernity. *Balik kampung* had taken on the importance of a group rite, the liturgy of which was, as much contemporary ethnographic detail in Malaysia is, reproduced on television.

During Hari Raya 1994 – the year that Prime Minister Mahathir felt he needed to remind Malays to remember their roots – a sudden proliferation of television advertisements appeared that accentuated the moral theme of *balik kampung* in sharp contrast to the individualism of modern *Melayu baru* city life. The year before, Hari Raya images of the *kampung* roots of Malay cultural identity came to the city primarily in the form of decorative and colourful *pesta* images: miniature *kampung* houses on display in shopping malls and convention centres, giant plastic *ketupat* (packages of rice) lit up and swaying from hotel façades, public presentations of traditional songs and dances, and evocative drawings of wooden houses on the Hari Raya cards my informants sent to each other.[11] But new in 1994 was a remarkable series of highly produced, emotionally wrenching television advertisements that explicitly addressed the pull of the *kampung* in the context of conflicts of modernity and traditional obligation. This kept the Prime Minister's holiday exhortation to 'remember' the traditional *kampung* holiday ways much on the minds of the modern citizenry, as the advertisements played over and over during the holiday season.

In my house, my landlady, Aziza, and I watched these advertisements and then later discussed them with friends. To them, such advertisements captured genuine Malay conflicts, underlining the sense of duty which they, often far from their childhood roots, felt they owed to their parents and culture. Below, I give two examples; the ones which Aziza and her friends said were 'best' in demonstrating important Malay values.

TELEKOM'S *MELAYU BARU* CORPORATE ADVERTISEMENT

In an advertisement produced by Malaysia's huge telecommunications conglomerate, a Malay businessman is shown in his elegant, corporate office. He has a small sports-car model on his desk. A woman calls on the telephone – she sits in shadows, her face old and worried. It is his mother. '*Bapak sakit* (father is sick)', she says, in a helpless voice. The son spins in his modern chair. '*Tak boleh balik kampung* (I cannot come home)', he says. The camera moves quickly around him – showing him from different angles, implying that business is fast, demanding, ever changing. The darkened scene again – father lies ill on a bed, tears streaming down his face. The mother is shown hanging up the phone helplessly. We see the businessman's face again, and a cut to sepia flashbacks – he is a boy, going to school. He passes his father pushing a tiller by hand on the *padi* fields. Then, the boy is older, getting on a train with his luggage (going to MCKK boarding school, presumably). His father is giving him a pen. The image cuts to the present. He picks up the pen on his desk – it is the same one. He slams his hand down on the desk. Suddenly, he is in his red sports car, driving up to an old wooden *kampung* house. The mother sees him, her faces melts into wrinkles and smiles. Then, in the darkness of the wooden house, he is on his knees, kissing his father's hands, the potent Malay Muslim symbol of asking for forgiveness, always replayed between children and parents on Hari Raya Aidilfitri. The father ruffles his hair. All is forgiven. The son has not forgotten his roots.[12]

JOHN PLAYER'S HARI RAYA ADVERTISEMENT

In this advertisement, for a major men's clothing manufacturer, we see a stereotypical *Melayu baru* in his elegant office, with computers and expensive executive paraphernalia around him. He has decided not to *balik kampung* this year, for deadlines must be near – his desk is littered with papers and files. But then, black-and-white images come to him: a *gotong-royong* (shared labour) event where he is shown rebuilding a house with villagers. He remembers a village friend admiring his watch, remembers giving it to him, and thinks about how happy the traditionally dressed

fellow was. He looks at his own watch – an even more expensive-looking
one than the one he gave away. He *can* afford the time – he races out of
the office, and the next scene shows him driving up to a wooden *kampung*
house, shown in black and white. His family all see him, and an old
woman's wrinkled face lights up. The friend with the watch is there and
embraces him. All his old village friends still love and accept him, even
though they are wearing traditional Malay *baju sarong*, and he is wearing
his stylish, sporty John Player clothes, really just a *kampung* boy at heart.

These rather heavy-handed messages suggest that a modern Malay in
Kuala Lumpur can – and is clearly obligated to – maintain or re-establish
simple and solid *kampung* values in the face of dramatic social and economic change. In the first example, respect for one's parents, and in the
second example, egalitarian relations among peers, accentuate the under-
lying importance of obligation and duty one Malay must show another,
themes which were discussed in the previous chapters. But a second
crucial theme emerges from the chiaroscuro: evidence that in popular consciousness, even the most successful economic actors in Kuala Lumpur
have all come from essentially the same starting-point as those left behind,
that humble Malay *kampung* that Dato Hassan and other entrepreneurs
claimed they came from and re-enacted in their urban social relations.

THE COLLECTIVE *KAMPUNG* PAST

Images of the *kampung* and the value system it is claimed to have espoused
imply that all Malays – rich and poor alike – are really just members of an
extended family with a shared past, Malay brothers and sisters symbolically
equal or at least potentially so. These images reject symbols of privilege and
revive commensurateness, providing Malay men and women, *anak-anak
kampung* (children of the village), a Malay identity that connects them to
one another and to their supposedly common and *commonplace* past. As
many more Malays seek to join the ranks of the economically privileged,
demonstration of its norms provides evidence that they are still very whole,
very connected social beings. What is being revived from the Malay past,
then, to the well-positioned Malays who represent it in the present, is not
about social difference, but putative sameness.

As indicated in the previous chapter, it is not the grandly ceremonial
and publicly displayed traditions of the sultans – now revealed, since
charges of corruption and even physical abuse were made against them, to
be imperious and even anti-human rights (Muhammad Ikmal Said 1993) –
which best serve today's need for establishing Malay cultural identity

among my informants. Now, to the *kampung*-boy-made-good, that elite tradition – another past which defined Malay culture – represents an ascriptive, non-democratic, anti-egalitarian society which NEP was intended, if not to break down, to create its opposite: a meritocratic system in which any '*kampung* boy' could become an entrepreneur, a rags-to-riches sultan in his own right.[13]

Indeed, when representations of the *kampung* such as the popular new restaurant described below came to Kuala Lumpur, they, like the very experience of lavish Hari Raya 'open houses', took on an increasingly valid character as contemporary, urban evidence of the simple, communally focused, egalitarian, humble Malay self, who beneath the modern costume of material difference was immediately recognizable as 'traditional'.

A '*KAMPUNG*' PLACE IN KUALA LUMPUR

During the time that I lived in Kuala Lumpur, a paradoxical symbol which embodied some of these ideas about Malay culture to my informants appeared in the form of what they described to me as a truly '*kampung*' place, an elegant and expensive restaurant called Sri Melayu. Over the course of my fieldwork, I attended Hari Raya open houses, lunches hosted by UMNO chapters, fund-raising and charity events, and Malay entrepreneurs' organization meetings at Sri Melayu. The restaurant, a showplace for Malay *pesta*-orientated culture, was financed and managed by a massive holding company that includes one of Malaysia's largest merchant banks under chairman Tan Sri Azman Hashim. Tan Sri (the term means 'lord') Azman Hashim is widely described as 'the top Malay entrepreneur' and 'leader of a new generation' of *Melayu baru* businessmen. Sri Melayu, people said, was especially built at the request of Prime Minister Mahathir to show off the best of traditional Malay culture in a place that was evocative of the *kampung*. An elaborate wooden structure built in the style of a Malaccan *istana* or palace, it was, Tan Sri Azman Hashim told me in an interview, a place where 'even the Prime Minister can feel like he is back in the *kampung*'. To me, Sri Melayu embodied a profound contradiction – it was a luxurious and expensive place which was affordable only to the political and corporate elite who, like all of my informants, disavowed their social differentiation by 'being *kampung*'.

Sri Melayu was first launched with a lavish Hari Raya open house in 1993. I was fortunate to be invited along by one of my informants, who was a business contact of the wife of Tan Sri Azman Hashim, herself a member of a royal sultanic line. The event was one of the most eagerly anticipated of that year's Hari Raya holiday season, and was attended by the top government figures, cabinet ministers, royalty, entertainers, and many successful Malay business leaders. Dato Hassan was there, and welcomed me to join his table for coffee. The Deputy Prime Minister and other government figures sat on the floor in special sections, eating *kampung*-style with their fingers. During dinner, we viewed a cultural show, with traditional Malay costumes and dancing, and then, Tan Sri Azman Hashim and his wife entertained the audience with karaoke, singing traditional Malay and modern Western songs against a pre-recorded instrumental background. Tan Sri Azman Hashim then gave a speech about how Sri Melayu was a place to feel 'truly Malay', to eat traditional foods 'in a traditional way', and most of all, to incorporate the values of the past into the needs of the present. Somewhat bafflingly to me at the time, it was Tan Sri Azman Hashim singing karaoke – a modern form of entertainment which had been introduced to most of Southeast Asia by Japanese businessmen – that most impressed the people I spoke to at Sri Melayu that night as exemplifying Tan Sri Azman Hashim's true Malay spirit or *roh*.

As I commented on their delighted response to his singing, one of the guests said to me that they enjoyed seeing evidence of Tan Sri Azman Hashim's traditional and simple Malay ways. 'It is because of his *kampung* spirit that he wanted to build Sri Melayu', my host explained to me, but further evidence of his openness, generosity, and simple spirit was to be found in the singing. Karaoke, as Dato Hassan – a great karaoke fan himself – explained to me, is a modern, 'corporate' way to express what he believed was a very traditional Malay manifestation: that even corporate leaders and Prime Ministers can be informal, simple, and down-to-earth people. To Dato Hassan and the other guests, giving a karaoke performance was proof that leading Malays were part of the family and community. They had not become too big or too proud, but were still *orang biasa*, ordinary and common men, ready to share a song. This was the Malay cultural virtue which the guests saw in Tan Sri Azman Hashim (a virtuoso). That representation had become '*kampung*'. As we have begun to see, it is increasingly the government-aligned businessman's image (cf. Yoshino 1992) of the *kampung* that determines of what modern Malay behaviour shall consist.

KORPORAT VALUES AS *KAMPUNG* VALUES

In my numerous interviews with top Malay corporate leaders – the politically well-positioned men who were referred to as self-made entrepreneurs and whose virtuoso 'know-how' ideology had reached into common discourse – I was encouraged to see that a distinct Malay corporate culture was emerging. The successful Malay business leaders I knew had long been exposed to Western and Japanese business culture and management theories, and, in many cases, had read the same popular management books and magazines which Wall Street executives I knew had also read. These included such books as *Megatrends, In Search of Excellence*, and *The One-minute Manager* and *Entrepreneur* magazine, as well as a favourite of both Dato Hassan and company presidents in America, books which revealed 'zen' and 'samurai' secrets of Japanese management culture[14] or discussed complicated problem-solving techniques such as De Bono's 'lateral thinking'. My informants freely explored Western and Asian corporate images as well as Quranically inspired ones to portray their experience of corporate life, often explaining that in the 'universal' and secular world of business (which they said could be found anywhere), there was a complementary and local corporate culture they had initiated or discovered. To understand the nature of this Malay corporate culture, let us briefly return to the subject discussed above, karaoke, and what, in all its multiplex symbolism, it implied to many of my informants.

Dato Hassan and Tan Sri Azman Hashim, rather than to associate karaoke with the Japanese, or even the Singaporean and Malaysian Chinese, who had appropriated it first in Malaysia, saw it as a potent symbol of a key and very local ideal: that the leader of an organization would be accessible, humble, and open, more like an equal or a wise brother than a ruler or a boss. While much of this view of leadership has an obvious Quranic source (Muhammad Nejatullah Siddiqi 1981), it is also believed that there is an innate Malay and *kampung* capacity for Malay bosses to be just, fair and brotherly, usually in comparison to what they describe as autocratic Chinese bosses (Nik A. Rashid Ismail 1988) – *towkays* and *taipans*. Through a particular traditional delineation of purported Malay '*kampung*' classlessness and egalitarianism, my informants had begun to articulate their model of Malay *korporat* culture.

As such, Tan Sri Azman Hashim told me he thinks of the thousands of employees at his conglomerate, Arab Malaysian Holdings Berhad, as his 'personal friends', and that they, in return, thought of him as a 'brother' and 'friend'. (This sentiment was, in fact, confirmed in interviews with various employees of his company. Malay loyalty to such 'brother-leaders' runs high.) The corporation, Tan Sri Azman Hashim maintained, must be run informally and openly, without hierarchy or domination. People must feel free to contribute to the larger whole because they want to, not because they are forced into submissive loyalty. He insisted that the workplace must not be impersonal, as it often is in the West, but must be 'like a *kampung* or a family'. He pointed to the 'first-names-only' policy at his corporation, and the enormous investment he had made in personnel training seminars and programmes involving community and national interests as evidence of these values.

The director of training in Tan Sri Azman Hashim's conglomerate told me that a key concept in management–employee relations at Arab Malaysian Holdings was to teach every employee that there are no barriers to success in corporate life. Using the 'rags-to-riches' story of Tan Sri Azman Hashim's own success, he explained to all new employees that the chairman is 'just a *kampung* boy' who crawled his way to the top. Now on top, the director of training told me, Tan Sri Azman Hashim uses his position primarily to help others humbly (a perfect delineation of a Weberian virtuoso), just as at the opening night of Sri Melayu, his luxurious restaurant, Tan Sri Azman Hashim received praise from my informants *not for how far he had gone in amassing individual wealth and prestige*, but, on the contrary, for singing karaoke, demonstrating *how simple his values remained*. Rather than establishing the power, class, and authority differences between managers and workers, or even between Tan Sri Azman Hashim and everyone else, the corporation, in the minds of its virtuosi, is a place of highly integrative and balanced relationships.

Dato Hassan explained his explorations of indigenous Malay corporate culture in similar terms. At his conglomerate, he had also implemented Western-style training and motivational programmes which he believed encouraged professionalism and discipline among the employees, as well as introducing Japanese-style corporate themes, contests, and group exercises. These, he believed, showed employees that the company was 'caring and responsible', like a 'family' or 'community'. He acknowledged that some of his management technique was borrowed from other cultures, but there was a profound localizing difference. 'Because our Muslim spirit is more fair', he explained, 'Malay development has come with greater caring and stronger values than in either America or Japan'.

Beyond this, Dato Hassan believed he was teaching workers Islamic lessons he himself had already learned, as described in the previous chapter: that group goals were more important than individual ones, just like in the *kampung*. These values were primarily established by such corporate events as *Hari Keluarga* or family days, 'unity days' devoted to building team spirit and loyalty, and other functions which enforced group feeling and interdependence (cf. Kondo 1990) such as treasure hunts. Often I was invited to such events, at which Malay corporate leaders took great pains to show that the organization 'cared' about employees and others far beyond the organization. 'Caring' events, including raising money for the orphans in Bosnia or helping flood victims in the poor *kampung* communities outside Kuala Lumpur, were written up in the local newspapers and prominently featured in the corporate annual reports of organizations such as Dato Hassan's and Tan Sri Azman Hashim's. Moreover, Dato Hassan and Tan Sri Azman Hashim played down the economic purposes of their companies, just as Arif, for example, played down the power of profit-seeking and played up the conceptualization of 'family' and commitment to the *ummah* in his entrepreneurial pursuit, EG2020.

The personalization of the corporation as a 'caring' and community-based organization modelled on ideal *kampung* relations had begun, during the time of my fieldwork, not merely to espouse traditional Malay social values, but to actually stage and re-enact them. Making a contrast to Chinese companies which tend to give annual employee dinner parties at luxury hotels and to *exclude* families and children and serve alcohol, Dato Hassan proudly told me that Malay 'caring' corporations build family values, *including* the family in the *korporat* community at a healthy outdoor location where people would socialize openly and simply, just like in the *kampung*.

Indeed, just as 'returning home' during Hari Raya Aidilfitri had become a powerful symbol for commitment to and renewal of traditional Malay values among my informants, Malay businessmen were attempting to reproduce the sense of *kampung* 'return' and all its moral injunctions in the corporation. In 1993, all three of the huge corporate 'family days' I attended had actually been given the same theme: '*Balik kampung*'. At each of them, '*balik kampung*' was symbolized by encouraging Malay, Chinese, and Indian workers and their families to wear *sarongs* and other *baju asli* (traditional clothes) and engage in activities such as making *bunga manga* (a traditional sign of village celebration), the recitation of *pantun*-style verses (a traditional poetry form), and the playing of traditional *kampung* games. The theme of 'returning to the village' was not intended to alienate the non-Malays, Dato Hassan told me when I expressed my feeling that it might, but include them. The simple ideals expressed by that 'return' could be shared by everyone in the nation, Malay, Chinese, and Indian alike, as they all became a *kampung*-like community nation-state with shared ideals, a subject we will return to shortly.

Many Malay corporate executives had other ways of demonstrating these values in their businesses. Some had instituted what they called *kampung*-style business meetings and *kampung*-style training programmes, where employees were encouraged to sit on the floor, talking and eating informally as in a 'real village'.[15] Just as in Malay ritual behaviour, confirming affective ties, sharing food, demonstrating informality, providing access, and symbolizing the putative impugning of hierarchy were, increasingly, ideas used by my informants to define and express unique Malay values in the corporation, so 1990s-style *kampung*-ized Malay Muslim *korporat* culture, to its creators, is egalitarian and fair. It represents the past and the present as classless and free of conflict.

In the Malay case, as we shall now see, the constellation of ideas around *kampung* does not only selectively represent the past and the present, it also has become, paraphrasing Malinowski, a mythic charter for the future. Indeed, by retrieving and reviving *kampung* values in corporate and civil life, Malays are frequently exhorted by no less than Prime Minister Mahathir, the first non-aristocratic – that is, as many Malays would say to accentuate the contrast to old, out-of-date forms of ascribed-status identification, the first *kampung* – Prime Minister Malaysia has had, to create the good society of the future by re-enacting behaviours from the past. *Kampung* values are increasingly represented as a Malay paradigm for the development of a modern civil society and the future of the multiethnic nation-state.

CIVIL VALUES AS *KAMPUNG* VALUES – VISION 2020

The 20-year deadline for NEP expired in 1990 with relatively little notice, aside from a somewhat ambiguously delineated programme to continue some of its mandates in what was now to be called the 'National Development Policy'.[16] Rather than announcing an explicit reinstatement of the system of quotas, privileges, and political sponsorship of Malay economic development, in 1991 Prime Minister Mahathir unveiled a concept which was intended to provide a cultural direction to national development, encourage rapid technological advancement and investment, and create the ideal Malaysian society of the future.

Prime Minister Mahathir argued that by the year 2020 Malaysia would have become a fully developed and industrialized nation, and called upon the citizenry to make themselves ready for its demands. Future citizens would need to behave as fully modernized, ethical, and caring members of a united Malaysian nation. He extolled such virtues as being computer literate, speaking several Asian languages and English, exuding confidence, and demonstrating locally defined morality. 'Vision 2020' became a clarion call and catchy, futuristic-sounding slogan supporting a somewhat vague set of norms and programmes that would bring Malaysians into the future by replicating traditional-style social relations in an increasingly sophisticated, highly technical, enterprise-based economy.

Key to Prime Minister Mahathir's vision was a concept of civil society that leaned heavily on a rhetoric of 'family', 'local', '*kampung*', and 'Asian' values in contrast to decayed and decadent Western ones, which included, to name a few, drug use, immoral sexual behaviours, violence, greed, and a welfare-state mentality. As such, Vision 2020 could be construed to mean that Malay economic ascendancy would continue to be supported by the sponsorship of the state, but modern ideals, values, and norms of the entire Malaysian civil society would be increasingly relegated to the realm of 'traditional values' from what he called a 'caring culture' (Mahathir Mohamad 1991a). Prime Minister Mahathir thus made it explicitly clear that in the year 2020, the 'welfare of the people will revolve not around the state ... but around a strong and resilient family system' (1991b: 405), a somewhat ironic position if one takes the view that NEP was a Malay-only welfare programme *par excellence* (Jesudason 1989), and an elite one at that (Guinness 1992; Jomo K.S. 1986), and that with Vision 2020 and NDP, pro-Malay affirmative action and economic trusteeship policies of NEP would not be abandoned, rather, they would, in all likelihood, be enhanced (Shamsul A.B. 1992a).

The general response to Vision 2020, after some initial confusion,[17] was overwhelmingly positive. In the minds of my Malay informants, it was additional evidence of the Prime Minister's own brilliant vision leading Malaysia into full development without losing its essentially traditional character,[18] a 'virtuoso' definition of the Prime Minister's enormous skills and virtues. For anyone resident in Malaysia in the early 1990s, Vision 2020 – given form in songs, logos, speeches, corporate campaigns, and daily discourse – had an enormous effect on everyday life. Again and again, in speeches and seminars, Prime Minister Mahathir articulated his idea for how to develop Malaysia fully by the year 2020, when *bangsa Malaysia*, the Malaysian nation, will live 'in harmony and full and fair partnership' (Mahathir Mohamad 1991b: 404). When I arrived in Malaysia, the very phrase 'Vision 2020' was on everyone's lips (cf. Kessler 1992).

In one sense, part of the appeal of Vision 2020 was its sheer vagueness. Some of my informants understood Vision 2020 primarily as an appeal for them to take better care of their own families, and Aisha, the co-owner of the Marchland company, explained that she had hired her own brothers-in-law and cousins as managers to demonstrate the crucial values of Vision 2020. 'It means helping your own', she said, 'just like we say, "charity begins at home"'. Dato Hassan believed that Vision 2020 was

Prime Minister Mahathir's instruction to modern Malay entrepreneurial leaders like himself to advance towards high-technology industries – while at the same time creating an indigenous and neo-traditional Malay business culture. Other people felt it was Prime Minister Mahathir's way of reminding them not to spend so much time thinking about materialistic concerns, and to think more about others instead. Other informants felt that Vision 2020 and its exhortation to 'care' about others meant they should remember to be more caring about the environment and world issues like the plight of the Bosnians and orphans in Palestine. Some of my informants said it was a way to show Malaysians how they could be different from the West and yet still be modern, proving that industrialization did not bring about a concurrent decline in values; soon, they said, Malaysia would not only prove that it was better than the West, but that its version of Islamic and civil modernity was better than what Arab-centric *dakwah* Islamization had extolled. They envisaged a society which was tolerant and open, in which everyone had the same chances for wealth.

VISION 2020, VIRTUOSI, AND THE ENTREPRENEURIAL ZEAL

However, what most characterized many of my informants' understanding of Vision 2020 was that they believed it asked them, almost as if they had been drafted into national service, to improve themselves both economically and spiritually. They felt Vision 2020 asked them to develop themselves and develop the nation, to be at once skilled, religious, and ambitious, to be honourable and respectful, and to offer help to others regardless of past ethnic enmity. Rokiah, who had attended several UMNO-sponsored workshops and seminars on Vision 2020, explained that behind it all was really a spiritual idea about serving others. She said the content of Prime Minister Mahathir's 'vision' as UMNO leaders had explained it was very simple – it just meant that Malays should be 'good, modern Muslims', but, of course, the Chinese and Indians could follow it, too. As good Muslims, Malays, in the style of hospitality and harmony for which they were known, would now open up the nation for everyone to succeed. She explained, 'Vision 2020 means the future can be perfect, and everyone can be affluent, or at least have an equal chance to be. People will be fair and balanced, and will be concerned about uplifting others. But we have to earn that perfection, by always showing that we care about others more than about ourselves'.

As I discussed and debated Vision 2020 with my informants – for indeed, there was not a day in my time in Malaysia when it was not mentioned – I became aware of how often they saw in it the universal expression of traditional Malay Muslim social ideals in which all Malaysians could benefit, a kind of secular paradigm of the good society envisaged by the Prophet at Medina, in which people of all religions could live in harmony. The future was also an expressly Malay place, the meta-*kampung* or open house, in which, as in their remembered childhoods, 'everyone was the same'. But crucial to their enthusiasm for Vision 2020 was its inherent message of virtuoso-style altruism which much paralleled their version of Islamic modernity, of its powerful proof that Malays always put the importance of the group before the individual.

To Rokiah, for example, a key feature of 'caring' about the year 2020 was that it was other-focused and virtuous because it was likely, as Prime Minister Mahathir himself pointed out, that 'we won't be here to enjoy it' (1991b: 409), which meant that it involved being selfless, a principle which she related to earning *pahala* (good behaviours counted up on Judgment Day) to get into heaven. Tan Sri Azman Hashim, equating Vision 2020 with fairness and equity (and using the popular 'know-how' language of entrepreneurship), said that it, like 'the Prophet himself' espoused a 'win/win business idea' – it ensured that the Chinese, Indians, and Malays would be able to benefit equally from development in a Malay-dominated country. As such, it was not 'selfish'. But not only did Vision 2020 frame a spiritual ideal for a modern enterprise-based society, it became linked to enterprise itself.

Again and again, my informants who sought to engage one another in entrepreneurial projects explained to one another the validity of their business ideas and schemes in terms of Vision 2020 – such as Arif, who, as we know, called his educational game 'EG2020' and appealed to the moral interests of Rokiah and Ishak to join in his altruistic mission to help others reach modernity. To my informants, Vision 2020 was the particular domain of the Malay entrepreneur. To economic actors ranging from Rokiah and her ambitious office clerk to millionaires like Tan Sri Azman Hashim and Dato Hassan, Vision 2020 emerged as a series of ideas which reminded them to improve themselves and others, to 'network', and to share modern economic opportunities with others. It was modern Malay moral economic development, precisely that congeries of virtuoso ideas which entrepreneurship itself demonstrated.[19]

To them, Vision 2020 required that they give evidence that their core values and behaviour had remained essentially the same as in the Malay past – to treat employees like family, to model their businesses and networks in the form of *kampung*-ized social relations, and to upgrade themselves on behalf of Allah, the nation, and others. My informants embraced

Vision 2020, and found in it a flexible guide to conceptualizing their economic and social obligations towards one another and the future. Moreover,
pointing to the 'futuristic' connotation of Vision 2020, many of the economically ambitious Malay men and women I knew looked primarily
toward entrepreneurship through *hi tek* – high-technology projects – computerization, electronic communications, and advanced machines – such as
the million-*ringgit* computerized sewing machine from Italy that was both
Marchland's pivotal entrepreneurial advantage and its downfall – as ways
to best implement Prime Minister Mahathir's directives.[20] If it involved
technology, computers, and advanced technological development of any
kind, my informants linked the powerful valorizations of Vision 2020 to
their very aggressive pursuit of a certain kind of economic opportunity. In
fact, when a high-technology electronic-communications project engaged
the entrepreneurial efforts of Rokiah and Ishak and many others in their
cross-linking social network for several weeks, they validated their activities in the name of Vision 2020 – through it, their very profitable
hi tek Malay entrepreneurship would help develop the whole nation.[21]

THE MALAYSIANIZATION AND UNIVERSALIZATION OF THE *KAMPUNG*

Through images of the idealized future, ultra-modern Malay economic life
is anticipated to be morally and socially similar to the idealized, communal Malay past. My informants tried time and again to show me how, in
contrast to the West, Malays, in a economically successful multicultural
nation, now – because of the success of NEP – made room for others and
happily shared resources. They pointed to their fair treatment of the
Chinese and Indians in Malaysia as the obvious example of this, ascribing
it to their ability to be tolerant and just, and ever hospitable. This was
given vivid form through their harmonious *pesta* culture. They pointed to
their interlinking networks of social ties in pursuit of economic activity as
evidence of the Malay tendency to share opportunities and engage others
in their success. They pointed to nascent Malay *korporat* culture as a powerful *kampung* model for modern social relations. Again and again, my
entrepreneurially focused informants explained their modern economic
culture in communal terms, claiming to act first on behalf of their Malay
brothers and sisters and next on behalf of the industrializing Malaysian
nation, which included everyone else.

  I have attempted to show in this chapter that a key concept in the revival
of images of the *kampung* was the sense that people in the *kampung* got

along and lived in a constant state of mutual consensus and social equity, with the doors to their houses flung wide open to everyone. In it, everyone was the same. Like the *kampung* they remembered before the ethnic riots and the highly structured economic policies of NEP, the Malaysia my informants claimed they were creating through economic development, corporate culture, and entrepreneurship was a harmonious, neighbourly, and affluent village-nation with enough wealth for all – Malays, Chinese, and Indian alike. Whatever else 'Malayness' is, in the very contemporary self-understanding of idealized Malay traditional and ritual culture, it is symbolized as incorporative and not appropriational, balanced and not hierarchical, tolerant and not absolute – all of which many social critics would dispute (see, for example, Jomo K.S. 1989a, b; Shamsul A.B. 1992a, b). What Tan Liok Ee calls Malaysia's Malay 'rhetoric of indigenity' (1988: 45) establishes a peaceful Malay-style model for the development of a modern, multi-ethnic nation-state and its civil society. Indeed, in Malaysia, in a social and political milieu which is today primarily characterized by differentiation – religious, ethnic, and economic – images of 'tradition' are invoked to fashion out of conflict and inequality an image of national cohesiveness, order, and justice in intra-ethnic and inter-ethnic social relations, portraying the core of Malay culture as essentially egalitarian, bucolically inspired, highly personalized, and humanitarian. The image of hospitable, balanced social relations in the Malay *kampung* projected by government and in the minds of my informants increasingly serves as a symbol for the Malaysian nation as a whole as it enters, in its local particularity, what my informants called the 'universal culture of modern business'. The *kampung*, which in the devalued economic sense and the backward intellectual sense, kept Malays back, redefined and invigorated, now moves them ahead, creating the good and just society for all.

PART II: NETWORKS

5 Networking: the Social Relations of Entrepreneurship

Malaysia has been given as an example of an economy dominated by a small handful of political elites in an increasingly polarized, class-based society in which the power of the state has grown simply to protect its interests (Crouch 1992). Shamsul A.B. (1986a) has argued that NEP is an elite patronage machine, in which the real beneficiary of NEP 'poverty eradication' programmes has been the state itself, comprised of Malay politicians and their 'clients'. Gomez meticulously outlines how politically connected entrepreneurial groups have formed in Malaysia, demonstrating how, 'through their abuse of the NEP and government enterprises as well as their rent-seeking activities, influential Malay politicians and a business elite with close links to UMNO leaders' became so-called entrepreneurs (1994: 6–7). As such, modern 'entrepreneurship' in Malaysia is generally seen as a mere reflection of privileged political access and largely ignored.[1]

However inevitable, the justification of hegemonic power arrangements is a crucial process of economic development and political leadership which I believe deserves more scrutiny than anthropologists generally tend to grant it. Cohen (1981) pointed out that any true anthropological understanding of the 'haves' in a society must take into account the complex cultural ways in which they see themselves tied to, and intricately bound to, the 'have nots', the legitimacy and valour they grant to their own destinies in service to others and the processes of acceptance throughout society which confirm their place. Indeed, codifying in modern terms their traditional sense of 'giving' to others, my informants had begun to resolve some of the issues which had haunted their claims to 'having' since the affirmative action and protectionist policies of NEP were put in place nearly a generation before. Entrepreneurship, to them, was proof that they had diligently and meritocratically learned what NEP was intended to teach – full participation in their own and the world economy – on behalf of the entire Malay group. Beyond that, part of the value given to entrepreneurship by Malays in the NEP cohort is that it seems to them *to diminish the effects of class and power*, or conversely, *to open the doors to power* to

119

nearly any '*kampung* boy' who can demonstrate worthiness. They did not see that today there were 'haves' and 'have nots' in Malay society. There were, however, 'know-hows' and 'know-whos', modern Malays and 'dark age' ones, economically active and economically passive Malays – but, according to my informants, all of them had been given the same opportunities in the *kampung* of their childhoods.

As the social rituals of daily life are portrayed by my informants as communal and inherently egalitarian social relations played out in Kuala Lumpur's food stalls and locations such as Sri Melayu, the '*kampung*' place for corporate leaders, networking actually does provide them with significant opportunities to link themselves to other modern Malays – sometimes accessing the power elite. Obviously, to participate in largely state-led economic development, my informants, who saw themselves as virtuosi, nation builders, civil citizenry, *kampung* children, and 'new Malays', needed to perform what Cohen calls an elite's 'difficult task of grafting' (ibid.: 60–1) itself onto the collaborative network of relationships at the uppermost reaches of the state. Yet, in all of their social, moral, and modern definitions, my privileged informants claimed that what they were doing to demonstrate their entrepreneurial capacity was expressly *not* about old, feudal Malay culture traits like 'know-who' patronage, and what they called *bumiputera*-ism, but *bona fide* capitalistic development, generously shared and available to all. Through its seemingly endless incorporativeness, through the enmeshing of material and affective ties, Malay entrepreneurship, to its actors, symbolizes diminished eliteness and classlessness, and implies shared power and access, claiming the opposite of what most determines it.

The paradox of successful Malay entrepreneurship is that my informants did not see in it the power or prestige of the state, but the power of society, of people and community. NEP may have once helped Malays when they most needed help, but now Malays saw themselves as self- and group-empowering, a modern, civil, meritocratic, capitalist society in its particular Malay Muslim *kampung* incarnation. The broad brush strokes of 'patron–client' relations may indeed explain the powerful Malaysian state, NEP macro-level development, and the creation of Malay millionaires, but it does little to express the assertion of community and modernity sketched out by the finely drawn lines of everyday experiences which connect contemporary Malays who socialize and seek to do business together in a highly interactive milieu – in their seemingly endless and overlapping networks. In this chapter, we will begin to consider how legitimacy and valour have come to feel real in the lives of Malays in the NEP cohort, and how those meanings are played out in social reality. In order to understand the local definition of entrepreneurship and capitalist development and how my informants saw in it a viable symbol of moral, modern, meritocratic citizenry, we must now look deeply into social relations, into those very personalized networks in which they operated.[2]

NETWORKING – THE KEY TO MALAY ENTREPRENEURSHIP

When my informants themselves described seeking relationships with other economically ambitious Malays as 'networking', they used the English word, which, in scholarly studies of Asian capitalism, on the Internet, and in popular business-magazine articles available in Malaysia and elsewhere, is much in vogue.[3] The *Bahasa* equivalent to a 'network' – *rangkaian* (literally 'a cluster') – is a term mostly used by government ministers who try nationalistically to establish a *Melayu* language for business and, somewhat in contradiction to that, also encourage Malays to create, like the Chinese, business *kongsi* or societies which replicate family solidarity (*New Straits Times*, 2 February 1993). My informants did not need to be told to act like the Chinese, as they increasingly saw their traditional society, as I have demonstrated in earlier chapters, as incorporative and inclusive, now transformed into modern reality through networking. Networking to them both maintained and developed Malay society in its varied modern contexts, translating idealized, egalitarian images of the *ummah* and the *kampung* into the modern locales of food stalls and hotel banquet halls.

Moreover, they were adamant that networking was a meritocratic correlative of 'know-how' entrepreneurship; if it brought rewards, they were well earned. For example, within the women's entrepreneurial association, Peniagawati, explicitly referred to by its members as a 'network' modelled upon the MCKK 'old-boys' network' (see Chapter 2), the story travelled that one of the members had received a multi-million-*ringgit* contract to produce mattresses for the Malaysian Armed Forces. How had she acquired this opportunity? In great 'know-how' style, people said, she performed outstanding network research. We learned how she had spoken to everyone she knew to uncover a good business opportunity, calling upon contact after contact to find an entrepreneurial niche. When she discovered that the Army would be ordering new mattresses by the thousand the following year, she became, *ex nihilo*, a mattress manufacturer, then 'networking' her way to actually winning the contract, then finding other Malays to help her fulfil it. To the other women in the association, an entrepreneur was, in this order, someone who networked well, then established a venture, for through networking one could ideally spring full-grown, like Athena from the head of Zeus, into business. As such, that great nineteenth-century resource that most defined Schumpeterian entrepreneurship – invention and innovation (1934) – had little value in their minds, unless we expand the concept of innovation to include social action, which indeed, as we shall see, in the Malay case was often highly ingenious, a kind of self-marketing creativity which would have impressed, in my opinion, even the most sophisticated marketers I knew on Wall Street.

Networks were not only used to uncover potentially lucrative business niches and contacts to fill them, as the mattress entrepreneur did, they were also important sources of normative information. Stories of who had succeeded and who had failed at one or another venture passed rapidly throughout Malay networks, until, at times, there were ten, even 20, stories about entrepreneurial action concerning one person, stories which often ended with the entrepreneur being bankrupted, morally and financially, because of serious entrepreneurial mistakes (greed, lust, and naïvety were favourite themes). I also heard many positive, and often contradictory, stories about such entrepreneurial paragons as, for example, Dato Hassan and Tan Sri Azman Hashim, which circulated among members of various networks, in which theories and rumours about their virtuoso attributes were passed into shared knowledge.

But most important of all network-gleaned resources were the multiple details of immediate-venture opportunities ripe for picking and possibilities for entrepreneurial alliance-making which circulated within social contexts. Again and again, the holder of business information, or, as frequently, *mis*information, passed along to others knowledge of a potential business deal available in the booming economy until it appeared and overlapped in many networks. An example of this was the 'meat deal'. For several months, various people I knew revealed that they had heard that several huge resort hotels on the recently developed east Malaysian island of Labuan were urgently seeking high-quality imported beef to serve in their restaurants. This story had spread quite widely – one of my informants had heard it from a contact in the agriculture ministry; another – unconnected to the first – had heard it from someone in the tourist ministry. Someone else heard it from someone at Sime Darby, a huge conglomerate which had interests on Labuan. Moreover, several different alliances had formed to attempt to capture the 'deal', groups with crucially different versions of the story. It was often uncertain to the members of such *ad hoc* alliances what the actual opportunity entailed; often, the very nature of the alliance was an agreement among the members to plumb within their individual networks for additional information until that very investigative action became defined as an entrepreneurial economic venture itself. I was to hear of the urgent meat deal off and on for nearly six months, long after I assumed it had been completed. Later on in Part II we will look again at the mobilizing effects the power of entrepreneurial *information* – and the power of the *holder* of information – has in social networks. For now, we must understand how ventures could be built on the power of possibility alone.

THE ENTAILMENT OF MALAYS IN THE COHORT

My informants referred to people within their networks with whom they had multiple social and economic ties as *kawan* or friends. The group of friends Rokiah networked among included people who had loaned her money or provided her with business opportunities, eased introductions to important people, and pursued her for access to her own high-level UMNO contacts. Sometimes, as with Arif who brought her the entrepreneurial venture EG2020, her network also included her cousins, and as often, her cousins' contacts and friends. But networking was never cast in a kinship idiom; indeed, its distinguishing feature was its seeming lack of discrete, definitional social-structural form among the cohort which saw itself, as we have learned, deeply entailed in what I have described as symbolic ethnic 'siblingship'. Often, Rokiah's networks consisted of people she deliberately sought out for their resources, or people who sought her out. She frequently participated in certain activities for the sole purpose of meeting and being seen with important people. Networking, seen from above, appears to take the form of highly purposeful and innovative cultivation of actual and implied friendship ties, a micro-strategy along the micro-structures of the corporate and political, status-based, NEP-privileged cohort – what the mattress entrepreneur described above appeared to have accomplished.

Aisha, the entrepreneurial co-owner of the Marchland company, was one of these friends who pursued Rokiah, relentless in her attempts to get Rokiah to 'put in a good word' with the *ketua* or head of the UMNO Wanita (the women's division of UMNO) district with whom Rokiah was instrumentally close. Aisha believed the *ketua* had significant pull in the business community. Back and forth between Aisha and Rokiah went invitations to open houses, charity dinners, high teas, and launchings of businesses at which entrepreneurs, government ministers, and corporate leaders were promised to be in attendance, people with any number of resources either of them could use. During the period in which Rokiah's friendship with Aisha was strong, she generously gave Aisha access to such events, and in return, Aisha provided Rokiah, and Rokiah's business partner Ishak, with invitations into her network. Rahim, Aisha's husband did as well. Their multiple relationships enmeshed ever more tightly and expanded ever more widely.

Ishak, Rokiah's business partner, spoke of the top executives and other employees at the company to which he provided consulting as his 'network' and, interchangeably, as his 'friends'. He also counted top government ministers among his friends. Often, and to great advantage, he 'name-dropped' such high-level friends, increasing his reputation as an entrepreneurial resource in the networks in which he participated. As such, people sought him out. Were such people – both those he sought out and those who sought him out – his friends? To him, absolutely yes. From such people Ishak received knowledge and information about economic opportunities, as well as invitations to weddings and Hari Raya *kenduri* to which he invited other people, offering all along the way to make introductions as a demonstration of his own affective and material links to others. (Below, I describe my own experience of the powerful, all-encompassing sense of social entailment – and indeed, community – such relations produce.)

Rahim, Aisha's husband, who had substantial elite connections within the huge UMNO-allied conglomerate where he worked, also spoke of very important men in both corporate and political circles as his 'friends'. He and Ishak – as did nearly all of my informants – offered to arrange introductions for me to some of the most famous and respected corporate leaders in Malay society – in a convincing claim that they did have close access to such men, a claim which in itself has social value in expanding one's networks.

But networking, to its participants, does not have the feel of manipulative deliberateness that I just have given it; instead, it feels random and open, unplanned, creative, even, as portrayed in Chapter 4, festive. Most often, it was at social events or locations that networking took on its greatest power. As such, network contacts or 'friends' in the lives of my informants appeared to come almost by a process of *bricolage*[4] – a like-minded former acquaintance or school friend met coincidentally at the food stalls late one night, at a charity dinner, or through a tie to someone else's network was suddenly enthusiastically incorporated into a major plan for a new business idea or was revealed, at a casual meeting, to be the one, most crucial link to getting an important government contract for oneself, or, convoluting even more, for another friend. In a spirit of great openness, excitement, comradeship, collegiality, randomness, and NEP-era cohort inclusiveness, points of confluence in networks are demonstrated and fixed in the free-flowing atmosphere of everyday life until one theoretically may ally oneself – and feels entitled to do so – to nearly anyone in social or economic life who promised, rightly or wrongly, to provide entrepreneurial resources of one kind or another. Among contacts and friends retrieved from social networks and established by chance, business meetings were swiftly arranged, promises made, and ambitious ideas for new enterprises sketched out – as in American movies about adventurous moguls – often on paper napkins, until the margins between social relationships and economic relationships were completely blurred. Development and economic opportunity in these settings appear to be interwoven with freedom, choice, and the sense of endless possibility for enterprise and alliance.

As such, networking, to my informants, did not imply an *exploitation* or invention of affective connections for instrumental purposes, but like instrumentality intertwined with affect in Malay families and marriages, seemed to make relationships material, expressly real. They saw themselves helping and sharing in networks. Indeed, they openly go about plumbing their networks for mutual, beneficial alliances as a consequence of all the types of relationships comprising their society, variously consanguineous, conjugal, sacramental, social, and professional and invariably informal, loosely knit, overlapping, and expectant. In networks, my informants established transactions and alliances that tested the legitimacy of others; evaluated social and economic costs and risks; learned of opportunities; attempted to create businesses; raised capital; and judged limits of trust and distrust among old-boy groupings, political comrades, professional contacts, potential investors, neighbours in the new housing estates, extended kin groups, and sometimes, even a visiting anthropologist, as we shall soon see. But crucial to all of this action was the belief that along the way, they were demonstrating their innate Malay selves, their traditions of egalitarian openness and balance, their version of moral and civil society in modern development, ideas which have taken on the powerful impress of government suasion, establishing a convincing, socially stabilizing portrayal of what my informants presuppose about Malay culture (cf. Pemberton 1994).

MOBILIZED RESOURCES, RECIPROCAL BONDS

My own participation in the social relations of entrepreneurship began to give me important clues about the nature and workings of network alliances in Malay society. For extended periods of time, I had almost daily contact with several newly established and still-on-the-drawing-board entrepreneurial businesses, their owners, managers, and employees, and, if they had them, their customers and vendors, generating experiences which will be elaborated in the case studies presented below. But I was not provided with privileged access to these companies automatically. My role in the business was first granted as an agreed-upon exchange for 'marketing' services which I volunteered, based on my own business knowledge (see Chapter 1). This function I served was key to my building an ongoing relationship to Malay entrepreneurs, a practice which perhaps exceeded the usual definition of 'participation' in participant observation.[5] But doing so brought me into Malay networks as a participant in entrepreneurial activity, just like my informants. Because of my contributory business relationship with my entrepreneurial informants, I was invited to the formal activities of their associations and charities, their *kenduri*, and their informal night-time food-stall venturing, just as any valuable and valued 'friend' might be. Invariably, I, like my informants, discussed business at such events.

Contributing valued resources to my informants' entrepreneurial pursuits or in anticipation that I would do so, I was given substantial access to their personal and professional lives. Indeed, I was often allowed to talk to people I otherwise would not have met: the Chinese printer printing a brochure; the Chinese vendor designing packaging; the *bumiputera* advertising agencies and magazine owners seeking business from my informants through their own interlocking Malay networks; the banker handing out NEP-funded loans; the potential 'big venture capitalist' my informants wanted to impress; a secret government source of equity capital behind a business. My contributions justified my spending endless hours in the place of business (as any job worth doing in a Malay-owned business takes many hours of discussion), talking, meeting others, listening to plans, watching, and when asked, suggesting ideas and listening to my informants' reactions. More importantly, it legitimated my role in their lives – I was perceived to be giving something in return for what resources they gave me: the riches of Malay access, hospitality, and openness.

As I became known in various networks, my reputation as a former 'Wall Street marketing executive' often preceded me, and opened doors. My status increased over time. Ishak and Rahim offered, as described above, to introduce me to top Malay corporate figures, partly to impress upon me the idea that their networks were very instrumental, but also because they believed I had something to offer contacts who were instrumental to them. I had value in Malay networks – and networks provided value to me. But just like my informants, I soon lost any sense of the planned manipulation of others – and their resources – that might emerge from such action. Indeed, during the course of my early involvement with 'CrossLinks',[6] Rokiah and Ishak's company, Rokiah and I became close friends, at which point my social and instrumental relationship with her, Ishak, and the other key people in their networks became nearly all-encompassing. I was a friend, anthropologist, and business resource with no clear lines demarcating any of those various roles (cf. Kondo 1990). Soon, they began to introduce me as CrossLinks' 'business consultant' from 'Wall Street and Oxford University', partly to assist my reputation as someone who should be spoken to by important business people and partly to assist theirs. Other times, I was merely introduced as a close and special friend. In either case, I had come to belong in their networks. Where my obligation to them left off and theirs to me began could no longer be traced. Before long, I was introducing them to people I had met through others, including them in networks of my own.

But finally, although I did not fully understand it at the time, participating materially and affectively was actually a very Malay-entrepreneurial thing to do, with normative and moral implications: *to anticipate being given access to information and contacts in exchange for something else* ultimately led me to my understanding of the nature of entrepreneurial action among Malays – that everything that happened in the large networks of friends and acquaintances ultimately had to do with an anticipated exchange of anticipated resources in social contexts, often generous exchanges that established friendship and alliance as well as success and failure. Networks were about possibility – and the arranging of it into potential results. By helping, by volunteering, by contributing (and sometimes mobilizing) information and knowledge, I was both participating in and earning validation in the entrepreneurial network system. Through my own close involvement, I stumbled into what was both the most obvious thing that was happening in networks and the most elusive concept concerning the social and cultural expectations of the Malays I knew – the degree to which one Malay is expected to help another, why he or she should or would, and, most importantly, the feeling of promise that networking gives, the great and often inflated sense of anticipation that people *will* help one another succeed, *will* participate in the entrepreneurial activities of their friends, and *will* trust one another's good will. Through networks, we established friendships and exchanged resources in no particular order – they ideally were one and the same and they implied one another. As such, my informants eagerly sought out relationships with nearly anyone in modern Malay society who seemed promising as friend or resource, and everyone they met seemed to be after the same things, contributing much resonance to the feeling of openness, generosity, and community they claimed to share. Whether that experience of the Islamic spirit of capitalism actually contributes to economic development is a thorny question we will consider later on.

The boom-town image of economic development in Malaysia does imply a spirit of generosity. With the greatest sincerity, my informants wished that everyone, rich and poor, Malay, Chinese, and Indian, would eventually share the benefits of development and, as demonstrated by their belief in the ideal, equitable, and essentially Malay society of the future which would begin, they hoped, in the year 2020, they worked towards it through their complex and inclusive entrepreneurial activities. Development, my informants said, helps everyone, everyone must help himself or herself, and everyone must help one another. They believed, along with their political leaders, that society, not the state, should provide the channels of economic opportunity to all citizens who wanted to uplift themselves, and knew that by Allah's will, there were enough resources and rewards in Malaysia for all who worked for them (see Mahathir Mohamad 1991b). Networks give eidetic form to this belief.

Remarkably, their valorized image of everyone helping one another, showing a capacity for Malay sacro-civil beneficence in economic development, momentarily came true during my fieldwork, when social relations – loyal, generous, and mutually trustworthy and profitable across class and ethnic lines – were transformed into a highly idealized and reciprocal form among all citizens. Momentarily, the boundaries around social differentiation and ethnicity opened, and Kuala Lumpur social life and its networks suggested no less than an economic paradise.

THE 1993 STOCK-MARKET BOOM

When the Malaysian stock-market reached astronomical heights in the latter part of 1993, the Malay men and women I knew stayed in the food stalls until late at night, sharing ideas, rumours, stories about how many millionaires were created that day, gossip, tips, and talking of fears of a 'crash'. In the spirit of a first-night party aboard a cruise liner, suddenly everyone had a context for immediate friendship and exchange. Strangers moved their tables closer to other strangers, passers-by were urged to sit down. People talking to friends on their hand phones at other food-stall locations suddenly found themselves talking on the phone to strangers, put on the line to share ideas and tips with people they could not even see.

During the day, at the offices of brokerage houses, Malays, Indians, and Chinese sat watching television monitors which broadcast buy-and-sell prices and openly discussed trends and tips among themselves, demonstrating a degree of intra-ethnic socio-economic participation that I had not seen before.

Nearly everyone knew someone who worked at one or another 'hot' company who gave them 'insider tips', which would then be shared openly, among outsiders. As people raced to the stockbrokers' offices the next day, believing that they had obtained, in networks of strangers-become-friends, information that was of the highest value, the market actually shot up, a process which was maintained for nearly three or four jubilant months. Everyone's information was also momentarily trustworthy – there was no misinformation in the market – because every rumour was proven 'true' by a subsequent price rise, what I knew from my Wall Street days as a charging (or mad) 'bull run'. My informants, giddy with the daily rises in their accounts, announced to me that this huge market rise was what modernized Malaysia was all about – that even a simple, humble stall-owner could gain at the same time as a millionaire. The interests of people could be served at all levels and across all races, they said excitedly. The bull market of late 1993 was a picture of how Malays dearly wanted to see themselves: hawkers, clerks, taxi drivers, and millionaires, Malays, Chinese, and Indians, all altruistic, all benefiting from information and generosity in development, merely at different levels. My informants compared the generous atmosphere in social settings to life in the *kampung*, where everyone shared what they had, regardless of social or ethnic difference. For me, and seemingly for my informants, the idealized concatenation of traditional Malay social norms to Malaysianized civil society in economic development was, at last, complete.

When the stock-market crashed in early 1994 – and coincidentally, a high-rise apartment building as well[7] – my informants felt suddenly very guilty: Allah, they thought, might be teaching them a bitter lesson about *ikhtiar* and *ikhlas*. Just as it was suspected that the apartment building fell down because its greedy developers had cut corners when laying the foundation, the falling stock-market reminded Malays of the importance of effort and sincerity in their pursuit of material wealth (see Chapter 3). While the stock-market boom served to confirm the idealized egalitarian spirit of a truly Islamic community and open exchange among the economically ambitious regardless of difference, it also reminded them that material wealth should not perhaps come so easily to Muslims. Creating a free-for-all affluent society was not enough, for it was uncomfortably like what my informants scorned as *mentaliti kampung*, the attitude ascribed to

Malays wishing for the fruit to fall instead of performing work. Even in the year 2020, Rokiah reminded her friends as the market dropped and dropped, using the 'know-how' language of the times, people will have to 'work smart *and* work hard'. Working the stock-market had been smart, but not hard enough; the lessons learned by its crash were surely hard, even sobering. Networking in the social milieu of Kuala Lumpur returned to its prior status of culling information and fostering relationships within the cohort, not a collective free-for-all. My informants had learned that while much could be shared in society, it must not be free. It *should* be hard. Indeed, what we will begin to see is just how much ingenuity, resilience, ambition, strategy, effort, time, trust, and money are invested in networking by Malay entrepreneurs – how much work it really requires, what is actually shared, and just how elusive and difficult success often is.

If we stopped the analysis here, we would only have learned how the Malays I knew saw themselves and how I interpreted their behaviour as purposeful, often ingenious, mutual, functional action – as good works and hard work. It should be obvious that in general, my informants and I agreed whole-heartedly on the rather Durkheimian sociology of their networks: networks are functional both in the sense of *mobilizing entrepreneurial possiblities* and in *demonstrating the bonds and responsibilities of members of Malay society.* As I have sought to establish throughout this analysis, built into their theory is the Malay Muslim concept of modern development, holding out a promise of wealth and social balance in a vast meritocratic landscape of opportunity for those who, quoting Rokiah, worked hard *and* smart. But obviously there is much more to learn about Malay networking. Do ideological, altruistic images of religious valour and *kampung* equity, given form in networks and fast friendships, actually provide Malay entrepreneurs with the contexts for economic success? Do Malays help one another establish mutually rewarding alliances through networks, providing and exchanging access to various social and economic resources? What, finally, happens in networks, when exchanges and ventures, constructed along a web of social relations and interwoven with ideals of self- and group interest, link the protagonists to other Malays in pursuit of shared resources and a modern image of their own idealized, anti-aristocratic society?

In order to answer these questions about the social relations of Malay entrepreneurship, economic development, and their consequences, we will turn, in the next three chapters, to three elaborate (and highly representative) cases of Malay entrepreneurial business among the many which I followed. But the way in which these will be presented needs some introduction. While I am concerned to show within these examples some of the business issues which were addressed by my informants, these are not case studies of 'enterprises', resource moblization, the functioning of capital networks, or even of individual 'entrepreneurs', but examples of *episodes within the complex unfolding of social and economic possibilities my informants sought to establish for themselves through social action*. We will see no charts and numbers about capital, sales, or profits (cf. Kondo 1990), and the reader will need to adjust, as I did, to the dawning realization that fundamental business issues are not the subject that mobilize entrepreneurial activity most among the Malays.[8] They are, then, cases of entrepreneurial alliances, the often ingenious, promising, and always ambitious consequences of social networking through which my informants attempted to facilitate their further transformation towards successful economic development and modernity as they defined it. Through them, I hope to impart some of the urgency, variety, and even drama of socio-economic activity in modern Malay life, how deeply it is intertwined with assertions and conflicts of community life among the NEP cohort, and how profoundly ideas about entrepreneurship shape and represent modern identity in social life. With them, I seek to provide a rendering of modern Malay social and economic experience in the world that NEP created, the Malay theory of modern meritocratic economic development in action. In the Conclusion, we will consider some of the contradictions and limitations inherent in Malay entrepreneurship, and tackle some of its problems.

First to be considered is the entrepreneurial alliance between Rokiah and Ishak, a dyad of financial and social interdependence formed to conduct what its participants defined as entrepreneurial activities. We will learn how two of my informants established and sought to profit from an alliance; how they capitalized their venture; what they sought to achieve in their entrepreneurial activities; and the way in which they appraised the potential of other entrepreneurs. We will examine their company CrossLinks as a way to consider a key theme in the social relations of Malay entrepreneurship – that entrepreneurs cultivate and use alliances to test their expectations of one another and to establish and harness perceived social and economic opportunities, often seeing in their alliances a definition of virtuoso entrepreneurship itself.

6 The Business of Alliances: the Social Emergence of a Dyadic Enterprise

CrossLinks had a somewhat dubious beginning as an enterprise, for it was started by Rokiah and her boyfriend, Ismail, in 1991 for the sole purpose of obtaining coveted 'MITI shares' or 'free shares'. The Malaysian Ministry of International Trade and Industry (MITI) allocated nearly 57,000 million shares of new publicly listed companies to over 2,100 *bumiputera* companies between 1991 and 1993. This programme was intended to provide an additional means to boost *bumiputera* ownership of the economy, one of the key components of NEP.[1] The intention of the MITI programme was to help Malay business people increase their capital base and establish a foundation for long-term growth. Companies that met certain requirements – 100 per cent *bumiputera* equity, 51 per cent of management and manpower classed as *bumiputera*, and paid-up invest-ment capital – could register with the government to receive their special allocation of newly listed public shares. Once a *bumiputera* company received a letter from the Ministry that it had been awarded such shares, its owners could take the letter to a bank and receive a 100 per cent loan at very favourable terms to purchase the shares, which is why many people called them 'free'.

Rokiah, who already had a *bumiputera* company, a real-estate busi-ness, therefore started a *second* company, CrossLinks, for the sole purpose of obtaining a double allocation of MITI shares. As such, she would get shares for her original company and for her new one. Many of my other informants also began what Malaysians call 'two-dollar compa-nies' in 1991 – companies set up quickly to capture an opportunity[2] – merely to obtain MITI shares. But this was not in itself perceived to be inherently wrong by the entrepreneurial men and women in the NEP cohort who expressed a heartfelt commitment to hard work. Rokiah – as well as many Malays I interviewed who started one or more extra compa-nies to increase their allocation of MITI shares – sincerely intended to fulfil the government's expectation that Malays use the 'free' shares responsibly, to advance Malay business interests (*New Straits Times*, 28 February 1994).

133

When Rokiah was first introduced to Ishak – whom she met through her boyfriend – they quickly established common entrepreneurial ground by talking about their mutual interest in entrepreneurial business: all the new opportunities which they heard about in their social and professional circles but did not fully know how to capture. Both of them were already in business for themselves, Rokiah in real estate and Ishak, somewhat more marginally, in consulting. They saw each other as highly professional, modern, 'know-how' business people; Rokiah had an established, profitable business; Ishak had a master's degree from an Australian university in engineering and years of service in the government sector. They both believed the other to be like themselves: highly ambitious and highly 'networked', with excellent contacts in Malay business and governmental circles and in large groups of like-minded friends. In their early conversations, like many I was to hear as I listened to other informants strike similar alliances, they generously offered to help each other improve their businesses through proffered and shared contacts and knowledge. Soon they began to think of each other as partners, entrepreneurs seeking the same goals who could act more powerfully together than they could individually.

They did not flaunt their resources to each other – they did not need to. Rokiah was already well known to Ishak by her reputation. As a real-estate agent specializing in business leases, Rokiah knew many top Malay businessmen and often socialized with them. She was also involved in the local UMNO Wanita chapter, and thought to be one of its rising new stars – a modern businesswoman, ambitious, generous, deeply involved with others. Once or twice her photo had appeared in the newspaper, as she had served on committees or been selected to receive or give an award. Rokiah was establishing a public identity as an entrepreneur.

Ishak did not need to boast about his assets to Rokiah – in their first conversation, she learned that he was consulting at a large company, that he knew a great deal about technology, that he had worked in senior posts for various government ministries, and one other key fact about him – that his wife was Dato Hassan's first cousin. Rokiah did not expect Ishak automatically to obtain business opportunities because of his connection to Dato Hassan – that would be nepotistically unIslamic – but she believed, quite rightly, that affective relationships were often expressed in material terms in Malay life. She believed also in the principle of propinquity: that connections among the meritocratically worthy would and should bring opportunity. This was not feudal 'know-who', it was modern, sensible, business 'know-how'. Ishak believed the same thing about Rokiah's assets.

Both of them described their fortuitous meeting as a gift from Allah – a process of both fate and effort – and interpreted their new-found partnership as a kind of 'reward' for having already learned, or wanting to learn more of, the many lessons and virtues of modern business. Rokiah began to think of CrossLinks and its explorations – not her thriving real-estate agency – as her primary business, for soon it took up nearly all of her time and became the locus of the combined efforts of her and Ishak. It was at that juncture that I first became involved with them and CrossLinks.

CAPITAL AND COMMITMENT AS ENTREPRENEURIAL RESOURCES

Rokiah had kept her initial allocation of MITI shares invested in CrossLinks for several years, but sold it at a substantial profit to fund the partnership she had set up with Ishak. Anticipating that the new venture would soon turn a good profit, she gave Ishak – whose consulting business was foundering in unpaid invoices – half the money generated by the sale · of the MITI shares, an advance against profits. As another early marker of the commitment and trust both of them felt towards each other, they restructured the organization of CrossLinks. Rokiah named Ishak as a 30 per cent partner in the business – at no investment cost to him. Rokiah offering free shares of her company to him – as well as giving him part of the proceeds of the sale of her MITI shares – was, for both of them, a significant measure of the alliance they were striking, demonstrating its seriousness and depth. Giving and accepting money and 'shares' was a potent symbol of trust, a confirmation of expectations of mutual ownership of anticipated profits and a validation of their venture.

The dyadic alliance formed by Rokiah and Ishak – formalized by handing over (and accepting) shares or capital, sacralized by the sense of conjoining in an agreement perceived to be made on common entrepreneurial ground – was an extremely common one. Indeed, at no point in my research did I uncover an entrepreneurial venture which was not an alliance of some kind, struck on the basis of an actual or promised exchange of resources, both material and affective. In the previous chapter, I described how my own experience of participation in Malay ventures provided important clues to how such exchanges, both real and anticipated, built relationships. Whatever else entrepreneurship is in Malay society, it is never monadic; it is always dyadic, inclusive, and additive – in a coined word, Malay entrepreneurship is socially and publicly *myriadic*. CrossLinks demonstrated that principle most of all in the businesses I studied because its protagonists actually conceived of their enterprise as being in the business of forming alliances.

CrossLinks did not really exist until this initial dyadic alliance was formed, but once it did, it was in business from that moment on. For nearly a year, Rokiah and Ishak plumbed their networks for other entrepreneurs with whom they could strike a similar kind of alliance and replicate the same fruitful relations. Was this a business? To them, absolutely. As we shall see, to them, it was the foundation of modern, 'know-how', virtuoso Malay entrepreneurship.

CROSSLINKS' ENTERPRISE AND THE MYRIADIC PRINCIPLE OF NETWORK ENTREPRENEURSHIP

During the year in which I tracked and participated in their entrepreneurial efforts, Rokiah and Ishak investigated, invested in, and explored ventures as varied as importing fruit from Dubai and meat from Australia; the educational board game EG2020 and tourist services; high-technology computer programs and business-support services. By casting their professional and social nets ever further, an endless series of potential interests and alliances came their way, were explored, and often were abandoned. Many people I spoke to expected great things of CrossLinks, for both of its partners were so visible and so visibly committed to success.

CrossLinks demonstrated a key feature of Malay entrepreneurial strategy: the variety of opportunities and contacts which its partners brought within its domain, the multifarious 'enterprise of entrepreneurship' which guided their pursuit. They sought a myriad of alliances with others like them, whom they intended to bring into their fold as members of the expanding CrossLinks 'portfolio'. Indeed, many of the Malay entrepreneurs I spoke to represented their perception of entrepreneurial success by what they called a *gabungan* – a conglomerate or 'holding company'. Rahim, the co-owner of the Marchland company which will be described in Chapter 7, drew a diagram of the future 'Marchland holding company' on a piece of paper the first time I interviewed him – he envisaged the Marchland *gabungan* comprised of multiple, elaborate subsidiary companies under one umbrella: textiles, furniture, clothing, import-export; wholesale, retail, and catalogue sales.

Other established entrepreneurs listed the multiple 'divisions' of their companies on the back of their business cards[3] in what seemed to me to be an unrelated (if not managerially difficult) series of ventures – one of the cards I collected at a charity dinner showed an entrepreneur's enterprise to be diversely comprised of a security-guard firm, a publishing company, a catering division, and a paper-box manufacturing firm; another card showed a *gabungan* that was comprised of a travel agency, an importing division, and a public relations concern. This was not at all unusual. Many of my informants, like Rokiah and Ishak, were not just content to establish an enterprise, but *enterprises*. Entrepreneurs envisaged such expansive businesses, established by making alliances and organizing others into bigger and bigger structures, that I began to see many of my informants as would-be conglomerateurs. Why did there need to be so much diversification?

The first reason is found in the way capitalist enterprise has emerged in Malaysia. Recent Malaysian economic history has imbued the image of the large, diversified holding company with a special importance. My informants responded to the potent NEP example of powerful *bumiputera* buy-outs and conglomerations at the uppermost reaches of the economy, which presented capitalist development and entrepreneurship as a process of massive corporate accumulation, often resulting in the grouping together of highly disparate companies (Gomez 1994). Holding companies have been defined as one of the primary NEP strategies of accumulating equity ownership on behalf of the *bumiputera* community.[4] In addition, Prime Minister Mahathir, perhaps to justify the huge mergers and acquisitions, corporate raids, and take-overs occurring under the name of NEP, asked Malays to emulate the huge conglomerates he so admires among the Japanese (Jomo K.S. 1990). Large companies are frequently diversified into nearly every sector of the modern economy, from banking to real estate and restaurants to entertainment. These are the models of 'know-how' virtuoso entrepreneurship which my informants wanted their ventures to follow; they believed in the principle of corporate multiplicity as one of the primary determinants of successful entrepreneurship; with a *gabungan* you could go after nearly any business opportunity.

Secondly, as described in Chapter 3, they saw such formulations as inherently 'Islamic' – for in size more could be shared. Conglomerates supported their definition of social and economic justice (cf. Nik A. Rashid Ismail 1988), and they looked upon the single-proprietor enterprise of the small Chinese businessman as 'selfish' and 'greedy'. This perception, that Malay business owners run businesses in more socially inclusive ways, was, as I have already pointed out, key to the virtuoso identity of such entrepreneurial leaders as Dato Hassan and Tan Sri Azman Hashim.

Many of my informants often already had independent (and sometimes substantial) access to capital – such as MITI shares and savings – but it was alliances they sought. Innovative expansion through networking – not economic intensification – had become the Schumpeterian (and perhaps

Islamic) symbol of Malay entrepreneurial success. Few Malay entrepreneurs saw the value in building something from the ground up. They believed that alliances made through networking were crucial to economic success.

Rokiah's own tendency toward corporate diversification began with her efforts to obtain double MITI shares – for then she was owner of two companies. At that moment, she put CrossLinks on her business card as a second venture, even though it was not a business as much as it was, at the time, a potential organization. Later, Rokiah and Ishak saw CrossLinks as a kind of *gabungan* holding company – a flexible structure of corporate resources ready to take on any challenges, from land development to computer consulting and from real estate to import-export. There was no particular business they sought to be in, but they wanted exposure in any of them. As with the mattress entrepreneur described in Chapter 5, whom both Rokiah and Ishak respected, networks would be ingeniously used to form alliances, and from alliances would come full-grown business. By looking more deeply into one of their attempts to strike alliances with other Malays, we can begin to see more clearly the objectives and limitations of alliances struck among entrepreneurial actors as they mutually appraised one another's legitimacy and assets.

ALLIANCES AND VENTURES I – CROSSLINKS AND THE LIMA COMPUTER KIOSKS

In July 1993, many of the Malay entrepreneurs I knew suddenly began a feverish pursuit of opportunities and alliances perceived to be available as a result of LIMA – the Langkawi International Maritime and Aerospace Show – which was to be held in December, on the newly developed resort island of Langkawi, far in the north of Malaysia. LIMA was endlessly touted by the Prime Minister in televised speeches as an all-encompassing symbol of Malaysia's progress on several fronts – it would provide participants from all over the world with information on modern transport technology; it would supply them – in a lush resort setting – with excellent accommodation and luxurious pleasures; it would demonstrate Malaysia's cultural diversity, ethnic harmony, and the single-minded, proficient interest in national development of its citizenry. In short, Prime Minister Mahathir wanted Malaysians to be able not just to host international LIMA guests in true, hospitable Malay style, but also to place Malaysia as a major power on the economic, technological, and cultural map, while at the same time demonstrating its local colour and character. The Prime

Minister enthused that Langkawi was the 'symbol of Vision 2020' because its 'five-star hotels' and the huge effort which went into building them represented the Malaysia of the future (1991a: 2). Indeed, the LIMA event itself was to represent the *hi tek* importance and know-how of Malaysian industry and entrepreneurship. A small rural island was to become, with LIMA, what my informants saw as a futuristic, international tourist boom-town which symbolized the economic benefits available to those who worked to earn them. LIMA – essentially a venue for international arms manufacturers – represented a complex convergence of nationalistic and visionary ideas to many of my informants, as well as a fountain-head of entrepreneurial opportunities.

Before long, nearly every ambitious entrepreneur I spoke to was trying to influence his or her chances to be included somehow in LIMA, no matter how marginally. Thus, Marchland's owners battled with other Malay manufacturers for the right to produce LIMA's batik T-shirts and baseball caps and sought out alliances with other entrepreneurs who had already obtained a contract with LIMA. One informant, Zaman, whose networking efforts will be described in Chapter 8, lobbied for the chance to provide computers to the business centre which was to be established for LIMA participants by seeking to form a sub-contracting alliance with the entrepreneurs who had already won the contract to manage the business centre. Jamil, whose entrepreneurial ambitions led him to night-clubs and discos in Kuala Lumpur (Chapter 3), called upon nearly every social and business contact he had ever made to enlist help in winning the shipping and mailing concession for LIMA, and ultimately found his way to a temporary alliance with Zaman, from whom he sought a sub-sub-contracting job.

None of these attempts at entrepreneurship was ill-founded, for opportunities poured out of Langkawi in 1993: 80 new hotels were built on the small island (*The Economist*, 18 December 1993); tourist amusements were hastily constructed; enormous contracts and concessions were distributed – from key-chains to baseball caps and from food stands to tour buses. Through LIMA, the government dramatically presented its position on economic development, implying that a modern citizenry must celebrate patriotism and development through economic pursuits. Many of my informants responded wholeheartedly to these valorizations, and soon, the nightly conversation at the food stalls resonated with tips on how one might win a piece of the LIMA pie. Rumours abounded, and various versions of different LIMA opportunities appeared in different networks; this was my first experience of how rapidly information on economic opportunities could pass through Malay networks until it reached nearly feverish proportions, and the effect it had upon my informants. Through CrossLinks, however, I began to understand the way in which alliances were formed in expectation of seizing those opportunities and couched in publicly demonstrable, virtuoso terms of duty.

Rokiah and Ishak had been well aware of promises to be found in LIMA opportunities when suddenly, the chance for a substantial venture fell across Ishak's path. As a sometime consultant to the computer technology division of a major company, Ishak was often privy to its new business ventures. Indeed, it became known that someone had approached the company with the idea to supply *hi tek* touch-screen, computerized tourist information kiosks at key locations on Langkawi during LIMA. These kiosks would give visitors menu-driven information on events, hotels, and services, and could advertise merchandise and products offered by LIMA exhibitors. The idea had already been presented to Prime Minister Mahathir, who reportedly embraced it enthusiastically. Two articles had appeared in the local newspapers about the LIMA computer kiosks, describing them, in the language of the time, as nothing less than 'visionary'. The Minister of Tourism was quoted on television saying the project had the full support of the government, which wanted *hi tek* computer kiosks to be placed all over the country for LIMA and for major tourism promotion thereafter. Kiosks, he said, would be a very big business.

Ishak and Rokiah wondered how, with his computer knowledge and her good management skills, they might be able to help the project succeed. Ishak told Rokiah that while the company he consulted to had already offered to supply the kiosk hardware and software, he believed there was a huge entrepreneurial space in the middle for CrossLinks. He had already spoken to Ramli, the entrepreneur behind the kiosk venture, who seemed interested in CrossLinks. There would need to be someone promoting the project, Ramli said, selling the idea of buying up time on the computers, and marketing the service to hotels, LIMA vendors, recreation facilities, and restaurants. Whoever was involved in the sales business of the kiosks would make a fortune, they reasoned. They set themselves to the task of translating an alliance with Ramli and his kiosks into a reality for CrossLinks.

AN ENTREPRENEURIAL ALLIANCE AND ITS MYRIAD SPIN-OFFS

Ramli, a Malay businessman, had, through his own high-level networking, been awarded the exclusive rights by the Ministry of Tourism for 'kiosking' LIMA and all future events of its kind in Malaysia. Ishak called Ramli and suggested a meeting with him, offering to give him valuable technical and marketing assistance with the project. Ramli agreed eagerly to the meeting, for Ishak represented himself as a computer expert with interests in a technology firm, CrossLinks.

At the meeting, which I was invited to attend, Ramli told us that he personally knew all the top people who would buy space on the kiosks, and that marketing to them would simply be a matter of making a few telephone calls. Already involved in tourist development and marketing on Langkawi, he insisted that the real reason the Prime Minister had been specially briefed on the kiosk project was because of his influence. He had, he reiterated, already obtained promises of exclusive and permanent rights to all future Malaysian kiosk projects from the Ministry of Tourism. He also had the support of the massive marketing organization which oversaw LIMA, and, he said, crucial ties to UMNO political alignments on Langkawi.

Ramli detailed even more of his assets. He told CrossLinks that his accumulated LIMA responsibilities were much bigger than the kiosks, for he was going to be responsible for all the information and communication needs of the event – a newsletter, an information directory, a promotional magazine, the local dissemination of all the tourist information, and so on. Most of all, he described how eager he was to obtain Rokiah and Ishak's help in establishing the various projects' great success. Rokiah and Ishak in turn spoke of their similar entrepreneurial goals – remarking upon how all three of them wished to serve the needs of the developing nation, to engage in new kinds of business, and to work together with other entrepreneurs to reach those goals. They agreed that they were on common ground. It seemed to me their alliance was already struck; and within moments, it had become very large indeed, as we soon shall see.

LIMA, they agreed, was best suited for the 'real' entrepreneur, not well-established 'corporate elephants' like the big company (Ishak's own client) which Ramli had already enlisted for help. Had not Prime Minister Mahathir urged entrepreneurs to show great initiative in helping to demonstrate their readiness for Vision 2020 through LIMA; did this not mean Ramli, Ishak, and Rokiah could try to succeed without a big corporation eating away all the profits? Ramli agreed to stop all negotiations with that company. 'Let's go it alone', they decided, by subcontracting various pieces of the project to other entrepreneurs like themselves. Rokiah announced that her cousin was in software development and could probably supply the technology to support the kiosks; in return, he could be offered a share of the kiosk venture. Ishak offered to include the technical resources of other people he knew, such as programmers and data-entry clerks. The venture was growing before our eyes. Ishak began to sketch out the divisions and resources available on a chalk-board. Rokiah and Ishak reported later that they had an exciting 'all systems go' feeling about the deal, and began to envisage tremendous opportunities unfolding for CrossLinks – computerization projects, tourism, advertising – not just for LIMA, but for many similar events to come.

Over the course of the next few weeks, Crosslinks went to great lengths to confirm its legitimacy in Ramli's eyes and establish its place in his venture. Ishak began to write up a proposal for the kinds of software and hardware the project would need, and made numerous phone calls to programming organizations in the United States for additional information on touch-screen technology. He called upon contacts he had at the Ministry of Tourism and mentioned his involvement with the project, receiving more information and tips. Rokiah asked her cousin to write up a software proposal and provide costs on the hardware. Ishak said that although Ramli had all the right contacts with the LIMA executives and Langkawi developers, he did not have a good understanding of the technology the project would require, and went about contacting friends of his who did, noting the way that 'Ramli's weaknesses were CrossLinks's strengths' and proceeding to establish various exploratory alliances to demonstrate them.

Rokiah, Ishak, and I came up with a sketchy marketing plan for contacting the potential advertisers. They requested that I prepare an 'advertising kit' which would promote the kiosks to big corporate sponsors, describing the benefits and costs. Rokiah temporarily released her office staff from their regular duties and assigned them various typing and pricing tasks, hinting that they might soon be able to shift all their responsibilities to the exciting project or even open up an office on Langkawi. Throughout the process, they thought up additional business ideas which they believed could result from their involvement with LIMA, and began discussing such ventures with contacts in their own networks and suggesting them to Ramli. Rokiah wondered if anyone was in charge of leasing billboard advertising space on Langkawi for LIMA and called a friend to her office to discuss the possibility. To assist with the newsletters Ramli had said he was commissioned to produce for LIMA, Rokiah contacted a friend who had a publishing business and enlisted his promise of help. My fieldnotes show that they spoke about the kiosk project in such promising terms to over 25 network contacts in one week. People were deeply impressed that they were involved with LIMA and were most willing to join the project.

SUCCESS IS BIG ENOUGH FOR ALL MALAYS

When Ramli came to Rokiah's office a few days later, he confirmed, to her great pleasure, that CrossLinks should think of itself as 'a full partner' in his kiosk enterprise. 'Think big', he advised Rokiah, 'for this project has the personal blessing of Mahathir!'

I had a chance to ask Ramli later why he was willing to be so generous with the opportunities which had been presented to him alone, something I said I had not seen in American business. He explained his motivation in terms of 'sharing' among the entrepreneurially minded. 'This project is substantial', he reminded me, 'and there is enough for everyone who wishes to take on the responsibility to make it work'. But I was still confused by the terms of his offer to involve CrossLinks. Were there not hundreds of people, I reasoned – equally ambitious Malay entrepreneurs – ready to supply Ramli with hardware and software, marketing assistance, and creative ideas, just like CrossLinks's partners? Rokiah and Ishak had been introduced to Ramli only days before. What bonds placed Rokiah and Ishak so fully into Ramli's ambit of 'mutual help'?

In an attempt to clarify this, I approached Rokiah and Ishak with my questions: 'Why does Ramli want to include CrossLinks in his venture? Why is he offering so much? Why is he so generous?' I explained to them that this was unusual to a Westerner, a statement they nodded at. 'But this is Malaysia', Ishak said, 'where we see such things differently'. Ishak, who had been coaching me in his theories of Islamic economics, reminded me of what I had learned. He suggested that Ramli's generosity was evidence of his Muslim *roh* or spirit, proof that he was concerned about others, not merely self-interested. Beyond that, paralleling Ramli's own answer, he felt that economic opportunity in Malaysia was infinite in its promises – LIMA was proof of this. 'There is so much to share in this project', Rokiah concurred, 'and too much for any one person'. Much, too, was said about what they felt they shared as modern economic actors with Ramli. 'Ramli feels he can trust our knowledge', Ishak speculated further, 'and I think he knows our entrepreneurial styles are well matched. He wants to help us, and he knows how much *we* can help *him*'. This was a nearly perfect alliance, they felt. We sent off reports, proposals, and organizational charts to Ramli, detailing all the ways in which CrossLinks could provide Ramli with knowledge and help in return for what he was sharing with them.

Yet as the days passed without proof, Rokiah and Ishak nervously speculated whether or not Ramli *would* give them the project. Had they demonstrated their capacities well enough? Had Ramli been completely sincere with them? Ramli had recently made some vague references to a mysterious 'new partner' he had spoken to, and Rokiah and Ishak began to wonder if someone else might be moving in on the project in which they already had made a substantial stake. They waited for Ramli to call ....

Ramli arrived unannounced in Rokiah's offices several days later, accompanied by someone neither Rokiah nor Ishak knew, a man named Usman. Ramli then proceeded to explain the 'partnership' he had struck with Usman, who had an organization 'ready to form' with 30 people – software specialists, marketing experts, hardware consultants, all the services CrossLinks had anticipated providing through contacts and sub-contracts of their own. As such, there was no need for them to do any of the hard work associated with the LIMA kiosk project, but he still antici-pated they could profit handsomely. In return for their participation in the enterprise's profit, Ramli explained, he now had to ask for an investment of at least 250,000 *ringgit*. He regretted that complex negotiations with other such investors required that the name of CrossLinks not be made public in the kiosk venture; they would be silent partners, but, in time, very, very rich ones. Rokiah and Ishak kept any shadows of emotion from crossing their faces, and allowed Ramli to continue talking, reiterating the rewards that all would share from the LIMA kiosks. Smiles frozen in place, Rokiah and Ishak listened to Ramli tell them how crucial they still were to the enterprise.

ENTREPRENEURSHIP AS A PUBLIC SOCIAL PROCESS

After Ramli and Usman left, Rokiah and Ishak exploded with anger. They felt cheated and exploited; Ramli had *deceived* them. Insincere, he had misrepresented his real intentions and motivations. Obviously, he had only wanted their money, right from the start. He had no interest in them as *people* or as entrepreneurs. Furthermore, Ramli was greedy. By closing out the original company (Ishak's client), they speculated, Ramli had intended to ensure that the profits would go mostly to himself. But by doing so, he had lost the significant capital contribution that this firm would have been able to supply; now he needed to get it from them. Money had always been Ramli's *only* goal, they said dismissively. He had been manipulating them. He had described himself as an entrepreneur – but he was not one. He had claimed to value them as entrepreneurs – but that was merely a deception.

They surmised that every meeting they had had with him had been built on a lie, for Ramli had made promise after promise of his willingness to share opportunities with them as valued entrepreneurial participants. This, they realized retrospectively, was Ramli's disingenuous attempt to make them feel important so it would be easier to exploit them, not an indication of any real esteem he had for them or their know-how. They had totally misjudged him, they realized, and fallen for his boastful grandiosity. 'We trusted Ramli too quickly', Ishak said sadly, 'we believed he sincerely wanted our help'.

They, in contrast, *had* sincerely represented their potential contribution to Ramli's business and future, and had sincerely tried to help him and demonstrate their commitment to his goals. But Ramli did not value these resources, for in the end he made it clear that he had only wanted capital. Worse, he wanted their role to be silent, submerged. Now they saw the *real* Ramli: he was merely a *bumi* 'handshaker' – good at manipulating people but not interested in real commitments. They stood to be secretly rewarded for such an alliance, but these were not the kind of entrepreneurial relations they sought to have. What Ramli represented, they concurred regretfully, was greedy, feudal behaviour in modern Malay economic life – the enrichment of oneself at the expense of others.

At first I was puzzled by their reactions. Many times in the past – and in many times yet to occur – Rokiah and Ishak were asked to make an investment of capital in someone else's entrepreneurial business or idea, such as when Arif approached Rokiah and Ishak for their involvement with his educational game, EG2020. Not dissimilarly, the alliance struck by Rokiah and Ishak – the very basis for their business relationship – was partly built on their highly utilitarian appraisal of each other's various entrepreneurial resources and largely supported by Rokiah's own capital. As if she were making an investment, Rokiah had handed money over to Ishak at the beginning of their venture and continued to do so for the better part of a year, with the intention of earning it back exponentially from their mutually profitable ventures. Why was the investment Ramli asked them to make in anticipation and promise of profit different from Arif's request, and different from the premise behind the utilitarian relations – exchanging 'shares' and capital for potential profit – that Rokiah and Ishak actually had with each other?

Rokiah and Ishak cultivated social *and* business alliances with other entrepreneurial Malays because they believed that in modern life one did not exist without the other. Moreover, to them, economic development and the entrepreneur's role in it was not merely about capital, it was about so much more. Indeed, Rokiah and Ishak's own alliance was a relationship in which, as Ishak had said about their presumed relationship with Ramli, each contributed what the other did not have, yet both contributed, and stood to receive, equally. Rokiah may have had money that Ishak did not have, but the fact that it passed between them, as it does in many other Malay relationships, implied that they felt a sense of obligation and bond-edness to each other, that they should trust each other and redouble their efforts to give more to their relationship. They were *friends*. Their tie was public, social, *and* economic, and implied a commitment to an on-going shared goal. Beyond that, and perhaps most importantly, it was demonstra-ble; everyone in their various networks knew about CrossLinks and Rokiah and Ishak's modern entrepreneurial commitments.

What, then, had they expected of the alliance with Ramli? They expected to be brought into Ramli's network of LIMA and Langkawi society and to invite others into it; they expected the public, social arrangements to intertwine with the economic ones. They had expected to profit handsomely from the alliance, but only in the context of valorized, virtuous economic development suggested by the government. They saw the name CrossLinks publicly associated with all the entrepreneurial power and virtuoso prestige that the development of Langkawi, LIMA, and its kiosks implied. They had assumed that Ramli shared their own image and expectations of what group-based entrepreneurship among Malay partners would entail. Indeed, they took Ramli at face value and thought he was a trustworthy, 'know-how' entrepreneur, quickly granting him the same degree of ambition, sincerity, and virtue which they initially saw in each other. As they did in their own alliance, Rokiah and Ishak put great faith in the present and future resources Ramli could provide to them and which they could provide to others in their networks by associating with Ramli. This was the alliance they had thought they were striking with him, and the substantial resources they were willing to offer and share.

By asking *only* for capital (a sum which, it should be noted, they did not have), Ramli disqualified himself as a potential entrepreneurial alliance, and suddenly he was untrustworthy, greedy, an old-style *bumiputera* busi-nessman. They decided that Ramli had no intention of engaging in a close business relationship with them which included engaging others from *their* network. They reviewed suspiciously their past interactions with him. He was seen as manipulative, concealing his real intentions, which were merely mercenary. Ramli, it seemed, had disregarded a premise of Malay networking and entrepreneurship that they, in contrast, demonstrated per-sistently, that it would be predicated upon an on-going, public, and socially exponential exchange of multiple resources and social entail-ments, not just money. Above all else, they assumed that their entrepre-neurial identities would be public, and that they themselves would be seen as social and economic leaders. Indeed, this is precisely what had enthralled them with EG2020. Without that context, the alliance was, to them, exploitative, untrustworthy, insupportable.

THE RESILIENCE OF MALAY SOCIAL AND ECONOMIC EXPECTATIONS IN NETWORKS

In December, after the LIMA event, Ishak learned through his network that the kiosk venture had been a failure. Instead of kiosks appearing all over Langkawi, there were only two or three. Very few advertisers had bought space on the computers. Hardly anyone even used the kiosks, much to the embarrassment of everyone in the Ministry of Tourism. Ramli, Ishak speculated, had been shamed. Perhaps Ramli had received his just recompense for being mercenary, because rumour had it that he had resorted to using a rich Chinese man to invest in his venture. The Chinese man, Ishak discovered, had somehow managed to manoeuvre his way into full ownership of Ramli's interests, and now had the sole rights to provide kiosks at all future events in Malaysia. Ishak shook his head at yet another example of how a Chinese can still outsmart even the most cunning of Malays.

Rokiah and Ishak could not help laughing a bit at Ramli's demise. This was further proof that Ramli was not an Islamically motivated businessman; greedy, Ramli lost everything in the end, an example, they pointed out to me, of how Allah works fateful lessons into life. But they were also reflective; Ramli had lost something and they had, too. Despite the Prime Minister's belief that LIMA would bring modern, world-class entrepreneurial opportunities to Malays, here was an example of how greed, insincerity, and backwardness could still exist among Malays. Through the kiosk venture, itself the essence of 'know-how', all of them could have learned much more about entrepreneurship, *hi tek* computer technology, high-power marketing, and project management, valuable modern skills; they could have profited handsomely and helped others profit, too. They had learned from their experiences with Ramli, but certainly not what Prime Minister Mahathir had intended Malays to learn from LIMA. They both hoped for a day when all Malays would be worthy of the opportunities which had been given to them, and renewed their commitment to make CrossLinks a worthy success.

Indeed, to the partners in CrossLinks, the LIMA kiosk venture was not a misadventure, but an episode in their on-going understanding of modern entrepreneurship, a resilient and trusting process that was sometimes swift and sometimes, as it had been here, painfully protracted, one which often dramatically engaged many network relations in the pursuit of mutual goals and sometimes provided difficult lessons about human nature. When all the parties were willing to demonstrate the right modern and spiritual values through entrepreneurship, they agreed success would come to CrossLinks.

As such, again and again, long after the kiosk venture, they enthusiastically pursued alliances with other Malays in an attempt to build the portfolio of CrossLinks, in ventures that formed as rapidly and as temporarily as the one they established with Ramli, searching for like-minded entrepreneurs in their networks. Several times they felt exploited to a greater degree than they had with Ramli; for example, when other entrepreneurially ambitious contacts engaged CrossLinks in a potential venture merely in the hope that Ishak would provide access to his wife's cousin, Dato Hassan. Most of their attempts to evaluate other people's expectations of them established that there was a mismatch in the alliance or that inflationary promises of potential had been made, and such tests usually ended, as did the LIMA project, in a crisis of suspicion and distrust. But they remained strongly committed to their virtuous image of national development and their participation through entrepreneurship and alliance with others, people culled quickly from their ever-expanding networks. That commitment was remarkably resilient.

Much to my amazement, some months after the LIMA kiosks venture, Ishak called upon Ramli to meet with a friend of his who was seeking to do business on Langkawi, in the hope that he could do them both a special favour by introducing them to each other. He spoke affectionately and warmly about Ramli to me, pointing out how willing Ramli was to help his friend. Ramli had proved himself to be an insufficient link in their network once, but perhaps not for all time. Ishak still hoped that Ramli might someday see the mutual social and economic benefits which could come of their sharing a real friendship together. Both Ishak and Rokiah said they would be willing to trust him again, and would be willing to test his progress in becoming what they called a 'real' entrepreneur – a highly skilled, socially and economically balanced virtuoso of Malay economic development – the goal they had for themselves.

In the next chapter, I shall continue to examine some of the social and economic consequences of networking, and how they both helped and hindered the progress of a new *hi tek* manufacturing business, Marchland. As in CrossLinks, we will see the way in which alliances became the primary focus of the Marchland entrepreneurs, taking precedence over the manufacturing or marketing process – partly by choice and partly by necessity. We will look carefully at another alliance made between two entrepreneurial actors whose networks converged, and seek to understand, as we did with Rokiah and Ishak and Ramli, the powerful social and economic expectations of people mobilized in an alliance. As with CrossLinks, much importance was granted to the public role and identity of virtuoso entrepreneurship which the participants sought to establish for themselves and their businesses. But with Marchland, different consequences emerged from the public demonstration of the entrepreneurial identity. We will begin to see that there are limits to networking, and limits to how far Malay entrepreneurial ambition can go before it is seen to overwhelm social relations and become anathema to what entrepreneurship, according to my informants, is supposed to serve: Malay development and the social group. We will see how the very networks and public identities some entrepreneurs seek to build for themselves can also emerge as a destructive force, especially, in this case, where they involve women.

7 Dangerous Business: the Social Limits of an Entrepreneurial Identity

Aisha and Rahim – the married co-owners of Marchland, a new manufacturing company – a photographic crew, and I drove through the streets of an upper-class community in Kuala Lumpur, stopping at a house with enormous white pillars and an elegant garden. Today they would photograph a series of magazine advertisements for Marchland at this house, which belonged to Aisha's wealthy friend. Aisha said it was a perfect location for the advertisements because the house was elegant and modern – exactly what the advertisements were planned to show about Marchland. Like many of the newly renovated Malay houses in Kuala Lumpur, it boasted a patio surrounded by columns, French doors, a waterfall fountain in the garden, and a stained-glass window in the entrance.

The Marchland company had been established to manufacture home-decoration accessories – bedspreads, sheets, table-cloths, and curtains. Aisha referred to herself as the 'Laura Ashley of Malaysia'; this self-styled sobriquet had been printed in the various newspaper and magazine articles which had recently been written about her, and, to her great pleasure, it had stuck, as had the tag *usahawan besar*, or top entrepreneur. As one of the few recipients of a prestigious million-*ringgit* loan from the *bumiputera* only New Entrepreneurs Fund scheme of the Malaysian development bank, Bank Pembangunan,[1] Marchland, but especially Aisha, who took on the role of promoting the company, was often featured in the media. She was described as a model of female Malay entrepreneurship, a paradigm of economic modernity, months before the Marchland factory had actually opened. In fact, on the day of the photo shoots, Marchland, running far behind schedule, still was not manufacturing its product yet, but the advertising space had already been ordered in the popular women's magazine *Wanita* (Woman) and, product or not, the advertisements would run. Aisha and Rahim wanted to advertise Marchland well in advance of the factory launch to establish its growing reputation even more solidly.

Aisha and Rahim's entrepreneurial idea was considered to be excellent by everyone who heard of it. They wanted to capture the growing trend in the lifestyle of modern Malays to decorate luxuriously. With their million-*ringgit* loan, they had ordered a huge, computerized, textile-stitching *hi tek* machine from Italy which would arrive soon. Articles which quoted Aisha talking about her modern factory and Italian machine implied that Marchland itself – one of the nation's few Malay-owned textile fabricating businesses in a Chinese-dominated sector – both represented and served changing Malay lifestyles and desires. Marchland, machine-less and factory-less, was already a well-known Malay-owned entrepreneurial business, a modern company formed to meet modern needs. The public, nearly transcendent, virtuoso content of the Malay entrepreneurial lifestyle was what Aisha managed to achieve – at least for a time – through the media, self-promotion, and the social relations of networking.

Up until the day before the photo shoot, there were still no prototype Marchland bedspread or curtains to photograph, but Aisha had finally come through with several hastily sewn samples. She had bought English fabrics in Singapore and had hired some workers who stayed up all night sewing duvets and pillow covers. As Aisha arranged props she had brought from her house – an elegant lamp, a lacquer box, a teddy bear for the bed – she riffled through Western decorating magazines to imitate the 'look' she wanted to achieve. But Hamzeh, Rahim's brother and Marchland's operations director, paced anxiously. His worries were not the advertisements, but what would happen after they appeared. He whispered urgently to me: how would Marchland provide product with no manufacturing facilities? What if hundreds of people called to order what the advertisements offered? What if they couldn't get more fabric from Singapore? No one had put any of these mechanisms in place, he said fearfully. But as he worried, the photos were taken; models arrived and put on costumes. Some of Aisha's friends and relatives dropped by during the course of the day, suggesting a change or two or offering a compliment, but mostly to stand around and watch. This was the first time any of the Marchland people or their visitors had seen a photographic shoot; the bright lights, camera equipment, and the famous models Aisha had hired suddenly made Marchland seem very formidable indeed.

The advertisement, when it first appeared in *Wanita*, was widely discussed by everyone in Aisha's circle. They noticed the image of opulence created by the setting and the flowered-print Marchland bed linens. The female model was immediately recognizable as a presenter on a popular local television quiz show, a fact which was quite impressive. Aisha passed the advertisement around at meetings of Peniagawati, the women's networking organization, and over cups of tea at the hotel coffee shops she frequented for lunch and at the food stalls she often went to at night.

This image was both compelling and infuriating to the people who saw it. In Aisha's network, comprised of other women seeking to engage in one or another version of important Malay entrepreneurial activity themselves, the advertisement elicited a considerable amount of envy behind her back. Marchland was a *hi tek* manufacturing firm, the essence of industrial modernity as extolled by the government. It was glamorous and important. By choosing television stars for Marchland's advertisements, Aisha had offered further proof that the business was already well capitalized. Furthermore, the glossy photograph appeared in the centre-fold of *Wanita*, what Aisha described as the 'most expensive location in a magazine'; this, too, was a symbol of her and Rahim's importance, which in turn implied the powerful and influential connections they were likely to already have.

From the start, it was assumed that Marchland did indeed have influence. Most people felt it was not easy to get one of the huge development loans made available to entrepreneurs without pulling a few strings. Aisha and Rahim did not deny that it was true that they had friends in high places, but also insisted that hard work had netted them the million-*ringgit* loan and all of the benefits that came with it: a new factory in a industrial park south of Kuala Lumpur with subsidized rent payable only after the company began earning, a subsidized marketing and promotion budget, as well as free publicity from MARA[2] in the form of elaborate displays in its grandiosely named 'Hall of Entrepreneurs'. At Aisha and Rahim's request, using the marketing subsidy, I had written and produced a glossy 12-page colour brochure for Marchland, its 'corporate image' piece, describing manufacturing capacity the company did not actually yet have. Aisha handed these brochures out to everyone she knew. Rahim stayed in the background, trying to organize the Marchland operation.

IMAGES AND REALITIES OF ENTREPRENEURIAL BUSINESS

Despite the positive impression other entrepreneurially ambitious Malays received of Marchland, from the outset it was plagued by internal problems. The biggest problem was cash flow, which began when the loan Marchland had received from Bank Pembangunan was delayed.[3] Because they could not pay for it until the loan money came through, the arrival of the computerized *hi tek* industrial sewing machine – on which all of their production depended – was delayed by many months. Indeed, Bank Pembangunan was behind on many of its promises – the factory was completed months later than had been anticipated, and when it was, the wiring was faulty. Marchland had been producing some small-scale sewing jobs on individual sewing machines in the batik factory of Aisha's cousin, and was generating, when I first began to spend time at the Marchland offices, a small, but nearly inconsequential, cash flow.

As such, Rahim's brother, Hamzeh, had not received his salary for many months, nor had other family members and friends who were employed in various Marchland functions. He was deeply worried about the organization on the day of the photo shoot, but his worries continued to increase. Aisha had ordered thousands of metres of cheap fabric from Pakistan which was the wrong size for the Italian machine; this faulty material had to be paid for, then stored in a warehouse, at substantial cost. Timing and operational problems got worse. Once the loan money finally came through from the bank and a cheque was forwarded to Italy, Marchland expected the industrial machine to come right away, but the Italian company – thinking its customer had reneged on the deal – had sold the machine Marchland ordered to another buyer. Meanwhile, Hamzeh had been told to hire and train a factory staff – 20 sewers, cutters, and machine operators – who had to be fired when it was learned the machine would be delayed again. Aisha, who had obtained a sub-contract to sew mattress covers from the well-known mattress entrepreneur (Chapter 5) she met at the networking organization Peniagawati, learned that the payment for the contract work would be delayed because of government red tape, and Marchland's cash-flow problems worsened.

Marchland had marketing and sales difficulties as well. Rahim had various ideas about how to sell the products once Marchland was up and running. He envisaged opening stores in all of Malaysia's biggest malls, selling through mail-order, and marketing through home-based direct-sales representatives, like Amway or Tupperware. (This form of selling has a long history in Malay life – see Chapter 8.) He discussed exporting bed linens to Indonesia and becoming the 'Laura Ashley of Southeast Asia'. Rahim leased several retail locations. Packaging was ordered in huge quantity, imprinted with the Marchland logo. Hamzeh attended seminars on direct-mail sales, and he and I wrote and had photographed a colourful four-page product catalogue which was ultimately never used. Six months after the *Wanita* advertisement had appeared, Marchland was still, unbeknown to most people, without a product, without a distribution system, and without an operational factory. What Marchland did have was, in addition to a wide reputation as a model entrepreneurial business symbolized by Aisha's increasingly public profile, a huge supply of unsuitable fabric, packaging, catalogues, a glossy corporate-image brochure, rising debts and negative cash flow.

NETWORKING ALLIANCES AND THE ROLE OF WOMEN

Throughout the months of difficulties, Aisha networked constantly. Like many of the women entrepreneurs I met, she was a nearly indefatigable networker. Often, more socially attuned and engaged, Malay women were *better* networkers than men and appeared to have more varied social contacts (cf. Lee 1986). Moreover, to Aisha, like many of the women I knew, was relegated the more visible entrepreneurial role within the structure of the alliance-based business, just as in time CrossLinks' 'marketing function' – networking – was intended to become Rokiah's alone. While they shared the economic interests, Rahim, Aisha, and Rahim's two brothers (who held smaller interests) felt that Aisha's ability to engage social relations in economic alliances was paramount to the company's success. Once Marchland was off the ground, Rahim intended to sell his construction business and take over day-to-day management of Marchland while Aisha would continue to 'network'. But this choice was to have complex consequences for Marchland's progress, as we will see.

Entrepreneurially ambitious Malay women such as Aisha and Rokiah often claimed that men actually have much greater social advantages than they do in modern life, such as old-boy networks, clubs, and their ubiquitous interest in golf. As such, women, in the spirit of retaliation, are formalizing their social interactions into associations and organizations for the express purpose of increasing their business contacts with other women. Most of the high-profile entrepreneurial organizations in Kuala Lumpur are, in fact, women's groups. Aisha was a highly visible participant in the women's entrepreneurial group Peniagawati, attending its meetings, dinners, factory tours, and lectures. But she kept her profile high in all contexts. She participated in government-sponsored entrepreneurship seminars on industrial development in manufacturing, and at them, revealed impressively that she had already become *hi tek*, describing her Italian machine to the other participants. As a recipient of a prestigious Bank Pembangunan loan, she was often invited by the Ministry of Trade to trade shows held in Kuala Lumpur and overseas. When television news crews came to photograph trade shows, Aisha was always on camera, talking about Marchland's successes and the role of women entrepreneurs in the Malay economy. She handed out the corporate-image brochure which I had written, and reprints of the *Wanita* advertisement. She attended the dinners and open houses of her friends, and mercilessly talked about her business. She booked expensive tables at charity dinners sponsored by UMNO and offered seats to contacts she had met through her networks – the woman who ran a large direct-sales organization who might represent Marchland's products and a woman with connections to a big resort hotel on Langkawi who might order bedspreads. When the LIMA event (Chapter 6) was announced, Aisha got the contract to produce its T-shirts, and she was photographed shaking hands with the LIMA director. In nearly every context, Aisha was a subject of public interest – a progressive, visible, energetic Malay businesswoman – whose entre-preneurial idea had been embraced and supported by the government.

While a great deal of complementary energy had been expended in the offices of Marchland and at Aisha and Rahim's house at night – where Rahim, Hamzeh, and their brothers were often to be found discussing how to produce, market, distribute, and export exclusive bed linens under the name of Marchland – the directors, by financial necessity and perhaps choice, eventually made a dramatic shift in organizational focus: seeking information on potential government and corporate contracts through informal and formal contacts became Marchland's sole venture, Aisha's domain. There was no more talk of retail stores or direct marketing. We put away the catalogue with its colourful pictures of non-existent Marchland products. All the loan money had been spent on starting up the organization and no substantial receipts were yet coming in. It was decided that Aisha, who was already out in public view, would spare no expense networking for alliances with other entrepreneurs who could bring business to Marchland through sub-contracting.[4] It came as no sur-prise to me when, at a charity dinner where she had purchased a table for 2,500 *ringgit*, Aisha met Sharifah, who represented an alliance which could not only save Marchland from approaching bankruptcy, but poten-tially bring in millions. This, she was to declare excitedly later on, had been the goal of all of her networking.

ALLIANCES AND VENTURES II – MARCHLAND AND THE LUXURY BUS CONTRACT

Sharifah and her husband owned what people in Malaysia call a 'trading company', a business which brokered merchandise and services to other companies.[5] I had met Sharifah at a party months earlier, and knew a little about her. As far as I could tell, she and her husband were in the business of supplying office furniture to large corporations. They were known to have excellent contacts throughout the Malay business community, because he was a former executive in a huge Malay-owned conglomerate. Like Aisha, Sharifah stayed in public view while her husband remained primarily in the background.

Sharifah reported to her friends at the dinner Aisha attended that she had just received a guaranteed multi-million-*ringgit* contract to supply a major corporation – Dato Hassan's company – with upholstery, curtains, and uniforms for its new transport division, a luxury bus line. Aisha, learning of this contract, immediately introduced herself to Sharifah, discovering, to her pleasure, that Sharifah was already familiar with Marchland, having heard about it through her contacts. In fact, Sharifah had intended to call upon Aisha and some of her competitors for quotes to produce the items for Dato Hassan's company. Aisha quickly spoke of how much greater Marchland's capacity, how much bigger her factory, and how much faster her machine was than anyone else's in Malaysia. Determined to get the job, Aisha described advantages Marchland actually could not be said fully to possess, and she intended, if necessary, to sub-contract portions of the project out to companies as needed.

It was obvious to everyone who knew about the contract that Sharifah would pick Aisha for the job. Indeed, their alliance seemed firm. For several weeks, Sharifah and Aisha were inseparable. Aisha invited Sharifah to be her guest at the annual Tun Fatimah awards, where the Queen awarded women who had served the nation most in the previous year. At Aisha's table – at which sat her various entrepreneurial friends who handed out business cards to each other – the luxury bus contract was discussed excitedly by Sharifah and Aisha while the other women sat silently, outdone by its importance. The two of them speculated that the following year, perhaps the Queen would give the Tun Fatimah service awards to them – the two top Malay women entrepreneurs. Sharifah invited Aisha to a high tea at the home of a relative of Prime Minister Mahathir, a most important event. (I describe this occasion in Chapter 8.) It seemed to everyone who saw them that much success would come from this alliance.

DATO HASSAN AND THE PURSUIT OF OPPORTUNITIES

Before long, Aisha had told nearly everyone she knew that she had secured a contract with Dato Hassan, often implying to her listeners that she knew him personally, and that her relationship to him would make Marchland rich. (Aisha had, in fact, never met Dato Hassan. She and Rahim knew I had, and begged me to 'put in a good word' for Marchland whenever I saw him.) Now, Aisha told her envious contacts that her job with Dato Hassan would be worth 5 million *ringgit* and she openly discussed what she would do with all that money – she would expand

Marchland into a *gabungan* (conglomerate). Sometimes, she hinted that Rahim, through his own connections, had obtained the project directly from Dato Hassan, neglecting to mention the role of Sharifah in securing the contract. She ostentatiously told some of her friends that she could not join them at a meeting because she was waiting for a call from Dato Hassan's assistant about price quotations. She told me excitedly that she intended to make an appointment to speak directly to Dato Hassan soon, to show him how deserving Marchland was of his projects; then he would introduce them to other top people who would give them other important jobs. She would enter his often-mentioned ambit of 'Malays helping Malays', at the highest reaches of the economy.

The luxury bus contract had immediately ramifying positive conse- quences for Marchland. On the strength of the new job, Aisha and Rahim decided to plan the public launch of the Marchland factory, and asked Rafidah Aziz, Minister of Trade and Industry, who officiated at only the most impressive business events, to cut the ribbon (to be sewn out of an appropriate flowery Marchland fabric). Hamzeh, Rahim's brother, in charge of the dormant Marchland factory, began to interview factory workers once again, in anticipation of the massive job Marchland would soon be doing. More than once, I sat in on a Marchland business meeting in which Aisha, Rahim, and Rahim's brothers almost danced with pleasure at how their luck had turned. All of Marchland's problems would be reversed, thanks to Allah. Indeed, Aisha and Rahim recalled the 'feeling' they had in Mecca when performing the *haj*, that Marchland would be a success. Moreover, to demonstrate further her sincerity and humility in Allah's eyes, Aisha immediately decided she would perform another pil- grimage as soon as the luxury bus job was complete, to offer tribute to Allah's greatness in bringing her luck. In this atmosphere of excitement, gratitude, and relief, there was an unexpected turn.

I was never to learn precisely what had happened, but several weeks later Aisha reported to me and to her friends that she was now signing papers for a huge contract with a Swiss duvet manufacturer and had regrettably been forced to hand the luxury bus contract back to Sharifah, for it was 'too small'. Hamzeh and Rahim both said privately that the bus job had simply 'died' – no one knew how or why. They never spoke of it again. Soon, all Marchland was scrambling to meet the demands of the Swiss contract, which, by the time I left Malaysia, had also failed to meet their expectations. A few people in Aisha's networks anticipated that Marchland would be bankrupt within the year, and it was hard to miss the note of satisfaction in such prognostications.

THE LUXURY BUS JOB?

Some time passed before I was able to ask Dato Hassan about his company's project to produce and outfit the luxury buses and how it was progressing. To my amazement, he insisted his company never had any interests in a project of this kind. Moreover, he claimed to have no knowledge of a woman named Sharifah or her husband, nor could he speculate when or why anyone in his organization had ever discussed engaging their services. '*What* luxury bus job?' he asked, raising in my mind a horrifying possibility that it had never actually existed. (This conversation with Dato Hassan and ensuing ones ultimately became a source of my understanding of the crucial determinants of entrepreneurial success in Malay society, discussed in the Conclusion.) At the time, I could only wonder what had happened. Had there ever been a luxury bus contract? Was Dato Hassan's conglomerate ever involved? Or, had Sharifah simply deceived Aisha? Had Aisha herself exaggerated the alliance she believed she was striking with Sharifah? I pored over my fieldnotes, trying again and again to unscramble the sequence of events in an attempt to understand what had happened. Regrettably, I would never know the answer to any of my questions.[6] Only later did I realize that understanding what had happened could not be traced, for indeed, networks are not anthropologically interesting because we might sketch them out on a computer until we could mechanically map the actual lines of information to ultimately discover who said what to whom and why. They are interesting precisely because, not unlike Fortes's 'web of kinship' (1969), networks are about shifting domains of social *relationships* that are often infinite in number, intent, and kind. In fact, networks demonstrate what physicists call 'chaos', and, as such, can produce ambiguous and discontinuous consequences which cannot be mapped.

What I could trace was the way in which entrepreneurial information, in its various channels and forms, profoundly affected the people I knew, and, in this case, pushed them into entrepreneurial overdrive. The advantages Marchland *appeared* to have and the alliances *assumed* to exist between Aisha or Sharifah and Dato Hassan had, as we have seen, a very powerful and transformative impact on everyone who heard of them. Aisha had always used an image of her success to sway her chances in social and economic settings. With the luxury bus contract, Aisha's entrepreneurial image implied 'know-how' at the highest, most impressive level of Malay socio-economic life. The luxury bus contract, and all it entailed, was about claiming and demonstrating – however exaggeratedly

– the existence of significant social and economic entailment in the innermost circle of Malay entrepreneurial virtuosi. It conferred enormous prestige on Aisha, whose business was already seen by the government and the media as a model of Malay economic development. To do work for Dato Hassan, a paradigm of Malay entrepreneurship himself, could only imply that Aisha, too, was what the newspaper reports and her own self-promotion said about her, a top Malay entrepreneur. It was proof that she belonged in the society of Malay entrepreneurial leaders.

Behind those claims, perhaps both premature and inflationary, an opportunity – the luxury bus contract – was claimed to exist; how real it was is less important than the fact that it was translated into information which was catapulted, with impressive consequences, into both Sharifah and Aisha's social and business networks. Where had the process begun? Perhaps someone in Dato Hassan's organization had indeed implied to Sharifah and her husband that they would be granted a huge project. This possibility was not unlikely, for again and again I heard government and corporate leaders, and, of course, many of my own informants, offer to 'help' one another generously as a virtuoso demonstration that they had the means to do so, an action which, as Mauss (1989) ably revealed, confers great prestige upon the giver.

As I have demonstrated with the example of CrossLinks (Chapter 6), alliances form among members of Malay social networks to test the expectations of such claims. Indeed, behind Aisha's 'test' of Sharifah and Sharifah's 'test' of Aisha, Sharifah was perhaps engaged in a legitimacy appraisal of her own to test the veracity of an alliance promised to her, and so on and so on until somewhere we might establish whether or not at some remote point in a network a 'real' opportunity actually existed. Aisha, it will be remembered, was already talking to other entrepreneurs about potentially sub-contracting part of the job to them, optimistically bringing others into the prestigious project. Rokiah and Ishak had done the same thing by speaking to their contacts about the LIMA kiosks. Such claims serve people well, as they confirm the efficacy of the entrepreneurial identity. For the myriad of Malay people who become entailed in them, however, the consequences, as should already be clear, are often profoundly unsatisfying.

As such, it is only demonstrable that Aisha and Sharifah made an alliance, quickly trusted each other, and together, increased their visibility at various dinners and meetings, until they exhibited the full impact of their alliance among those who knew of it, and allowed information concerning it to spread among those who did not. Wherever the idea of the luxury bus contract began, as the project was discussed in wider networks

– their own and others – it began to take on an eidetic force, until perhaps the job was bigger, more lucrative, more demanding than it first seemed, or, as in Aisha's case, more inclusive of Dato Hassan, more proprietary, more fulfilling, and more entrepreneurially validating than any of her previous efforts had been. In that way, although the alliance established in the episode proved to be miserably disappointing for Aisha, it provided a substantial, although fleeting, source of public validation and served as proof to many that her company was indeed successful and deserved to be even more successful. Presumably, Sharifah also benefited from the public alliance with Aisha and the alliance she claimed to have with Dato Hassan. In the Conclusion, we will examine the limits of such alliances in the larger context of Malay economic development. But now, we will look at the consequences for Aisha.

Glossing over the luxury bus job's demise, Aisha was not called upon by her friends to account for what had happened. Indeed, she spoke instead of the now *international* level of Marchland's alliances as evidenced by the contract with the Swiss company. This silenced her friends, but, as we shall see, also increased their growing jealousy. More than the disappointing alliances with other entrepreneurs like Sharifah and more than Marchland's operational problems, what others perceived as Aisha's lack of humility – of Islamic and Malay virtues – began to damage her, until the very networks she depended on began to slowly discredit her. Despite the virtuoso image of contributing to Malay industrial modernity she had been granted by the media, in her own networks people became less willing to see her virtues. She was increasingly seen to be self-interested, motivated only by greed, backward, undeveloped, and even dangerous. She was, in the minds of others, not really an entrepreneur at all.

Just as entrepreneurs like Aisha sought to ally themselves with legitimate sources of power like Dato Hassan, often, highly ambitious and overly competitive entrepreneurs were rumoured to have allied themselves with illegitimate sources of power, working against the collective social and entrepreneurial good, the subject to which we now turn.

ALLIANCES TO ILLEGITIMATE SOURCES OF POWER AND 'NEGATIVE NETWORKS'

I have attempted to show how my informants participated in networks in attempts to construct alliances with others; as often, they used networks in socially disintegrative and negative ways. Obviously, networks can have positive and negative consequences, and, as I have already suggested, destructive rumours, gossip, and normative information fly just as quickly through networks as does constructive information about economic opportunity. While I sat night after night in the food stalls, listening to the informal conversations of my friends and informants, a crucial normative pattern about entrepreneurs began to emerge. Malays – men and women alike – gossip more about successful women than they do about men. Indeed, powerful, ambitious women in Malay society appear to be the target of greater criticism, scorn, and jealousy more often than men (Shamsul A.B. 1986b). Successful Malay women are often seen as status-grabbing, corrupt, sexually manipulative, and *kasar* or rough. In contrast, the most ambitious men in Malay economic life – like Dato Hassan and Tan Sri Azman Hashim – are often admired for a virtuoso style which is *korporat*, Islamic, strategic, sophisticated, and *halus* or refined. In Chapter 2, we saw that the status level of male and female beneficiaries of NEP educational privileges is perceived as equal, and as such, both sexes theoretically enter the professional economy as equals. But now, we confront evidence that Malay women who appear to go too far in their public pursuit of economic and social status are often brought down by gossip and rumours about sex and sorcery – destroyed and negated by the same networks in which they seek to build positive relationships.[7] To understand how Aisha was discredited by her own networks, we need to briefly examine Malay Muslim attitudes towards sex and danger, and how these are reflected in gender categories.

DANGER, CHAOS, AND THE SEXUALITY OF WOMEN

During the time I lived in Kuala Lumpur, I often heard conversations about sex and sexuality, such as the use of such *ilmu* (knowledge) which could keep women sexually youthful. Women joke with one another about men's lack of prowess, and men and women sometimes 'spar' about each other's capacity for sexual pleasure and endurance (Wazir Jahan Karim 1992), often with a bawdiness which contrasts sharply with their modesty and propriety in other contexts. But while discussions of sexuality are permissible among mature women and men, overt display of sexual – even affectionate – feelings are discouraged, even between married couples, like hand-holding in public (Banks 1983; Wazir Jahan Karim 1990). Passion can be joked about; *acted-out* passion, unconcealed from the public eye, is considered embarrassing, uncontrolled, and dangerous.

Furthermore, when sexuality does veer out of control, it is generally women who are said to cause it (cf. Peletz 1996). My friend Aziz told a ribald story at the night-time food stalls he frequented. An old man (Aziz's uncle) had been married for 30 years when it was suddenly discovered that he was having an affair with his wife's younger sister. He divorced the wife and married the sister. The new wife bragged to the ex-wife (her sister), 'I just wanted him for sex! He's one of a hundred men I've had!' And then, as the story went, she stripped off her clothes, the husband appeared, stripped off *his* clothes, and they fell to the floor to have noisy sex in front of the poor woman. Again and again this story was told to men and women, who listened in amusement, women gasping in appropriate places, men shaking their heads as if to say, yes, they know about women like this. 'Some people have sex like animals', Aziz said when I asked him why such a thing had happened. Yet Aziz said that in his family, no one was really angry with the uncle, they were enraged with the younger woman; she was at fault, not he. She was the real beast.

Certain women are just 'that way', many informants claimed, unable to say no, needing lots of men, having a hunger for sex that cannot be satisfied. Normal women, my informants said, do not have such a powerful desire. Men, on the contrary, are perceived to be more sexual by nature, and according to many Malays, cannot be blamed for doing what comes naturally, although like all Muslims, should obviously demonstrate great effort in curbing *nafsu*, or their instinctive drives.[8] Aisha, it was said by many men and women who knew her, like the bestial woman in the story Aziz told, was 'that way'. The more successes she claimed and the more she appeared on television and in magazines, the more suspicious her behaviour ultimately seemed to be. At the same time that she was networking among government ministers and appearing at high-status charity dinners, networks nearly ululated with hushed rumours about Aisha, sex, and magic.

WOMEN'S CONTROL OF MAGIC AND POWER

In contemporary Malay life, just as in the classic studies of Malay 'magic' (Endicott 1970), women are claimed frequently to use love magic to control men's souls. Aisha was said to have had many adulterous affairs, which her husband Rahim, it was claimed, knew about. How could he *not* know, people asked, because Aisha flirted openly with men, right under his nose. But he could do nothing, because Aisha had gone to a *bomoh*, or traditional curer, to have a special charm placed on Rahim, making it impossible for him to leave her and magically silencing him. In fact, Rahim was often scrutinized by men and women in Aisha's network for evidence of this charm; his 'softness' and 'gentleness' were said to be a sign of how she had changed his nature from masculine to nearly feminine, as was his acceptance of the lesser role in the newspaper and magazine articles about Marchland. He was in the background not because he wanted to be, but because Aisha put him there.

People said Aisha had had special implants, *susuk*, placed in the skin around her lips which made everything she said sound sweet, even when it was not, so that Rahim could not hear her lies. It was rumoured, in fact, that Aisha had received the million-*ringgit* loan from Bank Pembangunan because she had magically 'sweet-talked' the bank officials. Eventually, people began to say that Aisha did not merely resort to the cunning resources of a helpful *bomoh*, but was described as having her own special *ilmu*, like a *bomoh* herself, an inheritance from a powerful non-Muslim uncle from Thailand. Aisha was then not just described as a woman who used magic, but dangerously possessed it.

FORCES OF THE UNKNOWN AND THE POWER OF GREED

When people claimed that Aisha had access to magical *ilmu* and powers that were not constrained by the teachings of Islam, they were making a sharp and frequently heard distinction between spiritual forces which are acceptable in modern life and those which are not. Paralleling the way in which Malays tend to see the sources of negative social behaviours arising from outside the boundaries of their own culture (Chapter 2), my informants believed that the most powerful and therefore most dangerous magic is used by non-Muslims in Thailand and mystically inclined Sufi-influenced Indonesian Muslims. This only begins to suggest the complex ideas about Islam and supernatural powers which influence Malays in everyday life, who believe deeply in the forces of the unknown, in Muslim *jinn* or spirits, and in the powers some people have to do unspeakable harm to others.

Despite the prevalence of such beliefs, Islamization in Malaysia has forced many Malays to examine the extent to which rituals which attempt to control the supernatural are part of their pre-Islamic heritage and go against the teachings of Islam (Mohd. Taib Osman 1989). As such, many traditional practices are performed by *bomoh* who now assert themselves to be 'Islamic healers'. My informants who visited *bomoh* expressly emphasized to me that they went to the 'Islamic *bomoh* – not the other kind'. Those *bomoh* who use verses from the Quran to appeal to the power of Allah and do good with their magic are said to be Islamic. No one objects strenuously to Malays who use Islamic *bomoh* to marshal spiritual and economic resources that do not cause anyone harm. (Increasingly popular among my informants, too, were 'corporate' *bomoh* – for it is well known that Malay businessmen at such modern corporations as Dato Hassan's and Tan Sri Azman Hashim's seek advice from well-paid *bomoh* who specialize in business success (Laderman 1991). Indeed, one only need glance at the advertisement which appears weekly in a Malaysian newspaper – which shows a 'traditional Islamic healer' in an Arab turban holding a hand phone who is 'on call' to homes and businesses 24 hours a day – to see an image which neatly illustrates the Malay belief that traditional supernatural forces can be both Islamic and *hi tek*. But horrifying consequences have also occurred when Malays have attempted – as it was ultimately said Aisha had done – to harness together the forces of the unknown and the power of greed in modern economic life. An extraordinary example of this emerged during my stay in Malaysia.

When a gruesome murder of a Pahang State assemblyman, Datuk Mazlan Idris, was alleged in newspapers to have been a ritual killing performed by a male *bomoh*, Nor Affandi, and his *bomoh* wife, national fascination – to the point of near-obsession – turned primarily to the wife, Mona Fandy. Stories were told about her using *susuk* inserted under the skin to make her beautiful. Mona Fandy, who looked 30, was really 60. Mona Fandy had sexual powers which had entranced Datuk Mazlan Idris. Mona Fandy was seen flying around Kuala Lumpur's Pudu Jail at night, after transforming herself into a bird. Mona Fandy was reported to feast on the blood of her chopped-up victims.[9] By the time Mona Fandy, her husband, and a third defendant went on trial, the newspapers and television reports referred to it simply as 'The Mona Fandy Trial' and the events were seen to be primarily about the dangers of an evil woman.

This is not to say that Malay men are not thought to use illegitimate sources of power or are not suspected of having done so; the male politician who was found chopped up in Mona Fandy's house had obviously attempted to influence his fate through her magic. But Mona Fandy was the one with real power, and the politician ultimately her victim. While it is well documented in anthropological literature that women's relationship to the forces of the unknown often results in a vivid embodiment of sexual and destructive inversions (for Southeast Asian examples, see Ong and Peletz 1995), there appeared to be almost no end to the grisly inversions about this woman who held my informants in nearly constant fascination.

Indeed, during the weeks in which Mona Fandy was in the news, the usual topic of discussion in the food stalls and other social settings –

entrepreneurship – was temporarily pre-empted. When I arranged through Ramli a coveted meeting with the head of LIMA, my interview with him rapidly shifted from the subject of Malay economic opportunities to Malay economic transgressions represented by Mona Fandy's and her clients' illegitimate empowerment over forces of disorder and greed. The power of greed became understood as the premise for Mona Fandy's activities. No one was shocked when it was revealed during the trial of Mona Fandy that some Malay businessmen and politicians had spent thousands of *ringgit* to purchase from her such things as *azimat Sukarno* (talismans which had, it was claimed, belonged to the late Indonesian president – one more example of the power of Sufi-induced Muslim outsiders) (*New Straits Times*, December 1994). The themes which were to be revealed by the murder case – business, politics, black magic, and sexuality – demonstrated how quickly danger and disorder could be generated by excessive greed, and how familiar Malays are with self-interest, the antisocial and sinister *antithesis* of altruism.

I was not particularly surprised, therefore, when it was revealed by some of my informants in hushed whispers in the food stalls that they thought Aisha *looked remarkably like Mona Fandy*. Was it because she had the same kind of *susuk* implanted in her skin, or was it because, like Mona Fandy, Aisha had recourse to Thai magical practices? Worse, was Aisha related through remote kinship ties to Mona Fandy? The themes of greed, self-interest, magic, and sexuality brought out by Aisha's numerous critics rapidly began to parallel the details in the Mona Fandy case. Aisha was greedy, just like Mona Fandy and her victims. Aisha thought only of her own success and power, just like Mona Fandy. Aisha appeared to exhibit peculiar powers over men, just like Mona Fandy.

The tricks of *susuk*, love magic, and sexual arousal – *ilmu* that Malay women are claimed to know and pass on as part of their *adat* heritage – appear not only to be evidence for Malay female independence and autonomy, as feminist researchers often suggest (Ong 1990; Wazir Jahan Karim 1995), but also a statement of women's often peculiar and terrifying powers to control men and the forces of danger. When Malay women, like Aisha, achieve substantial success or are too competitive, thereby exhibiting what Leach (1954) described as an 'unacceptable authority' over men, over social and economic outcomes, or over their own fate, they often come under attack as being the possessors of dangerous power, a conclusion about Aisha which was made over and over in the minds of my male and female informants and repeated again and again in their networks.

ENTREPRENEURSHIP AND THE GENDER OF VIRTUOSI

Accumulating wealth, or claiming to have accumulated it, is not enough to elicit accusations of witchcraft in or be marginalized by modern Malay society, for on the contrary, many of the richest Malays are said to demonstrate the most outstanding behaviours. No one ever speculated that Dato Hassan or Tan Sri Azman Hashim had earned their wealth through sorcery. The essence of their entrepreneurial identity, as well as that of other paradigms of Malay entrepreneurship, was a claim to membership in the primordial *kampung* to which all other Malays belonged, as well as the idealized *ummah*. Highly skilled and highly virtuous, Dato Hassan claimed, and was acknowledged to have earned, the virtuoso identity as defined by Weber, as well as the wealth it entailed.

Yet Aisha claimed the same identity. She took great pains in numerous magazine interviews to point out convincingly that she had grown up in a *kampung* and was a devout Muslim and a *hajah* (female pilgrim to Mecca) who fully credited her success to Allah. Indeed, she referred to herself time and again as a 'simple *kampung* girl', and like the sobriquet 'Laura Ashley of Malaysia', this description often appeared in magazine articles about her. Often she spoke of her mission to help Malays advance their modern economic participation, and her role in a predominantly Chinese domain – textiles – was strong evidence for this. Moreover, the government itself had embraced Aisha's zealous plans. Why then were Dato Hassan's successes deemed by other Malays to be the result of the processes of meritocracy and Aisha's of the processes of sorcery? Why was he more convincing in his virtuoso demonstration of ethnic goals and group concerns than she? Why was he a *kampung*-boy-made-good and she an example of *kampung* backwardness? To answer these questions, let us explore the example of how my informants described a businesswoman even more successful than Aisha.

The recipient of the award of 'Top Woman Entrepreneur' several years back, Mazneh Hamid,[10] was, perhaps to her great misfortune, portrayed by magazine articles as the epitome of success for a Malay woman. Photographed alongside her Mercedes, standing next to her warehouse-sized closet filled with handmade silk clothing, or pointing out the gold-plated taps in her enormous bathroom, Mazneh's public, media-bolstered image was one of the luxuries and rewards available to women who worked hard. She was described in articles and in her own words as 'self-made', 'a *kampung* girl', a simple, humble Malay who had learned modern business lessons. But, paradoxically, she had not earned the respect of any of my male or female informants, who described her as a representation of the 'lowest form of Malay entrepreneurship' and a fraud. My informants, male and female, said she was the epitome of *kampung* economic backwardness and of *bumi*-style greed.

They told me how she had paid for publicity, handsomely rewarding newspapers and magazines to give her coverage, handing out kick-backs and bribes for contracts, as had the bad *bumiputera* of the early NEP era. Nicknamed 'the Iron Lady' by the media, supposedly a comment on her strength and ambition, Mazneh was, to my informants, unfeminine, vulgar, and offensive. At the Peniagawati awards night, an important event in the female Malay entrepreneurial community, Mazneh appeared on stage with Prime Minister Mahathir, granted the privilege to hand out the award to the 1993 Top Woman Entrepreneur. The men and women at my table insisted that they had seen on the Prime Minister's face only revulsion for Mazneh. Even the Prime Minister, they claimed, knew how the Iron Lady had snared people into her web of greed and deceit; he acquiesced to her image only because he believed so deeply in supporting *all* Malay entrepreneurs.

When the Iron Lady appeared on television giving tips on how anyone could replicate her entrepreneurial success by working hard and remembering to thank Allah, my landlady, Aziza, mocked her, insisting she could see through her façade. 'She's a lazy fraud who knows nothing about business', she insisted, interested only in her own image and personal enrichment, not in helping others. By the end of my stay in Kuala Lumpur, the Iron Lady was rumoured to have destroyed herself through her excessive practice of black magic and sexual misdeeds – just like Aisha.

The claim ultimately made against Aisha's entrepreneurship was that it was self-interested to the extent that it could actually harm others in the Malay community. Aisha's story shows us that work or networking must never be seen by others in the Malay entrepreneurial community as being primarily for self-interest, but in all the tradition-affirming, socially and developmentally focused ways explored in earlier chapters. As such, Malays believe that unlike Western women – who rarely are business owners – certain Malay women may become top entrepreneurs frequently and easily. Indeed, my informants saw no limitations on how far a woman who showed the right qualities might go. According to my informants, Aisha did not fail because she was a woman, but because of her motives.

Aisha, like Mazneh Hamid, was seen to be working against, not for, the common good. Self-interest, not group interest, characterized her entrepreneurship. Aisha, despite all the public demonstrations that she was a model Malay entrepreneur, was perceived not to be an entrepreneur at all. She had helped no one but herself. Like *kampung* Malays, she understood nothing about real business. In spite of her magical powers, Aisha was eventually seen by her numerous critics as an imploded person, her business and her family life in disarray, her children delinquent, and her husband silent and weak. In the end, Aisha was said to be a victim of her own ambitions, greed, and the retaliative forces of the power of goodness which, my informants believed, usually won over evil. Although magic may have brought her temporary entrepreneurial success, her own backward nature – greedy and insincere, people said – would and did ultimately bring her down. We shall return to the crucial subject of women entrepreneurs and the image of the virtuosi in the Conclusion. For now, it is important to note that other entrepreneurs, women included, escaped being harmed by their own networks, like Rokiah did, who was always thought to demonstrate *tidak sombong*, the humble absence of what Aisha too often demonstrated – *sombong* – pride, conceit, and the most Islamically incorrect and dangerous of all, self-centredness. A model Malay entrepreneur – publicly valorized by the media and the government for her contribution to Malay modernity – was shown to have stood for none of the virtuoso moral, social, business, and spiritual qualities which Malays have harnessed to their theory of economic and national development.

In the next chapter, religious virtue and other-centredness figure prominently, as well as images of the Malay Muslim social whole; this next and final alliance was an attempt to sharpen, through a business, the updated boundaries of the Malay *kampung* spirit. Indeed, embracing key ideas from government and religious ideology, the protagonists of this enterprise sought to establish a virtuous business. They used their friends and family – Malay networks – to market a product that was meant to reconstitute and enliven the traditional, other-centred nature of the Malay community. Promises of great profits were waved before the investors in this venture, but unlike the profits sought by Aisha, these did not flout altruistic norms, but magnified them. While many of my informants increasingly represented their economic efforts as a moral endeavour on behalf of the development of other Malays, the entrepreneurs behind the Amanah Anak-Anak Melayu or the Malay Children's Trust took the idea one step farther, envisaging a business which – not unlike the Prime Minister's programme Vision 2020 – was to become a social, civil, and spiritual movement for all Malays.

8 Virtuoso Entrepreneurship: Development and Wealth for All Malays

I had been interviewing Zaman and his brothers about the trio of inter-related entrepreneurial companies they owned – a computer firm, an office-machinery firm, and an office-furniture firm – when I discovered, almost by chance, that they had a significant interest in another company, Amanah Anak-Anak Melayu – the Malay Children's Trust. Zaman told me this company was still in the planning phase and therefore remained under a veil of secrecy. But he none the less agreed to introduce me to its director, his close friend Halim, under the condition that if Halim were willing to openly discuss the Amanah, they would as well. My curiosity was piqued, for despite the reticence Zaman felt, I could not help but hear the pride in his and his brothers' voices when they spoke of this business alliance. Halim, it turned out, was more than willing to meet me, and we were ultimately to spend a great deal of time together. I was fortunate to have entered the ambit of Zaman and Halim's network at a crucial moment – precisely when their entrepreneurial alliance, the Amanah, was about to bear fruit. As with Aisha and Rahim and their company Marchland, this venture had been conceived, planned, financed, and organized; now, it was ready to begin operations. Moreover, like CrossLinks and Marchland, the success of the business would depend wholly upon the networking ability of its principals. But perhaps to an even greater degree than the other two businesses we have come to know, the Amanah needed Malay networks, for, as we shall see, in a crucial sense, its very 'product' *was* networking.

THE RISE OF A VIRTUOSO ENTERPRISE

My relationship to Halim had many parallels to my relationship to Dato Hassan, although the two men were in quite different segments of Malay entrepreneurial society. Halim was struggling to make his entrepreneurial vision real; Dato Hassan, of course, had already done so. But they shared a belief in the purpose of Malay economic development and their own

171

participation in it: through enterprise, they could show others the spiritual direction they themselves had taken and they could bring into being a particular Malay Muslim version of socio-economic modernity. In the minds of many of my informants, Dato Hassan was what I have called a virtuoso – someone who had earned his right to leadership and rewards through socially valorized economic and spiritual means; Halim, his friend Zaman, and Zaman's brothers and contacts saw their business as the means to a virtuoso identity, and indeed, structured a business that was itself of virtuoso intent. Like Dato Hassan, Halim wanted to teach me what he believed was special about the Malay spirit or *roh* as it intersected modern business. Moreover, to Halim, the Amanah was a 'truly Malay organization', built on traditional Malay values but updated to meet the demands of modernity. To Zaman and his brothers, each of whom had invested a minimum of 50,000 *ringgit* in Halim's organization along with some of Zaman's friends, it was also a highly devotional enterprise which would improve the lives of other Malays and, they thought, make them millions.

As I have already mentioned, Halim and his employees had been working to develop the Amanah for several years when I met them. The organization had been surviving on capital brought in by Zaman's fundraising. Halim was the entrepreneurial innovator behind the Amanah; Zaman was its entrepreneurial financier. Like the alliance struck by Rokiah and Ishak in CrossLinks and the alliance CrossLinks attempted to make with Ramli and his kiosks, Halim and Zaman saw themselves as representing a powerful combination of strengths that complemented one another's weaknesses. Halim had ideas, a deep spiritual knowledge, and charisma; Zaman had capital and the networking capacity to bring a myriad of alliances into the foundation of investment support which the Amanah required. They shared a belief that the primary obligation of a Malay Muslim entrepreneur was to demonstrate sophisticated business skills and religious virtue on behalf of others.

Halim and Zaman had both been managers in a multinational corporation when Halim had the idea to start a new kind of investment trust for Malays. It would provide, at a low monthly premium, an annuity which parents could use to pay for their children's education. Halim believed that the abundant NEP-era educational resources for Malays would not be around forever, and as the government seemed to require that Malays begin to take ever greater group and individual responsibility for their own development – what he felt was the message behind Vision 2020 – he believed that Malay parents would soon need to put away money to pay for university for their children. The free-for-all atmosphere of NEP, he predicted, would soon be over, for Malays had learned the lessons of economic modernity and their responsibility to economic development. Through the Amanah, Malay parents would learn to take responsibility for the educational development of their own children; by investing small amounts of money in the trust every month for 18 years, parents would be able to draw out a substantial sum when their children were ready for university.

But Halim did not want the Amanah to be merely an educational savings scheme. It should be a way to develop the modernity of Malays – indeed, this was the cornerstone of his entrepreneurial idea. As such, during the time in which parents were investing, the Amanah would provide services to help Malay children improve themselves – tutoring, testing, career and educational counselling, group activities, even 'entrepreneurship seminars' intended to interest young Malay boys and girls in competitive business life. Halim envisaged Amanah offices in every city and town in Malaysia, staffed with teachers, social workers, volunteers, and religious leaders who would help guide Malay children towards the future. At the same time, the money invested in the scheme would provide a guaranteed return of at least 12 per cent, matching the substantial results available to *bumiputera* investors in such government-management investment vehicles as Amanah Saham Nasional.[1] Like other trusts invested on behalf of *bumiputera*, the Amanah would earn its returns by investing in various Malaysian corporations, but also by investing in less-developed entrepreneurial ventures, thereby not only helping Malay children get a head-start in modern business life, but eventually also nascent Malay business people, like his friend Zaman and Zaman's brothers. Indeed, as we shall soon see, Halim saw in his entrepreneurial idea a way to bring his image of economic development to all Malays who participated in the Amanah. Not unlike the entrepreneurial idea EG2020 which was introduced to us in Chapter 2, the Amanah was a perfect construction of entrepreneurial means and virtuoso ends, of profits and rewards; it was what my informants called a 'win/win' proposition.

Several years back, Halim, who had a business degree, resigned from his corporate job to work on the Amanah idea full-time. Meanwhile, Zaman had started a business of his own, selling computers and computer software (this was the business I had been interviewing him to learn more about when I first heard of the Amanah). Over the course of several years, setting up the Amanah had become more complicated, and time passed, during which Zaman had to raise funds and make alliances in both his own business and also for Halim. As such, his networking efforts for his own business and for the Amanah often merged. Once, when I had earned the full trust of Zaman, Halim, and Zaman's brothers, they enthusiastically showed me a organizational diagram of their various business interests. Impressively complicated, their *gabungan* 'holding company' was composed of complex alliances representing various cross-cutting shares held by all of them in one another's enterprises and the Amanah, a theme to which I will return below.

As a financial instrument, the Amanah became increasingly complicated as well, for it needed to be structured in line with sophisticated regulations established by Bank Negara, the national bank of Malaysia, and managed under the complicated terms of a private trust. Zaman had no problem building a network around key figures in influential financial and banking circles; for example, Arab Malaysian Bank, under Tan Sri Azman Hashim, was extremely interested in the Amanah and, in return for a portion of its potential business, underwrote some of Halim's operating expenses in the form of a large loan. When Halim and Zaman met with bank regulators and asset managers, I was invited to come along; I was often struck by the financial parallels between their investment and those I had come to know in my years on Wall Street. But as Dato Hassan himself had tried to show me, the differences between Malay entrepreneurs and 'my Michael Milken and Ivan Boesky' (see Chapter 3) were also striking, as I was to understand more fully through the Amanah.

THE AMANAH AND THE MALAY MUSLIM SELF

Behind its increasingly sophisticated financial plan, the Amanah represented what Halim described as a 'truly Malay organization', both spiritually and communally focused. He believed that the enterprise demonstrated, in modern form, the Muslim principles of *zakat* – giving without any expectation of return. While parents investing in their children's future could not be characterized as giving them *zakat*, as providing for one's children is considered a moral obligation clearly separate from the terms of charity, one of Halim's primary concepts for the Amanah was that it was a selflessly 'giving' organization, itself devoted to the Malay community and the Malay future. In its regional and local centres, the Amanah would provide community services, guiding children, teaching them, raising them up to be good Malay citizens and entrepreneurs; as such, it was almost a miniature NEP – but in the hands of the community – where Halim, along with most of my informants, believed development now rested.

To emphasize its *zakat*-like features, Halim asked me to help write a motivational sales kit which would focus on certain key valorizations: 'An investment in Amanah Anak-Anak Melayu is an investment in the nation ... its children ... and the future of all Malays!', 'Help yourself and help others even more!', 'Malays must think about the future – "fate" *will not* provide!'

One night, Halim and Zaman and I debated the differences between the culture of Malays and the culture of the West. In the West, Zaman said, the individual comes first. This, he felt, was exemplified by the ease with which Western teenagers engage in sexual relations and use drugs, and then excuse such behaviour by saying, 'I'm hurting no one but myself', or 'It is my business what I do'. No Malay, Zaman insisted, could ever say such a thing, because in Malay life, 'a man is never just "myself" – he is his family and his community first'. In America, Halim added, 'Parents tell children, "Do whatever will make you happy" – while in Malay families, children know that it is their obligation to make their parents and their community happy with their behaviour'. Like Prime Minister Mahathir, who feared that Westernization and industrialization were diluting such Malay family and communal values, Halim and Zaman believed that traditional Malay norms needed to be bolstered up and sustained. The Amanah, they both declared, because it required that everyone involved in it – from the rich investor to the Malay child receiving entrepreneurial training in a remote *kampung* – 'put others first', reconstituted traditional Malay norms in the modern setting. As such, Halim and Zaman believed that Malay entrepreneurship was not 'a man acting for himself' but for the Malay group – this, they said, was the primary difference between my Western culture of individual profit and their Malay culture of group gain. The organization they sought to build, set up on behalf of children and entrepreneurs such as they, institutionalized social and moral values it was dedicated to preserving. To entrepreneurs such as Halim and Zaman, Malay economic success would emerge as a refutation of Western individualism and a paradigm of traditional altruism in modern settings – precisely the virtuoso definition of economic development which Dato Hassan, Tan Sri Azman Hashim, and most of my informants shared.

These cultural values were not merely to be emphasized in modern institutional form by the Amanah, for the entrepreneurial-virtuoso concept was even more complicated than that. The key idea which Halim and Zaman had was that the organization would grow – helping, serving, and caring along the way – at exponential rates, because people who invested in the Amanah would introduce others to the investment, demonstrating their Malay Muslim willingness to help others benefit from it. On one level, then, the enterprise was envisaged as a sophisticated financial investment. On a second level, it was a highly idealistic social- and educational-services agency, in which *kampung* and *ummah* values would be revived in modern contexts by visionary entrepreneurs. But on a third level, the Amanah was something Malays are quite familiar with – the ultimate networking organization, like Tupperware or Amway; it was a direct-selling organization, in which people's social networks are transformed into pecuniary structures and economic activity – selling – is represented as an act of caring (Biggart 1989).

To understand how the entrepreneurs behind the Amanah sought to engage Malay networks in their marketing opportunities – and saw this as a demonstration of altruism – we must look briefly in a seemingly unexpected place: the direct-sales phenomenon in Malay life and its traditional antecedents, the *arisan* and the *kutu*.

DIRECT-SALES NETWORKING IN MALAY SOCIETY

Direct selling is 'the face-to-face (salesperson to consumer) sale of products or services away from a fixed business location, usually in a consumer's home…. The sales people … earn an income by selling at a profit goods that they buy wholesale from one or more manufacturers or distributors' (Biggart 1989: 16). However, multilevel marketing companies, like Tupperware, Amway, and Avon, take this concept one major step further, for in these organizations, sales people also *recruit* other people into selling, exponentially increasing their revenue. In complicated pyramidal structures, according to Biggart, commissions flow in as sales people become both recruiters and distributors and new members are brought into the organization as sales people and recruiters themselves. Eventually, recruiting takes over from selling, for it is much more profitable.

Single-level and multilevel sales organizations like these had long made a significant impact on Malay life. Indeed, many of my informants' mothers became *jurujual* or 'sales experts' for Tupperware, which had enormous success in Malaysia in the 1960s and 1970s. I collected many stories of proto-entrepreneurship among Malay women, who in small towns and *kampung* communities displayed their merchandise to friends and relatives who then enthusiastically joined up to sell it in other communities. Many women in my informants' mothers' generation had once sold 'high-class *impot*' (imported) Avon cosmetics from America. In recent years, Shaklee, Amway, and other similar organizations have boasted thousands of Malaysian recruits, initially among the Chinese, who were traditionally more interested in extraordinary health remedies and miracle vitamins, but such companies were, by the 1990s, making significant inroads into Malay communities. By the time I arrived in Malaysia, hundreds of similar direct-sales *impot* companies from Australia, Britain, and even Switzerland, places from which many of my informants believed especially potent remedies for modern ailments like 'stress' and 'tension' could be obtained, had signed on thousands of Malaysians as sales personnel.

Moreover, interest in direct sales had so dramatically transformed economic life in Malaysia that major companies, like Dato Hassan's, had banned discussing or distributing products during working hours, and had set up a facility in the employees' cafeteria for the ubiquitous lunch-time sales presentations and membership drives. Despite the efforts of the Malaysian government to place some controls on the activities of direct-sales organizations by requiring licensing beginning in 1993 (see Direct Selling Act and Regulations 1993) and banning those which emphasized pyramid recruitment instead of product sales,[2] direct selling had seized the entrepreneurial imagination of Malays. Many of my informants almost addictively attended membership meetings where, amidst cheers and applause, million-*ringgit* 'entrepreneurs' were presented as models of how rich they, too, could become. Because Malays increasingly believed that having a business – any kind of business – was a marker of meritocratic participation in the economy and the key demonstration of their modernity, the entrepreneurial appeal of direct sales, which required no risk and no capital investment (aside from the often expensive 'membership fee' which was shared by the recruiter and the parent organization) was quite powerful (cf. Biggart 1989). As we shall soon see, this 'no risk/no investment' networking approach to wealth generation was crucial to the marketing of the Amanah.

MALAY DIRECT-SALES ENTREPRENEURS

While direct-selling organizations in America traditionally appeal to part-time workers and housewives (Biggart 1989: 19) as they had to my informants' mothers, in contemporary Malay life, it was not just in the 'gendered' margins of society that direct sales held great interest. In fact, Zaman, before he started his own computer business, and Aisha and Rahim, before Marchland began, had sold through such organizations all manner of products from American and Australian sponsors. Many of my informants who were starting entrepreneurial ventures of one kind or another still held membership interests in a direct-sales business. Other of my entrepreneurially ambitious informants and I attended 'introductory' meetings upon the invitation of their friends who were seeking to recruit them into a mutually profitable alliance to sell everything from vitamins to cleaning products to 'miracle-cure mushrooms' from China. The socially inclusive form that direct sales takes has appeal at all levels of Malay society. While nearly every lower-paid employee in Rokiah's office was a representative for Shaklee or Tupperware, so, too, at one time or another, was their boss Rokiah, whose entrepreneurial explorations also included seeking opportunities in the very top reaches of the economy. In a society in which the value of 'being in business' has such a powerful socially validating force, nearly everyone I knew had experimented at one time or another with the suasory entrepreneurial and networking ideology of direct sales, in which both the products and anticipated profits are represented as having the ability to 'transform lives in physical, emotional, and spiritual ways', a transcendent feature quite peculiar to the direct-sales industry (ibid.: 99).

Indeed, one of Aisha's best friends, who drove around Kuala Lumpur in a shiny red Mercedes and exuded confidence more dazzling than the massive diamond ring and necklace she wore, told me and some other women that she had once been 'shy and ugly, with red boils' all over her face. She cured the malady with a Shaklee skin preparation; selling it to others made her a huge success. It was a double miracle.[3] Now, she claimed, 'money just flowed in' as her 'downline' (recruits, distributors, and sales people she had brought into Shaklee) was extremely profitable. The story captivated everyone who heard it, and afterwards, Aisha told me she dreamt of a day when Marchland would sell its products just as Shaklee sold its remedies, similarly transforming the lives of everyone it touched and making millionaires out of those who believed in it. Indeed, for a long time, Rahim attempted to market Marchland's home-décor products through direct-sales channels (see Chapter 7), and we spent many long nights discussing the various 'prize levels' Marchland distributors could achieve, like winning a Mercedes emblazoned with a Marchland logo when they had sold several hundred thousand sets of bed linens. The way in which miracle products were increasingly associated with miraculous lifestyle transformations (which invariably included a Mercedes) held great sway among many of my informants, who, as should now be clear, were often searching for entrepreneurial ventures which would similarly 'remake' them and all Malays who were entrepreneurially inclined.

SELLING AND SAVING IN MALAY NETWORKS

One of the reasons direct sales had had such a powerful impact on Malay life, aside from its powerful, asset-building 'no risk/no investment' version of entrepreneurship, is that direct selling is often indistinguishable from the social settings in which it is pursued (Biggart 1989), blurring the line between 'social' and 'economic' in ways which, as we shall see, are quite familiar to Malays. Indeed, often, selling and socializing had become one and the same event in the lives of my informants. Displaying various products and remedies during social occasions was extremely common in Kuala Lumpur society, and more than once, I was invited to a *kenduri* to mark a ritual occasion such as the death of an informant's relative or a boy's circumcision which was seamlessly transformed into a sales presentation for a new kind of water filter or health preparation. When I was invited by Sharifah and Aisha to a high tea at the house of a relative of Prime Minister Mahathir – a highly coveted invitation – the guests were treated to a slide presentation delivered by the hostess's friend, which featured full-colour pictures of suppurating skin tumours cured with 'Aloe Vera Miracle Tonic'. Nearly all of the guests shelled out 100 *ringgit* to purchase a bottle as a 'favour' to the hostess or because, as Sharifah earnestly reported to me, 'I feel I should show my interest when someone tells me about something that might help me or someone I love', a vivid example of the widespread tendency among my informants to utilize social relations for economic purposes and demonstrate affective relations through instrumental actions (see Chapter 2).

Once, after sitting through a meeting of the women's entrepreneurial networking organization, Peniagawati, I was invited to come along to a corollary social event attended by many of its members – a 100-woman *arisan* or what researchers in Southeast Asia call a 'rotating credit society'.[4] At this party, where huge amounts of money were placed into the rotating kitty, women in various direct-selling businesses – jewellery, silks, and other luxuries – displayed their expensive *impot* items. Similarly, at the smaller *kutu* meetings of my informants, also economic-cum-social organizations with a long history in the Southeast Asian literature, various products were invariably presented by members, everything from country-club memberships to exercise machines.

As such, while the basic form of the *arisan* and *kutu* groups appears to have remained unchanged from earlier descriptions of traditional savings groups – members contributed a fixed sum every month and drew lots to determine who 'won' the total amount collected – among my informants, traditional savings groups had been transformed into time-consuming, expensive events with social and economic value far above and beyond the mere saving-and-socializing motive ascribed to them by their mothers.[5] Rokiah's mother, for example, remembered *kutu* groups she had belonged to in the 1950s which required a weekly investment of a few dollars and home-made *kuih* (sweets). Many of the *kutu* groups I followed required a monthly investment of 500 or even 1,000 *ringgit* and held luncheon meetings at such expensive restaurants as Sri Melayu. The new-Malay-style *kutu* was no longer simply a means for saving money and socializing, nor was it, like many such gatherings I attended, merely an opportunity to sell something expensive to a captive audience. To many of my informants, the *arisan* and *kutu* groups they belonged to were really, as they revealed to me, 'top networking events' where people could meet to establish contacts and discuss business. In fact, they often felt obligated to buy such things as expensive exercise bicycles and miracle health cures to show their commitment to people with whom they wanted to network.

Indeed, perhaps the key point of difference between traditional descriptions of *arisan* and *kutu* savings-and-socializing organizations and those which I observed among my entrepreneurially ambitious informants was the degree to which my informants arranged social events in nearly feverish convergence with their growing economic interests, and, conversely, saw in social life the sufficient means to achieve economic ends. In Chapter 5 I suggested that this functional utility given to networks was not experienced in exploitative terms by my informants, who also saw in social life implied by networking the essence of 'Malayness'. This is precisely how Halim and Zaman envisaged the exponential growth of the Amanah. The Amanah was a direct-sales organization in which Malays would solicit, among their social networks, members who would join the group and then bring in others, until, Pied Piper style and in a great pyramid of virtue and profit, everyone would be conjoined and everyone would benefit. Halim and Zaman saw this as an Islamic approach to economic success.

THE AMANAH – DIRECT SELLING AND CARING IN NETWORKS

Halim began to hold recruiting meetings for the Amanah several nights a week and on Saturdays. Zaman, his brothers, and their friends and families invited their friends and families to these meetings, promising information on an investment idea that was socially responsible, Islamic, and highly profitable. They had no trouble getting people to attend, for they appealed to the diverse concerns of contemporary Malays, and couched their offer in the evocatory idiom of entrepreneurial success. Once, I heard Zaman on the telephone describing the investment to someone as 'not a get-rich-quick scheme, but a no-risk idea which *will* make you rich – in this world and the next'. When I described the virtuous Amanah 'idea' in similar terms to people in my own social networks, such as Rokiah and Ishak, they, too, were eager to attend Halim and Zaman's meetings.

Halim's presentation for potential Amanah members was compelling, for he was a charismatic speaker who echoed ideas which Malays had already heard in speeches given by the Prime Minister and were often foremost in their minds, issues concerning moral and ethnic development intertwined with economic progress. He told potential members that Malays, despite 20 years of NEP, were still far behind the Chinese, largely because of their own lack of drive. Malay students, despite government initiatives, still fell behind Chinese students in national examinations. Drug use, delinquency, and unemployment were higher among Malay youth than Chinese youth, he said. Malays, he said, echoing Prime Minister Mahathir's well-known ideology (see Mahathir Mohamad 1970 and Chapter 3), still suffered from economic backwardness, a short-term *kampung* world-view. He spoke against Malays' passive acceptance of fate and their expectation that Allah or the government would provide for them and their children. He warned the audience that NEP would not always be around to ensure Malay success. 'Take the future in your own hands, for your children and all the Malay children of the future!' he exhorted. His tone almost reverent, Halim began to reveal all the virtuous rewards of the Amanah.

An investment in the Amanah would provide tutoring and training for their children and needy Malay children in other communities; it would provide after-school activities for Malay teenagers, keeping them off the streets; it would provide the means for changing the future of Malays, a project which was begun by NEP but by no means finished. An investment in the Amanah was also, he explained, profitable in a very concrete way – at a guaranteed 12 per cent rate of return, a small monthly subscription would provide every investor's child with a big sum of money for university at the age of 18. Children who did not qualify to attend university could *still become entrepreneurs*, Halim said excitedly, to the enthusiastic response of the audience, for the Amanah would have taught them how to think like entrepreneurs. They could use the money accumulated in the trust for entrepreneurial capital.

But beyond this, and most crucially, members would also become 'counsellors' – bringing their family and friends into the organization, spreading the idea through networks and offices, 'face to face, person to person, people helping each other reach their own and the nation's goals'. This was a way for everyone to participate in the virtues of the organization.

Halim then talked at length about how such an important product should be sold along lines of personal contacts, among people who trust one another and care about one another, demonstrating a community in the true spirit of Islam. This, he said, was what a 'caring society' could be in the year 2020 – just as the Prime Minister himself had envisaged. This was how Malays could bring about that vision, he said. As a 'counsellor' sold, or more accurately, caringly 'counselled' others to see the benefits of the Amanah and brought in more and more members, he or she could earn a tremendous commission. As such, both the virtuous product offered by the Amanah and the means of marketing it promised to transform the lives of Malays profoundly. At one level, the 'product' of the Amanah was actually its members' own networks.

ALLIANCES AND VENTURES III – THE AMANAH AS A HOLDING COMPANY OF 'BROTHERS'

Despite the early members bringing in small sums of money, the overhead of the Amanah was becoming almost unbearably heavy. One of the keys to the successful launch of the organization, Halim and Zaman felt, was that potential members must see that the services the Amanah promised – tutoring and training in entrepreneurship, for example – were ready to be delivered as soon as parents enrolled their children. As such, the enterprise needed substantial capital to establish these services. Enrolment forms had been printed, as well as the promotional material I had written. The organization had rented a large office space, put in multiple phone lines and computers, office machines and furniture. These fitments were largely supplied by Zaman and his brothers, whose own businesses, it will be recalled, dealt in them.

For nearly three years, Zaman's primary role had been to find capital for the Amanah. He had brought in his two brothers, a brother-in-law, and several of his close friends as investors. Many hundreds of thousands of *ringgit* had been invested in the Amanah in the form of shares. Many additional shares had been given on paper to Zaman and his brothers in exchange for the office fitments they had supplied, for like Rokiah's 'investment' of shares in her partner Ishak, it was anticipated by Zaman and his brothers that in short time they would profit exponentially on their investment. Many of Zaman's contacts were deeply committed to the organization and to its goals, but like the potential members in the Amanah product who hoped to get rich selling it, the shareholders in the Amanah business also saw a potentially enormous return on their investment capital.

All of the shareholders in the Amanah had businesses which they believed could directly and significantly benefit from the growth of the organization. As such, they saw the Amanah as a kind of meta-entrepreneurial alliance which would ultimately incorporate their own ventures. Zaman had a computer business, and envisaged supplying an endless number of computers to the various Amanah learning centres and offices all over Malaysia. One of Zaman's brother's office-machine business and another's office-furniture business would flourish alongside the Amanah as well. The shareholder who had a printing company would be able to supply the children to whom the Amanah provided services with hundreds of printed workbooks, lesson books, and newsletters. (I was offered, but declined, the opportunity to invest in the Amanah, then sub-contract a public-relations company to it.[6]) Zaman's brother-in-law, an accountant, resigned from his position in a major corporation to take over the financial operations of the Amanah and its potential subsidiaries and bought a significant share. Another friend joined the organization as a shareholder and director of marketing – his wife's advertising company would handle all the advertising business.

Halim and Zaman described this investment network *behind* the Amanah organization as a *gabungan* 'holding company'. The Amanah was thus an alliance in anticipation of future profits made by a network of entrepreneurial members who were deeply tied to one another's success, people who claimed to believe unwaveringly in one another and were, Zaman said, like *abang* – they were truly 'brothers'. Zaman was very selective about those whom he brought into the organization; shareholders had to be willing to give, in addition to capital and fitments or services, all of their entrepreneurial resources to the Amanah, tapping into their far-flung networks to find members, devoting time and energy to membership meetings, and so on. In return, he could promise them significant benefits – they would help Malays and profit handsomely for that commitment, a return which he, like many of my informants, increasingly believed Allah promised to virtuoso entrepreneurs.

Just as the organization would market its product through networks of Malays – 'counsellors' – who were moved by Halim's exhortation to demonstrate caring by introducing others to Amanah and, as a consequence, could anticipate current and future – as well as this-worldly and other-worldly – rewards, Zaman believed he was showing a commitment to 'brothers' in his network. Through this commitment, through its dissemination, everyone would successfully engage his or her Muslim *and* entrepreneurial self in a profitable future. To Halim and Zaman, to potential Amanah members, and certainly to the *gabungan*-minded shareholders, this was surely the way to give and receive help in modern Malay life, a 'win/win' alliance. To Halim and Zaman, above all else, networks were social tools that provided multiple rewards, instruments of a convergence of devotion to others and to Allah, the means to an exemplary virtuoso identity.

THE PROSPECTS FOR THE AMANAH

In the months before I left Malaysia, the Amanah began to exhibit signs that it was foundering. Many of the complex terms of the financial trust had still not been finalized, and key parts of the investment contract could not be worked out between Halim and the various financial institutions he had sought to sponsor his product. Arab Malaysian Bank, under the directorship of Tan Sri Azman Hashim, which had once seen great promise in the Amanah, suddenly pulled out, and demanded the return of the loan it had made to Halim. Halim insisted that the loan could easily be paid back with memberships he said would soon be forthcoming. But many of the people who came to membership meetings were reluctant to invest until the Amanah had a firm contract with an investment company which would manage the funds. Alarmingly, several banks in Malaysia came out with similar investment products, promising high returns on educational trusts for children; these were advertised on television and received substantial media attention. Zaman scrambled to bring in several more 'brethren' shareholders and took more money from existing ones. This money went toward past-due bills, rent, and current operating expenses, and – it was rumoured mutinously among some Amanah shareholders – because Halim had fallen behind on his home mortgage during recent lean months, directly to Halim's personal bank account.

Late one night, the last time I saw any of them before leaving Malaysia, several of Zaman's friends voiced to him the fear that they would not see the rewards of their commitment and demanded an explanation. Zaman held his hands out in front of him, and asked them for forgiveness, insisting that his intent in taking their money had been completely sincere and virtuous, as had Halim's. He begged them to remain loyal to the Amanah, again and again invoking their commitment under the compelling terms of Muslim trust and belief. Privately, later, he told me that there had been moments when he had ceased to believe in Halim, and was praying to Allah for guidance, for the reinforcement of his trust in Halim.

Long after I had left Malaysia, a friend I had made among the shareholders wrote to tell me that the Amanah was still in existence, and that despite many setbacks, some participants still had faith that all the complex promises and expectations it framed would ultimately bear fruit. As I read his words, far from the ripe, expectant atmosphere of Kuala Lumpur, I prepared to write the Conclusion to my study of Malay entrepreneurship, where I confront the issue of why, at least in the material sense, so often it does not.

PART III: *KORPORAT* VISIONS

9 Conclusion

The episodes of entrepreneurship and alliance which I have described in the previous chapters provide some insight into the diverse economic opportunities which are generated and pursued by Malay entrepreneurs in the enriched landscape of modern development in Malaysia. Yet, despite the differences in the enterprises of CrossLinks, Marchland, and the Amanah, certain similarities appear in the case studies, characteristic of Malay entrepreneurial ideology as a whole: the claim that in development, duty to others must be stated and shown; the belief that one must not seek greedily the fruits of success but must generously invite others to partake; the insistence that entailments – be they profits, contacts, or opportunities – must be rightfully earned through effort, sincerity, and hard work; and, perhaps most crucial of all, the perception that the entrepreneur is the cornerstone of modernity, possessing the ability to transform simultaneously both society and the economy into the image of development espoused by the Malay Muslim doctrine of virtue and the Mahathir government.

As such, in the infusion of 'good works' (Part I) into 'networks' (Part II), we have seen the Malay theory of modern entrepreneurial, economic, and social development in action. This theory holds out the promise of both wealth and social balance in a vast meritocratic and moral landscape of opportunity for those who best understand and demonstrate its entailments and obligations. It states that contributions to self- and economic development are both necessary and appropriate; indeed, they are sacraments and requirements of a modern citizenry. It states, as did my informant Ramli, who was obviously paraphrasing Prime Minister Mahathir, that 'success was big enough' for everyone in Malaysia who is willing to abandon the Malay economic past, both the passive, naïve past and the elite, feudal one. It provides direction on how to be modern, Muslim, and Malay in pursuit of material interests. The Malay theory of modern economic and social development requires Malays to revive and practice a traditional communal morality in both the present and the hypothetical future. Responding to its hortations requires, as we have seen, an ultramodern understanding of business 'know-how' and an ultra-traditional expression of obligation and community. Indeed, the future envisaged by the Prime Minister is a Malaysianized civil society as a *rumah terbuka* or open house to which all are welcome; deploying themes of both a *hi tek* modernity and revisionistic traditionalism, the state encourages its vision

189

of progress and national stability. In the minds of my informants, nothing accommodates this image of the future of Malaysia better than a demonstration of self-help and group help already sequestered in their traditional culture and their modern theory of entrepreneurship.

To its proponents, entrepreneurship is an acute, eidetic experience of belief and action in search of a just society and the rewards of virtue. Through their entrepreneurial episodes, I have tried to demonstrate how, in the social contexts of Kuala Lumpur, my informants rendered real their version of modern and responsible, conjoined economic development on behalf of the self, the ethnic group, and the nation. I have tried to evoke the social atmosphere of Malay economic development, which often seems charged, even overloaded, with energy, discovery, potential, and excitement, one which, as I have suggested, is overwhelmingly stimulated by the image and idiom of government development and modern interpretations of Islamic doctrine. Indeed, while I have allowed my informants to speak and act as individuals, I have tried to show that it is impossible to overlook the impress of government suasion, political alignments, and Islamic teachings in their collective voices and identities. As such, the entrepreneurs I knew, who shared their ideas and goals with me, can, through this book, be momentarily seen as I saw them and as they saw themselves: conjoined and yet separate, communal and yet individuated.

In the fields of anthropology, economics, and psychology, the subject of entrepreneurship has long generated both significant scholarly interest and a set of explanatory theories. It has been looked at as a personality motivation (Schumpeter 1934; McClelland 1961); a set of activities and transactions in search of profit (Barth 1963); a form of class mobilization in search of power or status (Geertz 1963b; McGaffey 1987); and a mystification and justification of self-interest and individualist intent in capitalist development (Hart 1975; Parkin 1972). These are reasonable theories in search of an explanation for the reasons entrepreneurs do what they do, but they tell us little about what entrepreneurs in a particular setting *think*, how they themselves understand the purpose of their activity, or what their theory of entrepreneurship is. My analysis refutes none of these explanations for what happens when men and women attempt to control their economic and social fates and why they would do so, but primarily seeks instead to show how in Malay life, entrepreneurship – as it is likely to be anywhere – is an inherently culturally patterned and elaborated set of ideas about change and human action. As such, it explores a Malay theory for economic and social development.

Obviously, in searching for a cultural interpretation of entrepreneurship, I benefited enormously from the framing of entrepreneurship as a

full-blown emic category in Malay life and from the remarkable experience of an ethnographic encounter in which one's informants refer to
themselves in precisely the same term as that of the analytic endeavour:
'Malay entrepreneurs'. In earlier studies of entrepreneurship, researchers
had to elaborate a theory of entrepreneurship partly to identify who was –
and who was not – an entrepreneur. My informants, however, identified
themselves as entrepreneurs to me, and then proceeded to enact the role as
they defined it – and, as often, included me in validating or assisting that
role, as they would any trusted or useful contact. If I took them at face
value, which I did, it was not my decision to decide who was or was not an
entrepreneur – it was, as I think it must be, theirs to make. I was further
blessed with an undertaking that opened doors and generated endless discussion and debate among informants who were eager to understand what
entrepreneurship meant in a modern economy and society. Put more
simply, my 'project' and my informants' 'project' appeared to merge;
surely this was what Malay entrepreneurs call a 'win/win' deal.

But this apparent good fit which I encountered in my fieldwork holds
somewhat less visible risks, submerging the difficulties in what anthropologists call 'understanding and representing the "other"' (Gewertz
and Errington 1991: 15) and demanding heightened attention to context
and meaning. The nature of 'otherness' becomes difficult to identify in
corporate settings, business meetings, and what Ishak called 'brainstorming sessions', for these were the very contexts of entrepreneurship I
had once experienced in my own society. Their words of entrepreneurship
are even the same as ours: 'marketing', 'corporate image', 'venture
capital', 'networking', 'know-how', and so on. Their heroes of entrepreneurship are often ours as well. Indeed, as Dato Hassan did, many of my
informants pointed to American entrepreneurs like Henry Ford and John
D. Rockefeller as their models (but not Michael Milken and Ivan Boesky).
Yet, it was my informants who also endlessly pointed out to me that they
have a different culture of entrepreneurship than I – a representative of
what Dato Hassan called 'the culture of greed' – had seen in the West. As
such, my ethnographic blessing appeared redoubled, for my informants –
'the other' – insisted upon an entrepreneurial otherness despite apparent
and acknowledged similarities. I have tried to present, then, their theory of
entrepreneurship, much of which also reflects back upon their theory of
Western entrepreneurial otherness, an experience which increasingly characterizes the ethnographic endeavour in modern, globalized contexts. But,
as my informants often remarked, they felt fortunate to have come rather
late to development, for this meant they could examine the mistakes of
others, pick and choose among the paradigms of capitalism, and engineer

their own. As such, they felt they had much to teach me about human progress; their understandings of the lessons of modern development – both those they felt they had learned in the episodes of entrepreneurship and self-improvement they engaged in, and those they taught me about the moral identity of a 'Malay' and 'Muslim' – have become the subject of my analysis.

If, however, we stand outside their theories to look at Malay entrepreneurship and networks in strictly functional and etic terms, very quickly we are forced to acknowledge a paradox: despite the energy, time, resources, hard work, and commitment which my informants gave to entrepreneurship, economic success was, as we have seen in the three case studies, often elusive and easily undermined. Indeed, although the buoyant air of economic development in Malaysia – as well as the on-going enrichment of the Malay middle class through various *bumiputera* investment, distribution, shareholding, and quota programmes – kept the optimism, capital, ingenuity, consumption, and resilience of my informants high, there were many moments in my year-and-a-half in Kuala Lumpur when it was apparent to me, as it should be to the reader, that the economic costs of Malay entrepreneurship were actually greater than the economic rewards, although the social rewards were often very high. How functional *are* Malay networks in organizing economic activity and producing nascent capitalist structures? Indeed, if they are not, what is really being served by all of this extraordinary activity and belief?

Certain things function well in the Malay entrepreneurial economy: networking obviously does, as well as its rewards – such as mobilizing resources like capital and information, accessing decision-makers and allies, plumbing for opportunity; so does the resilience of optimism and trust that allows dyadic, triadic, and myriadic alliances to form, disband, and form again. Certain things appeared to function *less* well: successfully winning and fulfilling a contract, completing a job or a project, getting paid for work done, earning profits. As profit-capitalists and surplus-accumulators – what observers of entrepreneurs generally point out entrepreneurs primarily are intent to become (Barth 1963; Hart 1975; Parkin 1972) – my informants, at least at the moment at which I left them, were not actually accumulating money or profits. Indeed, they appeared unlikely ever to do so (leaving aside for a moment the virtuosi figures of Dato Hassan and Tan Sri Azman Hashim).

During the period I participated in and observed the ventures described in the three previous chapters (as well as many more which I documented) success and profit, in the economist's sense, remained elusive. Investment capital was funnelled out of other ventures and sources – such as Rokiah's real-estate company, government-sponsored Malay enrichment schemes (MITI 'free shares'), and development-bank loans (Marchland); friends and family (as in the case of the Amanah); even the stock-market boom – but except for a few one-time sewing jobs which came into Marchland's ambit through Aisha's indefatigable networking, none of the entrepreneurial projects I studied had yet generated nor was showing any signs of real earning potential by the time I left Malaysia. Moreover, even paradoxically, the *products* each of these ventures was established to distribute – CrossLinks' *hi tek* consulting, Marchland's flowery textiles, the Amanah's altruistic financial vehicle and social services – did not, by any utilitarian measure, as yet exist. None of their products could be sold or traded. Would they at any time in the future?

As I was leaving Malaysia, Rokiah and Ishak had agreed to abandon CrossLinks, at least for the time being, and had decided to concentrate more on their original (and separate) businesses – Rokiah selling real estate, Ishak programming computers. Marchland, despite Aisha's ongoing and enormous networking efforts, was mired in financial (if not image) problems which appeared insoluble, although the government programme which had funded it proved to be increasingly flexible, so that Aisha and Rahim were able to transfer shares of their company back to the development bank in lieu of repayment on their loan.[1] This meant that Marchland would, in all likelihood, stay in operation, but, within a relatively short period of time, the majority share of the Marchland company would be owned by the government bank and not by its Malay entrepreneurs, Aisha and Rahim. Aisha was evidently not going to be the Laura Ashley of Southeast Asia, although Marchland would perhaps be maintained through sub-contracting and servicing government contracts supplied by the development bank which now owned it. Finally, the Amanah, as we have seen, was also foundering, eating up more and more of its shareholders' capital with no indication that its services, investment product, or any receipts were forthcoming. It remained a good idea, a mobilizing idea, but no more than that. Faith in others also remained high. Yet certainly, the dream of massive *gabungan* companies which all of my informants shared as their image of entrepreneurial success was still very far off. Because entrepreneurship, as we have seen, is a lapidary assertion of both identity and morality in modern Malay life, and a complex eschatological theory of Islamic reward and virtue, to my informants, its projects and episodes, by definition, were ever evolving and ever incomplete; as such, these enterprises were not described as 'failures' but as 'lessons'. But this does not reconcile, for the observer, the sense that despite all that entrepreneurship evokes and promises, neither successful enterprises nor saleable products arise amidst all this Malay optimism, drawing into question what all the activity is really about, what function it really serves. Amidst the activity, my informants paid very little attention to their actual businesses or potential products; although they had many ideas for success, they demonstrated a remarkable lack of interest and concern in running the operations they had established.

Moreover, when I offered what I perceived as business-minded suggestions concerning their enterprises or products, my informants invariably responded with impatience; that part of entrepreneurship was secondary, their primary work was networking. 'We'll just hire someone to run the business later', entrepreneurs told me, insisting that that was not what entrepreneurship entailed. Many times people offered me the ultimate function of their multi-ethnic society: Malays will do the 'marketing', Chinese will run the Malay businesses, and Indians, ever at the bottom of the organizational chart, will be the workers.

How can we begin to make sense of the entrepreneurial identity my informants enacted and their seemingly acute need to demonstrate it, to inflate it, finally to market it, far beyond its utility or function as economic action? Indeed, entrepreneurship in Malay life is more functionally comprehensible as a symbolic construction of identity and community than as *sui generis* economic action.

THE MALAY ENTREPRENEURIAL IDENTITY AND THE 'VISION OF THE ANOINTED'

Upon ideas and behaviours which imply cosmopolitan, universal business knowledge ('know-how') aligned with a paradigmatic definition of indigenous, communal, and religious ones (Malay Muslim culture), the two axes of the 'virtuosity' I have refashioned from Weber, my informants heaped multiple meanings, beliefs, and discourses about modern economic development and identity. But the theory, purpose, practice – and even the form – of what they call Malay entrepreneurship is, finally, inseparable from voices of conflict in contemporary Malaysia. Indeed, to a great extent, *Malay entrepreneurship cannot be understood without reference to rival claims to legitimacy, power, and piety in the NEP era.*

To my informants, closely aligned with and economically dependent on sources of social and political authority in the Mahathir government and the UMNO-based interests which have shaped the policies of NEP since its inception, modern Malay entrepreneurship implies a tangible victory over alternative and polemic forms of power – be they ethnic, political, class-based, religious, or even, espousing a universally applicable Malay Muslim entrepreneurial culture superior to Western capitalism, global. Obviously, demonstrating entrepreneurship holds tremendous legitimizing weight in 'new Malay' identity, to the point at which it has become almost overloaded, inflated with importance, meaning, and value, a kind of meta-symbol; to my informants, it is the contemporary *ur*-point at which Malay modernity and validity begin and morality most enlightens human action. Entrepreneurship is demonstrable proof that NEP – a series of government policies which funnelled and continue to funnel state resources primarily to middle-class and upper-middle-class Malays (of which my informants represent the cohort that benefited most of all) – was a resounding success. The very existence of Malay entrepreneurship, the ultimate demonstration of modern economic sophistication, validates pro-Malay policies and affirmative action *vis-à-vis* the Chinese, who are believed to have pre-viously monopolized entrepreneurship in the nation; indeed, to my infor-mants, the existence of Malay entrepreneurship levels the playing field, avenging an ethnic injustice.

But, scorning the culture of government hand-outs as a form of feudal-ism, my informants invoke the theme of meritocracy inherent in their theory of entrepreneurship. As such, they did not measure or define Malay economic progress merely in terms of state-provided assets accumulated *vis-à-vis* the Chinese, but as a consequence of much internal change. Practising entrepreneurship implies, to its proponents, *a vast intellectual transformation for Malays*, a self-generating move from the *kampung* to the metropolis. Entrepreneurship implies, too, *a vast spiritual transforma-tion*, one which establishes economic modernity in Muslim terms, and which, framed in terms of a concern for the worldly and other-worldly consequences of spiritual goodness and for the collective whole, is used by moderate pro-Mahathir Muslims as sharp critique of and challenge to the perceived backwardness of *dakwah* and the pressing contestations of Islamic political activists (Chapter 3).

Obviously, much is elided by this collective legitimization of identity and power. Indeed, complex contradictions and paradoxes will inevitably result when a privileged cohort of people – the political elite in any meri-tocratically defined society – attempts to demonstrate and inflate their wor-thiness for rewards and power already received and to validate their sectional interests in societal, holistic terms (Cohen 1981). NEP has trans-formed members of the Malay educated and professional society into a new elite, one which is perceived as meritocratically deserving. Whereas the new elite is, in reality, a quasi-hereditary group whose fathers were civil servants, the socially and economically privileged beneficiaries of an earlier form of pro-Malay government policy (Roff 1967), its members genuinely view themselves as having begun at the same ground-zero, socially undifferentiated starting-point as all other Malays, the *kampung* Malays. Practising entrepreneurship implies class mobility – *a vast social transformation* – the move from an elite and aristocratic ascriptive society to a meritocratic one in which any *kampung* boy or girl can succeed, as has the Prime Minister himself (Chapter 4). We have seen how my informants believed that with entrepreneurship they had destroyed the old feudal order and ushered in the new, breaking the ties of elite entailment and claiming a great genesis of commonality for even the most elite among them.

Recasting images of familial obligation, blessings on origins, and Malay sibling metaphors in the language of economic development (Chapter 2), my informants see themselves as a communal cohort, foot-soldiers in Malay economic development engaged in community and national service, when, in fact, they are socially and materially distinguished – from one another and from the rest of society – in ways that are increasingly competitive and class-based. Yet, Malays *always* help Malays, they assured me, again and again. As such, they view their networking as evidence of Muslim norms (Chapter 3) and envisage a hypothetical future in which all of civil society – Malay, Chinese, and Indian – share in Malay-style openness and justice, but do not see that the Mahathir-valorized multicultural *pesta* (festival) model they espouse does not contribute to unity and social cohesion across ethnic lines (Chapter 4) or class lines. Indeed, as should be evident, there is little cross-ethnic economic cooperation and much subtle disparaging of *kampung* Malays left out of NEP's riches. As such, entrepreneurship and its all-pervasive networks are, paradoxically, the opposite of what Malay society claims them to be, socially and economically imbalancing, exclusionary and not inclusionary. Entrepreneurship, crystallizing and manifesting alignments to sources of vast political, social, and economic power in Malay life, demonstrates closure, not openness.

Sure of the equity of entrepreneurship and the widely cast net of opportunity in Malaysia, my informants were not aware of the social and economic inequities in their formulation of entrepreneurship. Moreover, they did not view the state as the source of their validity, opportunity, and legitimization. They did not see how they had closed their ranks to many citizens of the modern nation, Malay and non-Malay alike, and were further closing ranks within the NEP cohort itself, as I will describe below. Malay entrepreneurial theory has produced the power of self-justification among the beneficiaries of NEP, explaining not only why they should be rewarded unequally for their efforts, but also giving primacy to the culture they themselves have created, perpetuating and protecting what the economist Sowell (1995) calls 'the vision of the anointed'. Entrepreneurship is an ideology which helps to organize, support, maintain, and justify the power arrangements of the modern nation-state. It is precisely those power arrangements which can be traced out in Malay networks, which present social and economic life to those entangled in them as egalitarian, open, and ripe with possibility.

THE ENTREPRENEURIAL IDENTITY AND THE PROBLEM OF GENDER

One of the paradoxes of entrepreneurship as it is construed by the NEP cohort is that its egalitarian ideology not only excludes by social class, ethnicity, and political alignment, but also, increasingly, by gender within the cohort itself. Often a diagnosis of *kampung* backwardness and entrepreneurial insufficiency was made about successful women entrepreneurs, who were said to be more greedy, more interested in the status inherent in the entrepreneurial identity than its responsibilities, obligations, and norms, a consequence we have already seen for Aisha and 'the Iron Lady' (Chapter 7). Rather than '*kampung*-girls-made-good', female entrepreneurial successes are frequently said by men and women to manifest a *mentaliti kampung*. Women do not appear to evidence often the necessary skills and virtues of virtuoso entrepreneurship; legitimacy ultimately eludes them, confirming the status of Malay men and the ideal and lesser role of Muslim women in development.

In contemporary gender studies of Malay culture, there is a tendency to suggest that this kind of male dominance over women's identity – of which I saw abundant evidence in the conflicts and ambivalence of married life – is a recent and imported pattern in Malaysia. Such analyses (Ong 1987, 1990; Wazir Jahan Karim 1992) argue that with recent intensification of Islamic principles and policy (*dakwah*) enforced in the daily life of Malays, the social and economic value of women – equal to men in the traditional norms and customs of Malay *adat* – has been sharply diminished. Many authors point to the work of Firth and Djamour (Chapter 2) as vivid evidence of what Malay life was like for women before this imported phenomenon. Once, Malay women were powerful, independent, self-determining, and in control of their own sexuality and money; relations between men and women were balanced and bilateral (Carsten 1989). All of this, researchers claim, abruptly changed with the imposition of neo-traditional, patriarchal, modern Islam, when women were stripped of autonomy and influence to become objects of sexual and moral ambivalence in a modernizing capitalist economy that commodifies their labour (McAllister 1990). I have already questioned the degree of financial independence the mothers of my informants actually had in their marriages (Chapter 2); now I question the level of social autonomy women in Malay society have ever been able to attain, long before *dakwah*.

Certainly it cannot be claimed that large-scale capitalist intensification and the recent absorption of key Arab-influenced Islamic values into the major institutions of the Malaysian state have not weighed heavily on the lives of Malay women, especially among the rural poor and urban factory workers (Norani Othman nd; 1994). Obviously, Islamization has dramatically changed the lives of women since the days of their mothers by exerting forceful mechanisms of control over dress, social behaviour, and self-determination (Chapters 2 and 3). Yet, in my view, such tendencies to control and marginalize women through modes of social enforcement are not mere grafts upon traditional Malay society, nor necessarily a new practice of social and economic dominance over the autonomy of women. While feminist positions on *dakwah* are theoretically compelling, they do not take into account the widespread social inequalities of gender, rank, and status which Malay *adat* itself perpetuated in the Malay past (cf. Peletz 1996).

Indeed, my informants' mothers vividly recalled stories about women in the pre-*dakwah* past who were pulled back by gossip and accusations of witchcraft when their social or economic ambitions reached too high, stories which still held their interest 30 or 40 years later. The same means for controlling the status-based, ambitious activities of autonomous women is still useful today, for Malay women who are too aggressively self-promoting invariably become the targets of slanderous rumours and cruel gossip, to a much greater extent than men ever do. Today, as in the past, Malay women who go too far in their autonomous pursuit of status and independence are socially unacceptable, and ultimately do not find legitimacy within the fields of state-based entrepreneurial power, despite the material demands of modern NEP-era lifestyles which often require that they work outside the home (Chapter 2). As such, contemporary Malay society, as Malay society always has, 'genders' success and prescribes an appropriate identity for Muslim women, allowing them to control – and provide material contributions to – the domain of the household, but to not move far beyond it to the virtuoso realm of the powerful.

Indeed, towards the end of my stay in Malaysia, I noted an emergent contrast to the vulnerable role won by Malay women entrepreneurs. Among my informants, there were several women – a computer scientist, an architect, and a chartered accountant – all of whom had been educated in Britain or America on NEP funds, who had recently quit their professional jobs to become, as had so many of my informants, entrepreneurs. The wives of Malay executives and entrepreneurs, they were discussing starting a home-based business to sell Indonesian-made English-style 'antique' furniture or make elaborate gift baskets for their husbands' business associates, direct-marketing activities which they described as more appropriate for them as wives and mothers, taking up much less time, allowing them to stay at home. Such women increasingly represented an idealized amalgam of a traditional and modern identity for Malay women: Islamic wives and mothers first and entrepreneurs second, women who are engaged in economic modernity and who maintain the entrepreneurial identity with one profound difference – access to reward and opportunity is provided by propinquity to their husbands' corporate and entrepreneurial status, and not sought independently of them. Increasingly, in a society which fears losing its family values in the face of Western-style modernity, this was the home-based enterprising ideal for women in the NEP cohort, not the socially and morally fragile autonomy sought by such women as Aisha and the Iron Lady.

But we must acknowledge that men in Malay society, too, are frequently closed out of the uppermost domains of status, which is why I resist casting my analysis of Malay economic power in the problematical terms of gender alone (cf. Kondo 1990). Today, as in the past, men and women suffer from constraint and control in Malay society in different ways; it is my position that while Malay society has long controlled the independence and status aspirations of Malay women, *Malay men and women alike are controlled by the limits to autonomy and power in a society which is predicated upon hierarchy.* Therefore, although it appears that only Malay men of the NEP cohort may become entrepreneurial virtuosi, we must account for the fact that only a few such men actually do.

THE VIRTUOSI IN MALAY ECONOMIC LIFE

My informants harnessed their entrepreneurial interests and alignments – indeed, their very lifestyles – to the culture of the virtuosi Malay leaders with whom they identified. As I indicated in Chapter 5, my informants did not perceive networking as their way to important government and cor-

porate figures as a form of clientage reminiscent of the feudal-*bumiputera*
society they so denigrated, but saw opportunity as a consequence of
proving and 'marketing' their legitimacy, 'know-how', and skill.

Even so, my informants knew that many Malays today, acting out old
feudal norms, often sought out connections to important people, especially
through UMNO, the dominant Malay political party. Just as 'know-who'
Malays in the historical and recent NEP past tried to establish themselves
as clients of the sultans and government leaders, some illegitimate entrepreneurs, my informants said, still tried to engage politicians and government ministers in a reciprocal relationship, providing bribes and pay-offs
for successful tenders for government contracts. Sometimes when I mentioned that I had interviewed one or another top Malay entrepreneur, a
close informant would reveal that he or she was not a 'real' entrepreneur,
merely a proxy for some unnamed UMNO politician, who really owned
the company. When a report in the newspaper revealed that the brother
of one of my informants was wanted by the police for the crime of
defrauding a woman of 500,000 *ringgit* – posing as head of an UMNO
Youth chapter (he had asked her to pledge good faith money for getting a
'guaranteed' government contract through his UMNO connections) – no
one was particularly surprised; everyone knew someone who had engaged
in an abuse of the system, either by bribing an official or making fraudu-
lent claims. No one I knew claimed that all Malays today were interested
in responsible and 'real' entrepreneurship, in working towards the good of
the community and demonstrating meritocratic and moral virtues – indeed,
my informants assured me, many Malays, men and women alike, were
not.

As discussed in Chapter 3, Malays believed, however, that widespread
use of access to patrons had occurred mostly in the NEP past, among the
first generation of *bumiputera* entrepreneurs, ex-civil servants who capitalized on government contracts – 'know-who' – to get business. They were
less willing to see examples of how virtuoso Malay entrepreneurs still
influenced their business success today through contacts with the state
and the dominant political party, or, as in the case of Aisha, Sharifah, and
the luxury bus project, through seeking contacts with powerful UMNO-
connected businessmen. There is much potent evidence of 'know-who'
among the new *mentaliti korporat* NEP generation of 'know-how' business people. But submerged in 'know-how' are the powerful lines of
UMNO access which nearly always determine entrepreneurial success in
Malay life. Just as the Malay theory of entrepreneurship denies the role of
the state, its capital, and social status in the success of the NEP cohort, it
denies the role of the state in creating vast economic opportunity for select

members of that cohort. UMNO, the party of NEP and all pro-Malay policy since the 1940s has been both the champion of the Malay middle class and the dispenser of all Malay business opportunity (Crouch 1992; Shamsul A.B. 1986a); to my informants who were active in UMNO networks or sought out people who were, it was a kind of Rotary Club, an organization one went to in order to demonstrate 'know-how' and meet influential people. Yet, none of my informants (apart from men like Dato Hassan, as we shall now see), had penetrated the upper ranks of UMNO; none appeared to be headed on the state-led road to virtuoso success. According to Dato Hassan's vision, it is because most Malays still exhibit a *mentaliti kampung*.

THE VIRTUOSI IN MALAY POLITICAL LIFE AND THE MYTH OF THE CIVIL SOCIETY

Very near to the end of my stay in Malaysia, I spent a day with Dato Hassan as he gave me a tour around his luxurious country home outside Kuala Lumpur. Rumours were circulating in various networks that his 'Dato' title would soon become 'Tan Sri' – he was indeed soon to go from 'sir' to 'lord'. It was on this day that I had the occasion to ask him about the luxury bus project his company was engaged in, the contract which had so feverishly concerned Aisha, Sharifah, and Marchland (Chapter 6). *'What luxury bus project?'* he asked, bewildered.

Dato Hassan said he believed this 'project' was merely an unfounded and illegitimate rumour of a business opportunity in *kampung*-minded Malay society. As I saw in dawning horror that the source of the alliance that had so engaged Aisha and Sharifah had never actually existed, a look of disappointment crossed his face. 'Patricia', he said in a low, deliberate tone, 'you have spent all your time in Malaysia studying the *wrong entrepreneurs*'. Dato Hassan, who had devoted a great deal of time trying to explain the difference between his culture of modern business and mine, who wanted me to see the generosity, openness, and altruism in modern Malay entrepreneurship and corporate life, insisted that I had talked to all the worst examples of Malay entrepreneurship, the *kampung* group of quasi-business people his *korporat* culture of Malay entrepreneurship was trying most of all to eliminate. According to Dato Hassan, there were approximately a dozen men in Malaysia who were *real* entrepreneurs; he called them 'men with vision'. He predicted that most of the Malays who called themselves 'entrepreneurs' and 'new Malays' would fail because they were still caught up in what he called '1970s-style "know-who", a no-work, feudal mentality', that is, a *mentaliti kampung*. In this dialectical construction of *mentaliti kampung* and *mentaliti korporat* which I had heard so often in Kuala Lumpur life, the real axes of economic power were being sharply defined by the handful of entrepreneurs who had benefited the very most from NEP – those men who had been selected to run the formerly state- and UMNO-owned companies which had been privatized in the late 1980s, one of the primary policy directives of NEP under Prime Minister Mahathir. Dato Hassan was a key member of the Malay *korporat* and UMNO-aligned elite whose entrepreneurship consists of providing services for privatized conglomerates of which they are majority shareholders (Gale 1981; Gomez 1992, 1994).

Denigrating Malays less successful than he, Dato Hassan saw himself as others saw him: as a virtuoso entrepreneurial leader who had escaped the mistakes of the *kampung* and feudal pasts and had earned the right to ascendancy. By valorizing and emphasizing the virtuoso entrepreneurialism and meritocratic Muslim *korporat* identity of such rare figures as Dato Hassan and Tan Sri Azman Hashim, the UMNO-dominated state and much of the Malay citizenry were able to deny the disproportionate political and economic influence granted to these men and many like them. For so, too, does the UMNO-dominated state provide substantial rewards to its less luminary followers.

There is little restraint on the power of politically aligned entrepreneurs (and entrepreneurially aligned politicians) who award contracts and inclusion to other Malays embraced by the circle of the virtuosi. My informants were not wrong to hope to bring such men as Dato Hassan into their network ambit of entrepreneurship primarily by demonstrating their own capacity as public 'know-how' entrepreneurs; they misunderstood, however, that the determination of entrepreneurial success was not really theirs to make. Despite all the claims of collective developmental responsibility made by Malay economic and political leaders, the citizens of Malaysia do not participate in a true meritocracy. As such, *entrepreneurship and networking among the less powerful remains a symbolic, legitimizing construction of identity and allegiance to power, but not a source of economic success*; the ultimate determination of who will achieve success remains in the hands of the UMNO-dominated state and its powerful 'right entrepreneurs'.

Paradoxically, entrepreneurship is presented as evidence that Malaysia *has* produced a modern civil society, defined as social and economic arrangements that counterbalance the power of the state by providing an alternative source of power and prestige to the state itself. In fact, Malay entrepreneurship serves the needs of the state by aligning and organizing

Malay political loyalty and justifying its system of economic rewards (surely a 'win/win' deal all round).

It is here, then, that my theory of Malay entrepreneurship and my informants' theory of Malay entrepreneurship must diverge. The Malay theory holds out the promise of wealth, salvation, and social balance in a vast meritocratic and moral landscape of opportunity for anyone who understands and demonstrates its social and spiritual entailments and obligations; it states that anyone has the same chances to become a virtuoso. My theory of Malay entrepreneurship is that it is essentially a complex and often contradictory legitimization of ethnic, 'gendered', elite, and political power. It denies the role of the state, status, and gender in the creation of Malay entrepreneurs. It denies the role of the state and its capital in the emergence of the 'new Malay' lifestyle. It posits an illusion of a Malaysianized civil society through social and economic arrangements – networks – which *appear* to counterbalance the power of the state but in reality do not. Finally, Malay entrepreneurship, as defined by the UMNO-directed state's own valorizations, grants privilege to and rewards most those who best demonstrate its pre-determined axes of legitimacy – the virtuosi – and aligns others to them and the spoils of their vision.

However, not unexpectedly, theories of entrepreneurship elsewhere are equally powerful tools for eliding the sources of social and economic privilege. My own experiences of entrepreneurship on Wall Street were not wholly different from the Malay episodes I have presented, showing a folk theory of common origins, of equality and meritocracy, tending to mute and even deny the presence of institutional power and elite routes to opportunity and capital. Entrepreneurship as I came to understand it in my own culture had a peculiar way of legitimizing quasi-hereditary rewards *ex post facto*, and claiming liberal, democratic, classless, race-less, and gender-less routes to success in obviously elite-based economic and social arrangements in the modern world of business. Indeed, the two cultures of entrepreneurship I have sought to understand confirm *established* relations of power, rather than allow new routes to power, yet both are claimed to do otherwise. The eidetically open, hospitable, egalitarian vision of entrepreneurial opportunity in Malay life demonstrates, finally, the complex interaction between deeply felt claims to personal power and the deep impress of power arrangements in human experience, the endless webs of relationships through which we ever seek to improve ourselves and our society, and in which we are ever caught.

Notes

1 INTRODUCTION

1. The 1990 population of Peninsular Malaysia was comprised of approximately 8.5 million Malays (58.2 per cent), 4.5 million Chinese (31.3 per cent), 1.4 million Indians (9.8 per cent), and the remainder, or 'other', less than 1 million (under 1 per cent) (*Social Development Trends Bulletin* 1991).
2. I was not able to obtain government statistics on the rate of increase in numbers of Malay businesses in recent years (see Chapter 6, note 2). One report demonstrates that the total number of Malay establishments increased ten times between 1971 and 1981 (Chiew Seen Kong 1993).
3. A crucial consequence of British rule after the nineteenth century was the entrenchment of ethnic occupational categories. Malays were concentrated in agriculture and colonial administration. Chinese and Indians were brought into the colony to work in British mines and plantations, and the Chinese also – as they did throughout Southeast Asia – flourished in trade; see Roff (1967). In 1969, the Chinese were still largely in trade and the Malays in the modern sector were in government service.
4. 'Special privileges' granted to the Malays by the British were written into the Constitution of independent Malaysia in 1957; see Chapter 4. These provisions became the basis for the increase in Malay privileges and quotas after 1969.
5. The irony of NEP 'national unity' policies, according to some observers, is that NEP, by advantaging the Malays alone, acutely disadvantaged non-Malays, especially concerning access to education (Jasbir Sarjit Singh 1991).
6. According to one observer, the term *bumiputera* was revived by NEP policy-makers 'so that the non-Muslim natives of Sarawak and Sabah could reinforce the Malays numerically, because otherwise the Malays would have been a minority' in the nation (Milne 1981: 128–9). This perspective states that in order for the state to allocate a disproportionate amount of resources to *bumiputera*, it needed to justify its actions by including a greater number of citizens.
7. The 30 per cent target was not reached by 1990. Government figures indicate that between 1971 and 1990, the rate of increase of *bumiputera* share ownership was 91 per cent, with *bumiputera* holding 20 per cent of all share capital compared to the Chinese, who held 44 per cent (Chiew Seen Kong 1993). Some observers believe statistics provided by the government on certain aspects of Malay development since 1970 are skewed to the low side, to justify continued Malay-only policy (Jesudason 1989; Mehmet 1986).
8. UMNO was founded to oppose British policy initiatives in the period after World War II, when the Malayan Union Plan was proposed to give equal

political participation to the whole population, regardless of ethnicity; this was perceived by the Malays as an attempt to abolish the system of Malay privileges. UMNO demanded – and achieved – retention of the sultan system and references to the special privileges of the Malays in the constitution (see Roff 1967).

9. For a discussion of the educational opportunities available within the hierarchy of the pre- and post-colonial Malay civil service, see Khasnor Johan (1984) and Puthucheary (1978). See Jasbir Sarjit Singh (1991) for a discussion of how the children of these families benefited most from NEP.

10. See Scott's (1976) pivotal 'moral economy' thesis, which argues that traditional cultures do not develop economically because of conservative social formulations; Geertz (1963a) argues a similar point.

11. The *ringgit* is the Malaysian unit of currency. At the time of my research, 1 *ringgit* was equivalent to around US$0.38. The enormous resources for development since 1970 have come partially from foreign investment and domestic and foreign debt, and primarily from offshore petroleum discovered in 1973 (Jesudason 1989).

12. Widely read authors McClelland (1961) and Hagen (1962) used Schumpterian theories. This model had a profoundly 'democratic' appeal to development banks in the 1960s and 1970s.

13. The two standard studies of Malay entrepreneurs define entrepreneurs in essentially Schumpeterian/Weberian terms. See Abdul Aziz Mahmud (1981) and Popenoe (1969).

14. There is a Malay term for entrepreneur – *usahawan* – but no one uses it.

15. An example is the American 'entrepreneur' Donald Trump. Upon his near-bankruptcy, no one began calling him an 'ex-entrepreneur'.

2 OBLIGATION AND IDENTITY: PARENTS, SPOUSES, SIBLINGS, AND MALAYS

1. I have given my informants pseudonyms except in two noted instances where individuals were public figures whose identities I did not feel bound to protect. I have also changed small details of some biographies or enterprises which I perceived were too revealing.

2. Chinese students do better on the national tests in both English and *Bahasa Melayu* than Malay students, a source of embarrassment to the government (Jasbir Sarjit Singh *et al.* 1989).

3. The '2020' came from 'Vision 2020', the Prime Minister's highly touted economic and social plan. See Chapter 4.

4. Throughout this study, I shall refer to the group of entrepreneurial Malays as a *status group*, more in line with Weber's conception of stratification based on symbolic-cultural value (1974) than as a class determined by economic role in the Marxist sense (see A. Kahar Bador 1973; Cohen 1981).

5. For a similar point, see Biggart (1989) and Cohen (1981).

6. For discussions of aspects of Malay matrifocality, see Banks (1983) and Wazir Jahan Karim (1992).

7. Arranged marriages were the norm in the generation of my informants' mothers; according to one study, the vast majority of women in that generation – 85 per cent – did not choose their own husband (Jones 1994).
8. In 1947, the median age at first marriage for Malay males was 23; in 1980 it was 26. For females during the same period, age at first marriage rose from 16.5 to 22.5 (Jones 1994).
9. Classics in this 'domains of balance' approach are the articles in Atkinson and Errington (1990).
10. Recent studies provide an increasingly sophisticated understanding of gender and its effects on social power and control in Southeast Asia. See Ong and Peletz (1995); Peletz (1996).
11. The 1984/85 Malaysian Population and Family Survey showed that double-income families constituted 44.2 per cent of all households in the country (*New Straits Times*, 15 May 1994).
12. Polygamy, the Prophet said, is intended to prevent such socially disruptive situations as widowhood and fatherless children as well as an excess of single women. In Kuala Lumpur I knew of no case in which a man took a widow as his second wife; polygynous men generally marry young, pretty women.
13. McKinley (1975, 1981) has provided the authoritative discussion on the creation of kinship bonds through adoption in Malay society.
14. Contrary to standard theory about a lack of economic ties between Malay brothers (McKinley 1975), Malay brothers today do enter businesses together. Two of the three case studies in Part II involve this pattern, a ratio I found to be quite common in the businesses I studied. My informants acknowledged that this form of association was 'new' for them – they had borrowed it from the Chinese. In each case, however, the partnership was eventually abandoned. See Sloane (forthcoming).
15. It is said that the former Finance Minister, Daim Zainuddin, now the Prime Minister's economic adviser, picks all of his rising Malay corporate stars out of the MCKK network.
16. See Kessler (1992) for a description of how the anomalous terms 'Malay', 'Muslim', and '*bumiputera*' actually make definitions of ethnicity, religion, and race nearly impossible in contemporary Malaysia.
17. It is estimated that 1.5 million workers in a workforce of 8 million in Malaysia is comprised of illegal and legal immigrants, mostly Indonesians, Filipinos, and Bangladeshis (*Financial Times*, 19 September 1995).
18. For a discussion of the consequences of Chinese 'new villages' upon Chinese modernity, see Hirschman (1975).
19. For more discussion of these Chinese–Malay businesses, see Chapter 3.
20. The term 'holding company' has great significance in Malay entrepreneurship. See Chapter 6.

3 THE ISLAMIC VIEW OF ENTREPRENEURSHIP: MODERNITY AND ITS REWARDS

1. In the 1980s, UMNO's corporate holdings and many state-owned corporations were privatized. Gomez (1994) describes how well-placed Malay

'entrepreneurs' were granted massive stock ownership of these companies. Dato Hassan (the name is a pseudonym) is the director of one of the newly privatized conglomerates.

2. The term '*dalang*' resonates with meaning in Malaysia, where the puppet master who controls the figures in the shadow-puppet play is a metaphor for one who has enormous power.

3. Biggart (1989) makes use of Weber's 'virtuosi' argument in a slightly different way. Mine implies, as Weber's did, a greater role for spiritual service to God.

4. See Jesudason (1989) for a discussion of how multinational corporations in Malaysia were required to meet quotas of *bumiputera* managers.

5. This is a crucial concept about social relations in Islam: person-to-person relations are ideally established in such a way that they reflect person-to-Allah relations, so that all worldly acts are tantamount to worship (Muhammah Syukri Salleh 1992).

6. My informants generally had not been involved in strict *dakwah* during their university days, where most young Malays are first exposed to it. In part, having attended university in the early and mid-1970s, they were not subject to the intense peer pressure of the late 1970s and early 1980s. In fact, many of them recalled beer-drinking and discoing in their university days, activities which would have been unheard of five years later.

7. Malays are loath to criticize the faith or piety of other Muslims, and generally believe that the more religious among them are better Muslims (Kamarrudin M. Said 1993). There is thus little open criticism of the *dakwah* movement itself, or public criticism of other Malays in general, for as Rokiah often said, 'Malays don't want the Chinese to think we are disloyal to our own group'.

8. In time, PAS came to criticize NEP itself as an 'unIslamic economy' – see Mehmet (1990) – which gave much resonance to its critique of UMNO, the champion of NEP.

9. Dato Hassan was alluding to the attempts by the state government of Kelantan, headed by PAS, to implement *hudud* punishments, requiring that certain offences such as adultery be subject to public stoning. Many of my informants were fearful that this would 'scare away' investors from Malaysia.

10. See M. Umer Chapra (1992) for an outline of this approach. See Muhammah Syukri Salleh (1992) for the 'Islamic entrepreneurial' approach of the Darul Arqam commune in Malaysia, a *dakwah* group which was ultimately banned by the Mahathir government for 'deviationist teachings' (*New Straits Times*, 17 July 1994).

11. For a discussion of NEP-era corruption, see Jesudason (1989).

12. See Kessler (1992), where he calls Malay feudal deference and loyalty 'followership'. Prime Minister Mahathir is increasingly 'followed' and beloved for his modernity.

13. A letter from the sultan or *surat tauliah* traditionally meant the holder had been granted a position of authority (Milner 1982).

14. 'Ali-Babaism' is a term widely used in Southeast Asia, describing a business arrangement between a Muslim, 'Ali', and a Chinese, 'Baba'; these are stereotyped nicknames. The arrangement implies that the Malay obtains the

licence or the permit for a business and the Chinese does all the work. See Jesudason (1989).

4 THE *KAMPUNG* AND THE GLOBAL VILLAGE

1. Tan Sri Azman Hashim is a highly public figure in Malaysia, whose ideas and opinions have been much subjected to analysis in print. Unlike the other names presented thus far, his is not a pseudonym. Except for an hour-long interview with him described in the text, my experience of him was as a public figure. As such, I feel his is an identity I need not protect.
2. See Guinness for a discussion of how this term has been used by the Malaysian government to stand for community obligations in economic development (1992).
3. See Nagata (1995) for a discussion of Malay women and the Islamization of their clothing.
4. The date of the fast varies from year to year.
5. *Dakwah* groups still criticize 'mixing' – in 1997, when Chinese New Year and Hari Raya coincided, the shopping malls advertised the shared *pesta* as 'Gong Xi Raya', merging Chinese and Malay words into a phrase that was a pun for '*kongsi raya*' – or 'shared festival'. Several *dakwah* leaders decried this as apostatic. The Prime Minister rebuked this atmosphere of *pesta* ill-will in his annual Hari Raya address.
6. Peletz (1996) has written persuasively on the subject of *nafsu* and its disciplined opposite *akal*, especially in relation to gender roles in Malay life.
7. The atmosphere of inclusiveness was further enhanced through the sending of holiday greeting cards across ethnic lines. My informants sent Chinese New Year's cards or Christmas cards to Chinese contacts and vice versa.
8. Issues of Malay harmony and classlessness as an ideal, not reality, are discussed by S. Husin Ali (1975) and Gullick (1981). See Shamsul A.B. (1986a) for a convincing claim that such idealizations have slipped into and distorted the anthropological research, making the subject of 'class' in traditional Malay life nearly invisible (Nagata 1975).
9. McAllister believes that it is a response to capitalist development that Hari Raya events have become status-orientated (1990), an argument that depends on a view that only in contemporary life have Malays become socially unequal or status-conscious. A colonial-era account written by a Malay reflected an idea that Hari Raya was the time for the higher-status host to welcome lower-status guests: 'One's own servants are received in the drawing room where they are served with food and drinks as guests of equality' (Muhammad Ghazzali, Dato' 1933: 283).
10. Frequently, Malay bosses provide an annual bonus to Malay employees just before Hari Raya Aidilfitri. Annual bonuses can range anywhere from 50 to thousands of *ringgit*.
11. Kahn has written persuasively on these symbols of 'revived traditions' in the Malay context (1992).
12. I thank Helene Tychsen for 'deconstructing' this advertisement.

13. Gutman dismissed the 'reality of the rags-to-riches myth' in nineteenth-century America, demonstrating that most of America's powerful businessmen came from 'families of upper- or middle-class status' (1977: 211). The American myth of meritocratic entrepreneurship obviously needs some rethinking, even though it has been taken on whole cloth by my informants.

14. Malay businessmen have been very interested in Japanese business culture since Prime Minister Mahathir first extolled the virtues of Japanese-style management in 1981 (Mahathir Mohamad 1989) – the 'Look East' Policy.

15. There is a growing literature on the development of a Malay and Malaysian corporate culture, both in the popular media and relevant Malaysian management literature (see, for example, Asma Abdullah 1992). For studies of workers who are the focus of such ideology, see Ong (1987) and Guinness (1992).

16. See *Mid-term Review of the Sixth Malaysia Plan* (1993) and Mohd. Sheriff Mohd. Kassim (1991) for a description of the NDP. For a critique, see Jomo K.S. (1989a).

17. News clippings following the 'announcement' of Vision 2020 indicate that it was met with a certain amount of confusion over whether it was to be a systematic implementation of policies, like NEP, or if it was merely a set of 'guides' (see 'Project 2020: the first three months' 1991). Another criticism levelled against Vision 2020 was that the phrase was not really 'Malaysian', as it was presented by Mahathir first in English, then rapidly translated into *Bahasa Melayu* as '*Wawasan* 2020', which did not have the same clever 'optically perfect' meaning as it does in English (Shamsul A.B. 1992a).

18. Having 'vision' has become associated with Prime Minister Mahathir as a quality that best represents *Melayu baru*. To most of my informants, the Prime Minister himself was an entrepreneurial visionary who had, since the publication of his *Malay Dilemma* (Mahathir Mohamad 1970), shocked Malays into the reality of modern times. At times, my informants spoke of his visionary powers not unlike traditional descriptions of Malay leaders' *daulat*, a nearly magical capacity to rule (see Khoo Kay Kim 1991; Khoo Boo Teik 1995).

19. See, for example, the essays in the government-sponsored volume *Caring Society* (Cho Kah Sin and Ismail Muhd. Salleh 1992), which argue that caring qualities can be best fostered in the business setting.

20. The Mahathir administration recommends that Malaysia skip developing its huge stratum of resource-based industries and instead follows the South Korean/Japanese high-technology models. Malaysia does not possess a large technologically skilled labour force, however. For a review of Malaysia's Industrial Master Plan, see Anuwar Ali (1992). In 1996, when I conducted additional fieldwork in Malaysia, Mahathir's 'cybervision' for a 'multi-media high-technology super corridor' (MSC) had become the apex of Vision 2020's *hi tek*.

21. Both the Marchland machine and the *hi tek* project which Rokiah and Ishak were engaged in are discussed in Part II.

Notes 211

5 NETWORKING: THE SOCIAL RELATIONS OF ENTREPRENEURSHIP

1. There is a recent literature on the relationship between the state and the new economic elite in Southeast Asia (for example, Robison and Goodman 1996).
2. In the interests of space, I cannot discuss the field of 'network studies' or compare the Malay case to others, but a few details are necessary. The study of 'networking' in Asia is largely the study of *Chinese* networks, which Redding describes as highly functional and pragmatic (1991). He further argues (1990) that the Chinese networking system demonstrates an *Asian* capitalism, so that 'social networks' – which were first studied by social scientists as a functional, proto-industrial, *informal* response (Hart 1973) to disruption and hardship in third-world economic development (Douglas and Pederson 1973) – are now described by one economist as the 'world's fourth economic power' (Kao 1993). Using the Chinese model, entrepreneurship is now seen to be densely personalized socio-economic action at the level of firms, networks, and even nations (Chen and Hamilton 1991; McNamara 1990). It is a paradox to me that many of the positive, functional attributes of Chinese networks – social linkages, political alliances, patrimonialism, trust-building in closed groups – are negatively attributed to the Malays, where economic personalism in capitalist development is seen merely to be a function – indeed, a dysfunction – of the patronage-dispensing state. The Chinese, usually seen as politically disenfranchised minority entrepreneurs thriving in economic margins *in spite of* the immense power of the state, have been less frequently studied in modern, corporate organizations or *in collusion with* the state. When they have, there appears to be an overwhelming presence of close business–state ties, such as in the Korean *chaebol* or 'financial clique', what one researcher calls 'dependent entrepreneurship' (McNamara 1990). While I know little of small-scale entrepreneurship among the Chinese in Malaysia, it was clear to me that much of the success of larger-scale Chinese business in Malaysia is extremely dependent upon its entrepreneurs' collusionary relations with Malay and Chinese political power (as many entrepreneurial enterprises are similarly dependent on sources of elite power in America, a point which Mills [1956] made long ago). In Malaysia, a study of high-level Chinese networking would be as much a study of seeking access to 'virtuosi' as I will demonstrate it is in the Malay case. But somehow the Chinese escape the critique to which other business groups in Asia are subjected – see, however, Gomez (1994) – as researchers have a tendency to generalize the overseas Chinese as victims of hardship and inventors of economic paradigms, thriving in economic margins, even when they are not. It is my position that dependent entrepreneurship is a relatively uniform characteristic of modern, rapid, state-directed capitalist development in the Asian 'miracle' economies, Chinese and otherwise.
3. Anthropologists interested in entrepreneurship and economic action have long understood the importance of networks, before they came into vogue.

See Carroll (1965) for one classic in this genre. Barth's concept of 'bridging' transactions and his view of entrepreneurship as social action (1963; 1967) have had a lasting impact on theories of networks and alliances. Most non-ethnographic studies of networks are highly mechanistic, borrowing language from computer and management science which has little relevance to social analysis (see Larson and Starr [1993] for an example of this as well for a bibliography of similar studies). Bott's (1957) early study of social networks in England captures the importance of networks and personal entailment in modern, urban, industrialized social and economic settings which I perceived in Malay society. For references to Chinese networks, which are mostly analyzed in functionalist language reminiscent of early British social anthropology or management-school texts, see note 2 above.

4. The image of economic development presented by the Malaysian government to which my informants responded suggested a fount of opportunities for Malays, and, as such, '*bricolage*', which implies to anthropologists a kind of non-rational '*ad-hoc*' mentality (cf. Geertz 1963b; Hobbs 1988), had a very rational purpose as entrepreneurs scrambled to access them. I would also argue that to market Wall Street investments is also often a process of *bricolage*.

5. For examples of other anthropologists who performed a role in local Asian businesses, see Cooper (1980) and, a paradigm of the genre, Kondo (1990).

6. Company names in my case studies are pseudonyms with which I have attempted to capture the flavour of the actual names.

7. Just before the market fell, a block of condominium apartments called Highland Towers collapsed, apparently a result of faulty construction. This disaster rapidly became seen as a moral crisis. Many of my informants felt that Allah was punishing Malaysia with Highland Towers for putting 'easy wealth' before humanistic concerns, and in retrospect, they realized it was a foreshadowing of the stock-market crash in which they were to recognize themselves guilty of the same sins.

8. Malay entrepreneurs whom I knew were rather like Schumpeter's entrepreneurs in that they thought little about organizational business issues, perhaps intending to leave them to those less inventive, whom Schumpeter called 'managers' (1934).

6 THE BUSINESS OF ALLIANCES: THE SOCIAL EMERGENCE OF A DYADIC ENTERPRISE

1. Among other programmes were Amanah Saham Nasional and Amanah Saham Bumiputera. These programmes distributed to *bumiputera* who invested in them an enormous quantity of shares in government-owned companies. See Mehmet (1986) for a critique.

2. It is easy to incorporate a company in Malaysia. A Private Limited Company (*Sendiran Berhad* or Sdn Bhd) must lodge articles of incorporation with the Registrar of Companies, show proof of minimal paid-up capital, and pay appropriate fees. The process can take as little as five days. Many of the *bumiputera* companies I became familiar with were started as

'two-dollar companies' to claim MITI shares. I must note that my attempts to obtain statistics from the Registrar of Companies concerning the number and capitalization of *bumiputera* companies incorporated in the past seven years were fruitless. In my experience, it is impossible to examine statistics of this kind in Malaysia.

3. Business cards have an almost semiotic importance in Malaysian business; the same phenomenon appears elsewhere in Asia, particularly in Japan.

4. Other writers have noted that business groups in late-industrializing countries generally lack the technical or marketing expertise needed to grow, and, as such, tend to diversify widely into unrelated markets to increase capability (Gomez 1990; Zeile 1991). The two colossal conglomerates which began the Malaysian 'merger-and-acquisition' system of growth on behalf of *bumiputera* in the NEP period were PERNAS and PNB. See Gale (1981) and Mehmet (1986) for an analysis.

7 DANGEROUS BUSINESS: THE SOCIAL LIMITS OF AN ENTREPRENEURIAL IDENTITY

1. Marchland received approval for its million-*ringgit* loan in 1992, when a total of 132 loans with an aggregate *ringgit* value of 21.4 million was provided to *bumiputera* enterprises under the scheme (*Bank Pembangunan Annual Report* 1992). The loans were part of a massive programme called the 'New Entrepreneurs Fund' which was launched in 1989 to 'encourage new Bumiputera entrepreneurs to venture into various fields of business, in particular, manufacturing, agriculture, tourism and export-oriented businesses' (Bank Negara Annual Report 1993). Marchland, perhaps because it was a manufacturing enterprise in an area dominated by Chinese, received significant support from the Bank. Bank Pembangunan has been providing entrepreneurial loans since 1973, when it, along with many other institutions, was set up to ensure a constant flow of development funds to Malay capitalists (Jesudason 1989).

2. MARA (Majlis Amanah Rakyat) was set up, among other purposes, to provide loans and support to small *bumiputera* enterprises, a pre-NEP programme to develop Malay entrepreneurs which was dramatically expanded after the introduction of NEP (Chee Peng Lim *et al.* 1979). Its role in the creation of small-scale Malay entrepreneurship, despite enormous expenditures, was negligible. Its role in providing other funds for Malay development, such as in tertiary education, however, was enormous, as all of my informants had been funded totally by MARA for advanced studies.

3. All of the recipients of large loans from Bank Pembangunan that I interviewed complained bitterly about such delays and of the poor administration of their loans.

4. The sheer importance given to sub-contracting in Malay entrepreneurship is inestimable.

5. A trading company is also known as a company whose principals obtain corporate and government contracts and then broker or sub-contract them to others.

6. Months later, when going through issues of a local Malaysian business magazine, I came across an article which might have provided some of the answers I had been seeking. Apparently, Dato Hassan's conglomerate had proposed a series of projects to the Ministry of Transport to help reduce Kuala Lumpur's traffic congestion; among those suggested was a bus line. It is conceivable that the luxury bus job had its genesis in rumours or discussions about this project.
7. See Li (1989) for a discussion of witchcraft and business jealousy among Malays in Singapore.
8. Men are said by Muslims to be more able than women to control their passionate natures through reason. For a definitive discussion of reason and passion, see Kessler (1978); for one that confronts the complex issues of gender in Islamic Malay society, see Peletz (1996).
9. This sort of female *hantu* or ghost is common in Malay communities; Peletz (1996) analyzes it symbolically in terms of ambivalence for women's blood.
10. This name is not a pseudonym. Mazneh Hamid was a public figure I did not know personally.

8 VIRTUOSO ENTREPRENEURSHIP: DEVELOPMENT AND WEALTH FOR ALL MALAYS

1. See Chapter 6, note 1. This unit-trust scheme had supplied its *bumiputera*-only investors with annual returns of 12 to 20 per cent since its inception in 1981.
2. True pyramid schemes had been illegal in Malaysia since the 'Holiday Magic' scandal in the 1980s, when thousands of people lost money subscribing to a direct-selling scheme which involved outright fraud. When the Direct Selling Act and Regulations 1993 banned 'pyramid' recruitment in Malaysia, it was understood that somehow products had to *exist* in the organization, whether they were sold or not.
3. Anyone who has attended a membership meeting for such organizations will understand the concept of what I call the double miracle – that the very product that cured you can change your life and the lives of those you love by making you rich. The definitive study of direct-sales marketing, to which I owe a great deal of my understanding, is Biggart (1989).
4. For a cross-cultural analysis of this phenomenon, see Ardener (1964). See Freedman (1959) for a Chinese example; Geertz (1962) for an Indonesian example. My informants belonged to smaller groups of ten or twelve which they called *kutu*, while they reserved the term *arisan* for larger groups of 50 to 100 members.
5. I was also aware of more traditional-format *kutu* groups in Kuala Lumpur, especially among government clerks and schoolteachers, where the group did not have a social context but merely formed to save and distribute money. This is closer to the description of a *kutu* in Carsten (1989).
6. This was the only time I was offered a chance to invest in the business of any of my informants. Usually, my informants offered to make an investment in *me*, for they believed that the skill I had in writing up marketing lit-

erature was one which Malaysia sorely needed, and many people suggested that I return someday to start an entrepreneurial business with them.

9 CONCLUSION

1. Bank Negara, the national bank of Malaysia, has devoted significant funds to an Enterprise Rehabilitation Programme, a source of refinancing of 'ailing Bumiputera enterprises' (*Bank Negara Annual Report* 1993), which in many cases rehabilitates by first taking over the majority ownership and then the full management of bankrupt businesses that had been funded by the New Entrepreneurs Fund, the scheme which had provided the capitalization of Marchland.

References

BOOKS AND ARTICLES

A. Kahar Bador. 1973 'Social rank, status-honour and social class consciousness amongst the Malays'. In *Modernization in Southeast Asia*. Hans-Dieter Evers (ed.), Singapore: Oxford University Press.

Abdul Aziz Mahmud. 1981 'Malay entrepreneurship: problems in development – a comparative empirical analysis'. Occasional Paper No. 7, Yunit Penyelidikan Sosioekonomi, Jabatan Perdana Menteri, Kuala Lumpur.

Abdul Maulud Yusof. 1986 'Culture change in Malay society – from peasantry to entrepreneurship'. *Akademika: Jurnal Sains Kemanusiaan dan Kemasyarakatan* 29, 35–47.

Alexander, Jennifer. 1994 'Are market cultures gendered? Female traders in Javanese marketplaces'. Unpublished conference paper, SSRC conference, October, Boston.

Anuwar Ali. 1992 *Malaysia's industrialization: the quest for technology*. Singapore: Oxford University Press.

Ardener, Shirley. 1964 'The comparative study of rotating credit associations'. *Journal of the Royal Anthropological Institute* 94: 2, 201–29.

Asma Abdullah. 1992 'The influence of ethnic values on managerial practices in Malaysia'. *Malaysian Management Review* 27: 1, 3–18.

Atkinson, J.M. and S. Errington (eds). 1990 *Power and difference. Gender in island Southeast Asia*. Stanford, CA: Stanford University Press.

Azizah Kassim. 1984 'Women and divorce among the urban Malays'. In *Women in Malaysia*. Hing Ai Yun, Nik Safiah Karim, and Rokiah Talib (eds), Petaling Jaya, Malaysia: Pelanduk Publications.

Bailey, Conner. 1976 *Broker, mediator, patron, and kinsman: an historical analysis of key leadership roles in a rural Malaysian district*. Ohio University Center for International Studies, Southeast Asia Series No. 38.

Banks, David J. 1983 *Malay kinship*. Philadelphia: ISHI.

Barth, Fredrik. 1963 'Introduction'. In *The role of the entrepreneur in social change in northern Norway*. Fredrik Barth (ed.), Oslo: Universitetsforlaget.

——. 1967 'Economic spheres in Darfur'. In *Themes in economic anthropology*. Raymond Firth (ed.), London: Tavistock.

Berger, Peter L. 1987 *The capitalist revolution*. Hants., UK: Wildwood House.

Biggart, Nicole Woolsey. 1989 *Charismatic capitalism. Direct selling organizations in America*. Chicago: University of Chicago Press.

Bott, Elizabeth. 1957 *Family and social network*. London: Tavistock.

Carroll, John. 1965 *The Filipino manufacturing entrepreneur: agent and product of change*. Ithaca, NY: Cornell University Press.

Carsten, Janet. 1989 'Cooking money: gender and symbolic transformation of means of exchange in a Malay fishing community'. In *Money and the morality of exchange*. Maurice Bloch and Jonathan Parry (eds), Cambridge: Cambridge University Press.

217

218   *References*

Chee Peng Lim, M.C. Puthucheary, and Donald Lee. 1979 *A study of small entre-preneurs and entrepreneurial development programmes in Malaysia*. Kuala Lumpur: University of Malaya.

Chen, Edward and Gary G. Hamilton. 1991 'Introduction: business networks and economic development'. In *Business networks and economic development in East and Southeast Asia*. Gary Hamilton (ed.), Hong Kong: Centre of Asian Studies, University of Hong Kong.

Chiew Seen Kong. 1993 'Ethnicity, economic development, government intervention and social class in peninsular Malaysia'. Paper presented at the ASEAN Inter-University Seminars on Social Development, November, Singapore.

Cho Kah Sin and Ismail Muhd. Salleh (eds). 1992 *Caring society: emerging issues and future directions*. Selected papers from the First National Conference on the Caring Society, 1990. Kuala Lumpur: ISIS.

Clutterbuck, Richard. 1985 *Conflict and violence in Singapore and Malaysia 1945–1983*. Boulder, CO: Westview.

Cohen, Abner. 1981 *The politics of elite culture*. Berkeley: University of California Press.

Comber, Leon. 1983 *13 May 1969: a historical survey of Sino-Malay relations*. Kuala Lumpur: Heinemann Asia.

Cook, Scott. 1982 *Zapotec stoneworkers. The dynamics of rural simple commodity production in modern Mexican capitalism*. Washington, DC: University Press of America.

Cooper, Eugene. 1980 *The wood-carvers of Hong Kong. Craft production in the world capitalist periphery*. Cambridge: Cambridge University Press.

Crouch, Harold. 1992 'Authoritarian trends, the UMNO split and the limits to state power'. In *Fragmented vision: culture and politics in contemporary Malaysia*. Joel S. Kahn and Frances Loh Kok Wah (eds), Asian Studies Association of Australian Southeast Asia Publications Series No. 22. Sydney: Allen & Unwin.

Derossi, Flavia. 1971 *The Mexican entrepreneur*. Paris: Development Centre of the Organisation for Economic Cooperation and Development.

Djamour, Judith. 1959 *Malay kinship and marriage in Singapore*. London School of Economics Monographs on Social Anthropology No. 21. London: The Athlone Press.

Douglas, Stephen A. and Paul Pederson. 1973 *Blood, believer, and brother: the development of voluntary associations in Malaysia*. Ohio University Center for International Studies, Southeast Asia Series No. 29.

Endicott, K.M. 1970 *An analysis of Malay magic*. Singapore: Oxford University Press.

Firth, Raymond. 1967 'Themes in economic anthropology: a general comment'. In *Themes in economic anthropology*. Raymond Firth (ed.), London: Tavistock.

Firth, Rosemary. 1943 *Housekeeping among Malay peasants*. London School of Economics Monographs on Social Anthropology No. 7.

Fortes, Meyer. 1969 *Kinship and the social order*. Chicago: Aldin.

Freedman, Maurice. 1959 'The handling of money: a note on the background of the economic sophistication of overseas Chinese'. *Man* 59. Reprinted in *Readings in Malayan economics*. T.H. Silcock (ed.), Singapore: Eastern Universities Press, 1961.

Gale, Bruce. 1981 *Politics and public enterprise in Malaysia*. Singapore: Eastern Universities Press.

Geertz, Clifford. 1956 'Religious belief and economic behavior in a Central Javanese town'. *Economic Development and Cultural Change* 4: 2, 134–58.

——. 1962 'The rotating credit association: a "middle rung" in development'. *Economic Development and Cultural Change* 10, 241–63.

——. 1963a. *Agricultural involution: the process of ecological change in Indonesia*. Berkeley: University of California Press.

——. 1963b. *Peddlers and princes: social development and economic change in two Indonesian towns*. Chicago: University of Chicago Press.

——. 1973 *The interpretation of cultures*. New York: Basic Books.

Gewertz, Deborah and Frederick Errington. 1991 *Twisted histories, altered contexts: representing the Chambri in a world system*. Cambridge: Cambridge University Press.

Gomez, Edmund Terence. 1990 *Politics in business: UMNO's corporate investments*. Kuala Lumpur: Forum.

——. 1992 'Corporate involvement of political parties in Malaysia'. Unpublished PhD dissertation, University of Malaya.

——. 1994 *Political business: corporate involvement of Malaysian political parties*. Townsville, Australia: Centre for South East Asian Studies, James Cook University of North Queensland.

Granovetter, Mark. 1992 'Economic action and social structure: the problem of embeddedness in the sociology of economic life'. In *The sociology of economic life*. Mark Granovetter and Richard Swedberg (eds), Boulder, CO: Westview.

Guinness, Patrick. 1992 *On the margin of capitalism: people and development in Mukim Plentory, Johor, Malaysia*. Singapore: Oxford University Press.

Gullick, John. 1981 *Malaysia: economic expansion and national unity*. London and Boulder, CO: Ernest Benn, Westview.

——. 1987 *Malay society in the late nineteenth century*. Singapore: Oxford University Press.

Gutman, Herbert G. 1977 *Work, culture and society in industrializing America*. New York: Vintage Press.

Hagen, Everett E. 1962 *On the theory of social change: how economic growth begins*. London: Tavistock.

Hart, Keith. 1973 'Informal income opportunities and urban employment in Ghana'. *Journal of Modern African Studies* 11: 1, 61–89.

——. 1975 'Swindler or public benefactor – the entrepreneur in his community'. In *Changing social structure in Ghana*. Jack Goody (ed.), London: International African Institute.

Hirschman, Charles. 1975 *Ethnic and social stratification in peninsular Malaysia*. Washington, DC: The Arnold and Caroline Rose Monograph Series of the American Sociological Association.

Hobbs, Derek. 1988 *Doing the business. Entrepreneurship, the working class, and detectives in the East End of London*. Oxford: Clarendon Press.

Horii, Kenzo. 1991 'Disintegration of the colonial economic legacies and social restructuring in Malaysia'. *The Developing Economies. Journal of the Institute of Developing Economics* 29: 4, 281–311.

Hussin Mutalib. 1990 *Islam and ethnicity in Malay politics*. Singapore: Oxford University Press.

Hyman, Gerald F. 1975 'Economics in Krian: meaning and behavior in a free market economy'. Unpublished manuscript.

Jackson, James C. 1979 'Retail development in third world cities: models and the Kuala Lumpur experience'. In *Issues in Malaysian development*. James C. Jackson and Martin Rudner (eds), Asian Studies Association of Australia Southeast Asian Publications Series No. 3, Singapore: Heinemann.

Jasbir Sarjit Singh. 1991 'Multicultural education, social equity and national unity in Malaysia'. In *Education, politics and state in multicultural societies: an international perspective*. M.I. Alladin and M.K. Bacchus (eds), Needham Heights, MA: Ginn Press.

Jasbir Sarjit Singh *et al*. 1989 *Socio-economic environment, academic achievement and occupational opportunities in Malaysia*. Report prepared for the Educational Planning and Research Division, Ministry of Education, Malaysia.

Jesudason, James V. 1989 *Ethnicity and the economy: the state, Chinese business, and multinationals in Malaysia*. Singapore: Oxford University Press.

Jomo K.S. 1986 *A question of class: capital, the state, and uneven development*. Singapore: Oxford University Press.

——. 1989a. *Beyond 1990. Considerations for a new national development strategy*. Kuala Lumpur: University of Malaya Institute of Advanced Studies.

——. 1989b. 'Mahathir's economic policies: an introduction'. In *Mahathir's economic policies*. Jomo K.S. (ed.), Kuala Lumpur: Insan.

——. 1990 *Growth and structural change in the Malaysian economy*. Basingstoke: Macmillan.

——. 1993 'Introduction'. In *Islamic economic alternatives: critical perspectives and new directions*. Jomo K.S. (ed.), Kuala Lumpur: Ikraq.

Jones, Gavin W. 1994 *Marriage and divorce in Islamic South-east Asia*. Kuala Lumpur: Oxford University Press.

Kahn, Joel S. 1992 'Class, ethnicity and diversity: some remarks on Malay culture in Malaysia'. In *Fragmented vision: culture and politics in contemporary Malaysia*. Joel S. Kahn and Frances Loh Kok Wah (eds), Asian Studies Association of Australia Southeast Asia Publications Series No. 22. Sydney: Allen & Unwin.

——. 1996 'Growth, economic transformation, culture and the middle classes in Malaysia'. In *The new rich in Asia*. Richard Robison and David S.G. Goodman (eds), London and New York: Routledge.

Kamaruddin M. Said. 1993 *The despairing and the hopeful: a Malay fishing community in Kuala Kedah*. Bangi, Malaysia: Penerbitan Universiti Kebangsaan Malaysia.

Kanafani, Aida. 1993 'Rites of hospitality and aesthetics'. In *Everday life in the Muslim Middle East*. Donna Lee Bowen and Evelyn Early (eds), Bloomington, IN: Indiana University Press.

Kao, John. 1993 'The worldwide web of Chinese business'. *Harvard Business Review* March–April, 24–35.

Kessler, Clive S. 1978 *Islam and politics in a Malay state: Kelantan 1838–1969*. Ithaca, NY and London: Cornell University Press.

——. 1992 'Archaism and modernity: contemporary Malay political culture'. In *Fragmented vision: culture and politics in contemporary Malaysia*. Joel S. Kahn and Frances Loh Kok Wah (eds), Asian Studies Association of Australia Southeast Asia Publications Series No. 22. Sydney: Allen & Unwin.

Khasnor Johan. 1984 *The emergence of the modern Malay administrative elite*. Singapore: Oxford University Press.

Khoo Boo Teik. 1995 *Paradoxes of Mahathirism*. Kuala Lumpur: Oxford University Press.

Khoo Kay Jin. 1992 'The grand vision: Mahathir and modernisation'. In *Fragmented vision: culture and politics in contemporary Malaysia*. Joel S. Kahn and Frances Loh Kok Wah (eds), Asian Studies Association of Australia Southeast Asia Publications Series No. 22. Sydney: Allen & Unwin.

Khoo Kay Kim. 1991 *Malay society: transformation and democratisation*. Petaling Jaya, Malaysia: Pelanduk Publications.

Kondo, Dorinne. 1990 *Crafting selves. Power, gender, and discourses of identity in a Japanese workplace*. Chicago: University of Chicago Press.

Laderman, Carol. 1991 *Taming the wind of desire: psychology, medicine, and aesthetics in Malay shamanistic performance*. Berkeley: University of California Press.

Larson, Andrea and Jennifer A. Starr. 1993 'A network model of organization formation'. *Entrepreneurship theory and practice* Winter, 5–15.

Leach, Edmund. 1954 *Political systems of highland Burma*. London: G. Bell & Son.

Lee, Raymond L.M. 1986 'Social networks and ethnic interaction in urban Malaysia'. *Sojourn* 1: 1, 109–24.

Li, Tania. 1989 *Malays in Singapore. Culture, economy, and ideology*. Singapore: Oxford University Press.

McAllister, Carol. 1990 'Women and feasting: ritual exchange, capitalism, and Islamic revival in Negeri Sembilan, Malaysia'. *Research in Economic Anthropology* 12, 23–49.

McClelland, David. 1961 'The achievement motive in economic growth'. Reprinted in *Entrepreneurship and economic development*. Peter Kilby (ed.), 1971, New York: Free Press.

MacGaffey, Janet. 1987 *Entrepreneurs and parasites: the struggle for indigenous capitalism in Zaire*. Cambridge: Cambridge University Press.

Mackie, J.A.C. 1976 *The Chinese in Indonesia*. West Melbourne: Thomas Nelson.

McKinley, Robert. 1975 'A knife cutting water: child transfers and siblingship among urban Malays'. Unpublished PhD dissertation, University of Michigan.

——. 1981 'Cain and Abel on the Malay peninsula'. In *Siblingship in Oceania: studies in the meaning of kin relations*. Mac Marshall (ed.), Ann Arbor: University of Michigan Press.

McNamara, Dennis. 1990 *The colonial origins of Korean enterprise, 1910–1945*. Cambridge: Cambridge University Press.

Mahathir Mohamad. 1970 *The Malay dilemma*. Singapore: Times Books.

——. 1989 'New government policies'. In *Mahathir's economic policies*. Jomo K.S. (ed.), Kuala Lumpur: Insan.

——. 1991a. Dialog from seminar on 'Towards a developed and industrialized society: understanding the concept, implications and challenges of Vision 2020'. Reprinted in *Malaysia's Vision 2020*. Ahmad Sarji Abdul Hamid (ed.), 1993, Kuala Lumpur: Pelanduk Publications.

——. 1991b. Malaysia: the way forward. Seminar speech from 'Towards a developed and industrialized society: understanding the concept, implications and challenges of Vision 2020'. Reprinted in *Malaysia's Vision 2020*. Ahmad Sarji Abdul Hamid (ed.), 1993, Kuala Lumpur: Pelanduk Publications.

Mauss, Marcel. 1989 *The gift. The form and reason for exchange in archaic societies*. New York and London: W.W. Norton.

222 *References*

Means, Gordon P. 1991 *Malaysian politics: the second generation*. Singapore: Oxford University Press.

Mehmet, Ozay. 1986 *Development in Malaysia: poverty, wealth and trusteeship*. London: Croom Helm.

——. 1990 *Islamic identity and development: studies of the Islamic periphery*. London: Routledge.

Mills, C. Wright. 1956 *The power elite*. New York: Oxford University Press.

Milne, R.S. 1981 *Politics in ethnically bipolar states*. Vancouver: University of British Columbia Press.

Milne, R.S. and Diane K. Mauzy. 1978 *Politics and government in Malaysia*. Vancouver: University of British Columbia Press.

Milner, A.C. 1982 *Kerajaan: Malay political culture on the eve of colonial rule*. The Association for Asian Studies Monograph No. XL, Tucson, AZ: University of Arizona Press.

Mohd. Razali Agus. 1992 'Spatial patterns in a growing metropolitan area: Kuala Lumpur, Malaysia'. *Malaysian Journal of Social Research* 1: 1, 33–48.

Mohd. Salleh bin Abas. 1986 'Traditional elements of the Malaysian constitution'. In *The constitution of Malaysia: further perspectives and developments*. F.A. Trindade and H.P. Lee (eds), Petaling Jaya, Malaysia: Penerbit Fajar Bakti.

Mohd. Sheriff Mohd Kassim. 1991 'Vision 2020's linkages with the Sixth Malaysia Plan and the Second Outline Perspective Plan'. Seminar speech from 'Towards a developed and industrialized society: understanding the concept, implications and challenges of Vision 2020'. Reprinted in *Malaysia's Vision 2020*. Ahmad Sarji Abdul Hamid (ed.), 1993, Kuala Lumpur: Pelanduk Publications.

Mohd. Taib Osman. 1989 *Malay folk beliefs*. Kuala Lumpur: Dewan Bahasa dan Pustaka Kementerian Pendidikan Malaysia.

Mokhzani, B.A.R. 1965 'The study of social stratification and social mobility in Malaysia'. *East Asian Cultural Studies* 4: 1, 138–61.

Muhammad Ghazzali, Dato'. 1933 'Court language and etiquette of the Malays'. *Journal of the Malayan Branch of the Royal Asiatic Society* 11: 2.

Muhammad Ikmal Said. 1993 'Nationalism and national identity'. Paper presented at the ASEAN Inter-University Seminars on Social Development, November, Singapore.

Muhammad Imran. 1979 *Ideal woman in Islam*. Lahore: Islamic Publications.

Muhammad Nejatullah Siddiqi. 1981 *Muslim economic thinking: a survey of contemporary literature*. International Centre for Research in Islamic Economics, King Abdul Aziz University, Jeddah.

Muhammah Syukri Salleh. 1992 *An Islamic approach to rural development: the Arqam Way*. London: ASOIB International.

M. Umer Chapra. 1992 *Islam and the economic challenge*. London: The Islamic Foundation.

Muzaffar, Chandra. 1987 *Islamic resurgence in Malaysia*. Petaling Jaya, Malaysia: Penerbit Fajar Bakti.

Nagata, Judith A. 1975 'Perceptions of social inequality in Malaysia'. *Contributions to Asian Studies* 7, 113–35.

——. 1984 *The reflowering of Malaysian Islam. Modern religious radicals and their roots*. Vancouver: University of British Columbia Press.

——. 1995 'Modern Malay women and the message of the "veil"'. In '*Male' and 'female' in developing Southeast Asia*. Wazir Jahan Karim (ed.), Oxford: Berg Publishers.

Naipaul, V.S. 1981 *Among the believers*. New York: Alfred Knopf.

Nik A. Rashid Ismail. 1988 'Value systems of Malay and Chinese managers: a comparative study'. In *Economic performance in Malaysia: the insider's view*. Manning Nash (ed.), New York: Professors' World Peace Academy.

Norani Othman. (nd) 'Shari'a law and the rights of modern Muslim women'. Unpublished paper.

——. 1994 'The sociopolitical dimensions of Islamisation in Malaysia: a cultural accommodation of social change?' In *Shari'a law and the modern nation-state: a Malaysian symposium*. Norani Othman (ed.), Kuala Lumpur: Sisters in Islam.

Ong, Aihwa. 1987 *Spirits of resistance and capitalist discipline. Factory women in Malaysia*. Albany, NY: State University of New York.

——. 1990 'State versus Islam: Malay families, women's bodies and the body politic in Malaysia'. *American Ethnologist* 17: 2, 258–76.

Ong, Aihwa and Michael G. Peletz (eds). 1995 *Bewitching women, pious men. Gender and body politics in Southeast Asia*. Berkeley: University of California Press.

Oo Yu Hock. 1991 *Ethnic chameleon: multiracial politics in Malaysia*. Petaling Jaya, Malaysia: Pelanduk Publications.

Packard, Vance. 1957 *The hidden persuaders*. London: Longman.

Parkin, David J. 1972 *Palms, wine, and witness*. San Francisco: Chandler.

Parkinson, Brien K. 1968 'The economic retardation of the Malays – a rejoinder'. *Modern Asian Studies* 2. Reprinted in *Readings on Malaysian economic development*. David Lim (ed.), 1975, Kuala Lumpur: Oxford University Press.

Peletz, Michael G. 1993 'Sacred texts and dangerous words: the politics of law and cultural rationalization in Malaysia'. *Comparative Studies in Society and History* 35: 1, 66–109.

——. 1996 *Reason and passion: representations of gender in a Malay society*. Berkeley: University of California Press.

Pemberton, John. 1994 *On the subject of 'Java'*. Ithaca, NY: Cornell University Press.

Popenoe, Oliver. 1969 'A study of Malay entrepreneurs'. *Quarterly Journal of the Institute Technoloji MARA* 1: 3. Reprinted in *Readings on Malaysian economic development*. David Lim (ed.), 1975, Kuala Lumpur: Oxford University Press.

'Project 2020: the first three months'. 1991 *ISIS Focus* 74.

Puthucheary, Mavis. 1978 *The politics of administration: the Malaysian experience*. Kuala Lumpur: Oxford University Press.

Rabushka, Alvin. 1973 *Race and politics in urban Malaya*. Stanford, CA: Hoover Institution Press.

Raja Rohana Raja Mamat. 1991 *The role and status of Malay women in Malaysia: social and legal perspectives*. Kuala Lumpur: Dewan Bahasa dan Pustaka.

Redding, S. Gordon. 1990 *The spirit of Chinese capitalism*. Berlin and New York: Walter de Gruyter.

——. 1991 'Weak organizations and strong linkages: managerial ideology and Chinese family business networks'. In *Business networks and economic development in East and Southeast Asia*. Gary Hamilton (ed.), Hong Kong: Centre of Asian Studies, University of Hong Kong.

Robison, Richard and David S.G. Goodman (eds). 1996 *The new rich in Asia*. London and New York: Routledge.

Roff, William R. 1967 *The origins of Malay nationalism*. Kuala Lumpur and Singapore: University of Malaya Press.

References

Rosen, Lawrence. 1984 *Bargaining for reality. The construction of social relations in a Muslim community*. Chicago: University of Chicago Press.
Rutten, Mario. (nd) 'Asian capitalists in the European mirror'. Unpublished paper.
S. Husin Ali. 1975 *Malay peasant society and leadership*. Kuala Lumpur: Oxford University Press.
——. 1984 'Social relations: the ethnic and class factors'. In *Ethnicity, class and development in Malaysia*. S. Hussin Ali (ed.), Bangi, Malaysia: Universiti Kebangsaan Malaysia.
Schneider, David. 1980 *American kinship: a cultural account*. Englewood Cliffs, NJ: Prentice-Hall.
Schumpeter, Joseph. 1934 *The theory of economic development*. Cambridge, MA: Harvard University Press.
Schweizer, Thomas. 1989 'Economic individualism and the community spirit: divergent orientation patterns of Javanese villagers in rice production and the ritual sphere'. *Modern Asian Studies* 23: 2, 277–312.
Scott, James C. 1968 *Political ideology in Malaysia: reality and the beliefs of an elite*. Kuala Lumpur: University of Malaya Press.
——. 1976 *The moral economy of the peasant: rebellion and subsistence in Southeast Asia*. New Haven, CT: Yale University Press.
——. 1977 'Patron–client politics and political change in Southeast Asia'. In *Friends, followers, and factions: a reader in political clientelism*. Steffen W. Schmidt, Laura Guasti, Carl H. Lande, and James C. Scott (eds), Berkeley: University of California Press.
Sen, Amartya. 1981 *Poverty and famines: an essay on entitlement and deprivation*. Oxford: Clarendon Press.
Shamsul A.B. 1986a. *From British to bumiputera rule. Local politics and rural development in peninsular Malaysia*. Singapore: Institute of Southeast Asian Studies.
——. 1986b. 'The rise and demise of a Malay woman politician'. *Sojourn* 1: 1, 220–30.
——. 1992a. *Malaysia in 2020, one state many nations?* Bangi, Malaysia: Department of Anthropology and Sociology, Universiti Kebangsaan Malaysia.
——. 1992b. 'Vision 2020, Malaysia as a developed nation: old ideas, new proposal?' *Satiawacana* 5.
Sharifah Zaleha Syed Hassan. 1986 'Women, divorce and Islam in Kedah'. *Sojourn* 1: 1, 183–99.
Siegel, James T. 1986 *Solo in the New Order*. Princeton, NJ: Princeton University Press.
Skinner, G. William. 1963 'The Chinese minority'. In *Indonesia*. Ruth McVey (ed.), New Haven, CT: Southeast Asian Studies, Yale University.
Sloane, Patricia. (forthcoming) 'Families, networks, ethnicities, and communities: social relations among the Malay middle class'. In *Apa yang dikejar? Budaya moden kelas menengah Malaysia*. Norani Othman, H.E.A. Rahman and Rustam A. Sani (eds.), Bangi, Malaysia: Universiti Kebangsaan Malaysia.
Sowell, Thomas. 1995 *The vision of the anointed*. New York: Basic Books.
Stewart, Alex. 1991 'A prospectus on the anthropology of entrepreneurship'. *Entrepreneurship Theory and Practice* Winter, 71–90.

Stirrat, R.L. 1989 'Money, men and women'. In *Money and the morality of exchange*. Maurice Bloch and Jonathan Parry (eds), Cambridge: Cambridge University Press.

Stivens, Maila. 1992 'Perspectives on gender: problems in writing about women in Malaysia.' In *Fragmented vision: culture and politics in contemporary Malaysia.* Joel S. Kahn and Frances Loh Kok Wah (eds), Asian Studies Association of Australia Southeast Asia Publications Series No. 22. Sydney: Allen & Unwin.

Strange, Heather. 1981 *Rural Malay women in tradition and transition*. New York: Praeger.

Swift, Michael. 1963 'Malay peasants'. In *The role of savings and wealth in Southern Asia and the West*. Richard D. Lambert and Bert F. Hoselitz (eds), Paris: UNESCO.

Tan Chee Beng. 1984 'National culture and national integration'. *Aliran Monthly* January, 12–4.

Tan Liok Ee. 1988 *The rhetoric of bangsa and minzu: community and nation in tension. The Malay Peninsula, 1900–1955*. Centre of Southeast Asian Studies, Monash University, Working Paper No. 52.

Veblen, Thorsten. 1957 *The theory of the leisure class*. London: Allen & Unwin.

Wazir Jahan Karim. 1990 'Prelude to madness: the language of emotion in courtship and early marriage'. In *Emotions of culture: a Malay perspective*. Wazir Jahan Karim (ed.), Singapore: Oxford University Press.

——. 1992 *Women and culture: between Malay adat and Islam*. Boulder, CO: Westview.

——. 1995 'Introduction: genderising anthropology in Southeast Asia'. In *'Male' and 'female' in developing Southeast Asia*. Wazir Jahan Karim (ed.), Oxford: Berg Publishers.

Weber, Max. 1974 *From Max Weber: Essays in sociology*. H.H. Gerth and C. Wright Mills (eds) London: Routledge & Kegan Paul.

Wilder, William. 1968 'Islam, other factors and Malay backwardness: comments on an argument'. *Modern Asian Studies* 2. Reprinted in *Readings on Malaysian economic development*. David Lim (ed.), 1975, Kuala Lumpur: Oxford University Press.

——. 1982 *Communication, social structure and development in rural Malaysia: a study of Kampung Kuala Bera*. London School of Economics Monographs on Social Anthropology No. 56, London: The Athlone Press.

Wilson, Christine S. 1986 'Social and nutritional context of ethnic foods: Malay examples'. In *Shared wealth and symbol: food, culture, and society in Oceania and Southeast Asia*. Lenore Manderson (ed.), Cambridge: Cambridge University Press.

Yoshino, Kosaku. 1992 *Cultural nationalism in contemporary Japan*. London: Routledge.

Yusof Ismail (ed.) 1994 *Muslim women in organizations: a Malaysian perspective*. Kuala Lumpur: A.S. Noordeen.

Zainah Anwar. 1987 *Islamic revivalism in Malaysia*. Kuala Lumpur: Pelanduk Publications.

Zainal Abidin b. Ahmad (Zaba). 1949 'Malay festivals, and some aspects of Malay religious life'. *Journal of the Malayan Branch of the Royal Asiatic Society* 22: 1.

Zeile, William. 1991 'Industrial policy and organizational efficiency: the Korean *Chaebol* examined'. In *Business networks and economic development in East and Southeast Asia* Gary Hamilton (ed.), Hong Kong: Centre of Asian Studies, University of Hong Kong.

MALAYSIAN GOVERNMENT PUBLICATIONS

Bank Negara Annual Report 1993
Bank Pembangunan Annual Report 1992
Direct Selling Act and Regulations, 1993
Mid-term review of the sixth Malaysia Plan 1991–1995. 1993. Kuala Lumpur: Government Press.
Social Development Trends Bulletin 1980–1990. 1991. Kuala Lumpur: Socio-Economic Research Unit, Prime Minister's Department.

NEWSPAPERS AND MAGAZINES

Berita Harian (Kuala Lumpur)
The Economist (London)
Financial Times (Kuala Lumpur)
New Straits Times (Kuala Lumpur)
Star (Kuala Lumpur)

Index

Index

ethnic
  complementarity 4
  connectedness among Malays 44,
    45–6, 56
  conflict 4, 50, 53
  groups in Malaysia 49, 50, 205n
  riots (13 May 1969) 4, 50, 81
ethnicity 21, 49–50

families 23, 24, 26, 37, 196
  corporate 108–9
  remittances to 27
  symbolic 54
  see also 'siblingship'
fasting (*puasa*) 65, 93–4
fate (*takdir*) *see* Muslim belief and
    identity
feasting *see kenduri*
festivals *see* Hari Raya, Malay
    tradition and customs
'feudal' culture 78, 84
Firth, Rosemary 33
food
  emotional sustenance of 25
  stalls 19, 36, 162
  see fasting
Ford, Henry 47

gabungan (conglomerate) companies
    136, 158, 183, 193, 207n
Geertz, Clifford 9, 57, 206n
general elections 1969 4

haj (pilgrimage) 61, 65, 66, 158
hajah (female pilgrim) 167
Hari Raya (Muslim holiday) 91, 93–4
  balik kampung (returning home to
    the village) 101–4, 109
  bonuses 101, 209n
  communal relations during 94–6,
    209n
  Hari Raya Haji 28
  hospitality culture 95–97
  national culture 91–3
  Prime Minister's speeches 62, 64,
    95, 209n
  'showcase of culture' during 97–8;
    open houses 98–101
  television advertisements 103–4
  see Malay tradition and customs

Hart, Keith 9, 11
Hassan, Dato *see* Dato Hassan
Highland Towers 212n
high-technology (*hi tek*) projects and
    entrepreneurship 8, 114, 139,
    140, 153, 155, 210n
holding companies *see gabungan*
    (conglomerate) companies
houses and homes
  decor 151
  displays of status 95, 97
  and Malay definitions of culture
    96–98
  renovations to 27, 98
  women's domain 31

ikhtiar (free will) *see* Muslim belief
    and identity
illegal immigrants 207n
ilmu (knowledge) 162, 164
incorporation of businesses 212n
International Islamic University (IIU)
    69
Islamic
  corporate culture 59, 76–77
  economics 64–8, 69, 73–7 180,
    208n; investing in stock-market
    74, 128–131
  fundamentalism 35, 198; *see also*
    dakwah
  notions of fate and reward 62–3,
    64–7
  theory of capitalism 128
  Treasury (*Baitulmal*) 75
  view of poverty 63
  view of work 63
  see also Muslim belief and identity
Islamic Religious Department, Pusat
    Agama Islam 38
Islamization *see dakwah*

Japanese business culture 107, 137,
    210n

kampung *see* Malay tradition and
    customs, 'Malayness' theories
'*kampung* (village) boy' 86, 89,
    105
'*kampung* (village) girl' 167, 197
karaoke 106, 107, 108